THE GIRLS OF SUMMER

THE GIRLS OF SUMMER

OF SUMMER

An Ashes Year with the England Women's Cricket Team

David Tossell

First published by Pitch Publishing, 2016

Pitch Publishing
A2 Yeoman Gate
Yeoman Way
Worthing
Sussex
BN13 3QZ
www.pitchpublishing.co.uk

A CIP catalogue record is available for this book
from the British Library.

ISBN 978-1-78531-135-2

Typesetting and origination by Pitch Publishing

Printed by Bell & Bain, Glasgow, Scotland

Contents

For the Girls of Summer. Thank you for the lifts and the laughs.

For my own girls of every season: Sara, Amy, Sarah, Laura and Karis.

Thank you for the love and the life.

About the author

David Tossell is the author of 13 previous sports books, including five nominations in the British Sports Book Awards and two for the MCC/Cricket Society Book of the Year. A sports journalist for more than three decades, he has been the head of the NFL's public relations in Europe for the past 20 years.

Cover pictures by Press Association: Katherine Brunt (main picture and back) and Georgia Elwiss (right) celebrate Test wickets and one-day victory, while Charlotte Edwards (left) and Sarah Taylor (bottom) lament their dismissals and the England girls suffer the pain of defeat (back).

Foreword

By England Captain Charlotte Edwards

MANY times in the weeks after the 2015 Women's Ashes I saw little girls picking up a bat and ball. Their parents would come up to me and say how much their children had enjoyed watching the series and that it had been a trigger for them to start playing the game. That is so pleasing and it is an indication of what an important, historic summer it was for the women's game. Having reflected quite a bit on it I realise that, even though the result was not what we wanted as an England team, when you look at the success of the series, the attendances at the matches and just where the game finds itself now, then it was a brilliant series to be a part of. It was amazing the way the ECB marketed the games, the manner in which all the counties got behind us, the level of social media interest. It was an incredible feeling walking into grounds for the games.

But disappointment is always going to be the overriding factor for me. It was a wonderful summer in general for women's sport and we really wanted to carry on the momentum from the England bronze medal in the football World Cup and the success in the hockey European

Championship. It was great that we were supported and profiled as much as the other sports and got as many headlines.

The fans who came to our games were remarkable; so passionate and positive. There were very few negative comments from the people who followed us throughout the summer – and they kept on coming. One group, from Didsbury in Lancashire, were testament to that, showing up at every single game. But that just made it all the more heartbreaking that we weren't able to give them the results they wanted and were unable to retain the Ashes against a strong Australian side.

We felt like we had let a lot of people down. What makes it doubly frustrating for me is that there wasn't much between the two teams at all. I keep thinking how we played poorly at times yet nearly won. We just needed only a slightly better performance and we would have got over the line. But that is the cruelty of international sport.

There were so many small turning points. In my mind I see Heather Knight's run-out in the second game at Bristol quite a lot. It seemed such a small thing at the time but it was a massive shift in terms of momentum when we were chasing a target to win, having already gone ahead in the series. You could see the impact it had on the Aussies just when they were thinking that England were going to cruise home. Suddenly the whole summer changed, certainly in terms of where the Australians were at mentally.

But at no stage in the multi-format series did we feel like we could not retain the Ashes. The Test match was disappointing and the way we played meant we never really deserved to do well, but we still believed, especially with the way we came out in the first Twenty20 game at Chelmsford. But then we batted really poorly in the next game at Hove, even though we had an unlucky run-out at another crucial moment. Going back further there was a vital dropped catch against the Australian captain Meg Lanning and a missed run-out. They were crucial moments within the series and we didn't quite grasp them when we should have done.

I have had a lot of disappointments and I don't take them well at all, even though I have got other experiences to fall back on, like when we lost in the 2013 World Cup and immediately went on to win the next two Ashes series. To be honest, I think the defeats get worse and hurt more as you get older because you know you only have a few more years to play and you want to win every series you contest. I am a pretty proud person and losing the Ashes still cuts deeply. If it didn't feel like this I would be slightly worried. It is a good sign for me that I still have the inner drive to want to put it right.

But when I look at the sport overall it blows me away to think where it has got to so quickly. Every week during this past year there seemed to be some kind of development, whether it was the establishment of a Big Bash League for women or increased prize money given by the ICC to the international women's game, or even my England teammate Sarah Taylor becoming the first female to play Grade cricket in Australia. It has been one thing after another. For any young player, women's cricket is now a really good career option. It is unbelievable how you go places now and people know who you are, although it has taken a little bit of time to adjust to everything. Hopefully the England girls are going to be very much stronger for everything that happened in the summer of 2015. I know we are all energised by the thought of what is lying ahead.

It is an incredibly exciting period to be involved in women's cricket, and therefore a great time for someone to be writing a book about the England women's team. When we heard that we were going to have someone following us about all summer we wondered what to expect, but we welcomed David with open arms and got used to having him around – and he never encroached on our space! It could have been such a great story if we had won the Ashes on the final day, but I know that with the characters we have in the dressing room, and the ups and downs of the summer, this book will be a fascinating read.

Introduction and Acknowledgements

'It is difficult to avoid prejudice, following one team and concentrating on what they do. Naturally this leads to seeing life through their eyes, which is permissible perhaps in a book about the year in the life of one team'
– Hunter Davies in *The Glory Game*

I'D wondered when it would happen, if it happened at all. That moment when my wish to see the girls triumph on the field exceeded the natural desire of an English cricket follower to witness Australia beaten; advanced beyond an author's concern for the most appealing narrative. I'd known such a phenomenon on a couple of occasions and could recall specific tipping points. Neither, I hasten to add, in connection to Arsenal, lifelong fandom of whom I had been able to easily forget in favour of reporting deadlines. They were my team but I'd never been close to them on a personal level. It had been different, though, covering Slough Town for the local newspaper I worked for, riding the team bus to away games and getting to know the players' personalities and peccadilloes. When they had gone two goals up in an FA Cup match at Orient – a tie they contrived to lose in a replay – I'd been on my feet at the back of the Brisbane Road media area. Likewise, fellow writers and I who had hopped back and forth across the Atlantic with the London Monarchs American football team in the early nineties elicited, and ignored, a 'no cheering in the press box' warning as we watched a stirring comeback in a play-off game in New York's Giants Stadium.

Having asked, and been allowed, to follow the England women's cricket team at close quarters during what promised to be a historic year, it didn't take long for me to become aware of my partiality. About half an hour of the first match, in fact.

Somerset's ground at Taunton was already close to being full as I made my way from the England dressing room, where I had watched the early overs, to the press box, where I knew I could make myself a cup of tea. The buzz and chatter around the boundary made it feel like a grand occasion, an atmosphere befitting the first morning of the Ashes, regardless of the gender of the participants. England had already taken a wicket, a catch by Charlotte Edwards, and as I stood by the kettle Katherine Brunt, the quick-tempered and fiercely passionate fast bowler who I had quickly realised was the emotional heartbeat of the team, was bowling the ninth over.

Few sports can provide the split-second elation that cricket offers up in that moment when, often after a long period of inactivity, a wicket suddenly falls. In rugby and football, tries and goals are built over a matter of seconds, with even a shot out of the blue taking its time in finding the net. When a batsman is bowled it is instantaneous, no warning, no mounting inevitability. At least that is my excuse for shouting 'Yes' and, in the action of pumping both fists, almost sending a cup of boiling tea down the necks of those in the back row of press seats when Australian batter Jess Jonassen played across the line and had her stumps flattened. I returned sheepishly to my place on the end of one of the front rows. At least now I knew where I stood.

I pondered long and hard about whether this would be a problem; should I take a more detached view when it came to writing about the games? In the end I decided it wasn't and I shouldn't. In any other fly-on-the-wall type book I had read it was obvious that the author ended up rooting for his team. After all, if he or she didn't care, why should the reader? It is the author's role to create empathy, after all.

In one of the best examples of the genre, *The Glory Game*, published in 1973, Hunter Davies decided that he had no need to remove himself emotionally from the Tottenham team to which he had attached himself. Having written the words that appear at the start of the chapter, he argued that neutrality was the domain of the press men. Another writer, Pete Davies, had unashamedly called his book about a season with Doncaster's female footballers *I Lost my Heart to the Belles*. I might never be able to match the effortless excellence of those particular books, but at least I could use them to justify my own approach.

The fact that I felt close enough to the England girls to be so bothered about their fortunes owed a lot to many people. Firstly, Clare Connor, Director of Women's Cricket at the England and Wales Cricket Board, had welcomed the idea of this book from our first meeting in a coffee shop down the road from Lord's. She had even insisted that 'it shouldn't be sanitised' and immediately set about ensuring the cooperation of all those whose support would help it come to life.

Foremost among them was Paul Shaw, whose responsibility in overseeing elite performance in the English women's game included, but was not confined to, the role of head coach of the national team. Over the course of several months of regular conversations I was only very rarely aware of him being cagey about what he told me and not once did he ask me to leave the dressing room. Anything he did hold back was for the sake of the confidentiality of his employers or out of concern for the feelings of others.

From the outset I was aware that having the support of team captain Charlotte Edwards would be vital and in our first encounter she had appeared somewhat non-committal. In the end, I need not have worried. When I had my first proper chat with her, she could not have been more charming and enthusiastic. At first it felt over-familiar to call her Lottie, as everyone else did, but quickly it became unnatural to consider using any other name. She was never less than engaged and engaging, suggesting different elements of the team I should witness and experience, showing interest in my writing process and always willing to share her thoughts, even when they were not happy ones. It pained me to hear and read some of the stick she would take during a difficult summer.

From a logistics point of view I was lucky that the England women's team was blessed with one of the most efficient and accommodating PR professionals I have ever encountered in media manager Beth Wild. The speed of her responses to questions and requests was consistently impressive. In fact, all the members of the England coaching and background staff, in particular assistant coaches David Capel and Carl Crowe, deserve my gratitude for the way they quickly got used to having me around and never appeared to mind as I pestered them about what they were up to.

Various other people were helpful in many different ways. At the risk of missing someone out, I must thank: Harriet Jackson, Lorraine Burlinson, Chris Watts and Steve Richardson at the ECB; the BBC's Charles Dagnall for support and encouragement; Ebony Rainford-Brent; Don Miles for his photographs; women's cricket followers Raf

Nicholson, Syd Egan and Martin Davies; and, of course, Paul Camillin, Jane Camillin, Duncan Olner, Derek Hammond and everyone else at Pitch Publishing. The Chance to Shine charity deserves mention in any book about women's cricket for the outstanding work they have done in introducing so many young children of both sexes to the sport over the past decade. I am delighted that a percentage of royalties from this book will go towards their work, details of which can be found at www.chancetoshine.org.

But back to the England girls. As the father of four daughters whose ages mostly fitted within the range of the team, I found myself becoming more protective towards them as the summer series wore on, even more so when results and fortune began going against them. I loved their passion for the profession into which they felt so privileged to have been welcomed. None had expected to be paid to play cricket – certainly not so soon – and their determination to wring every ounce out of their sport without taking it for granted, and to give back in return, exceeded anything I had witnessed.

I saw the team spend most of a washed-out day at Worcester circling the stands signing autographs for those fans who were huddling for shelter. I noted the genuine enjoyment they took from introducing youngsters to their sport, many of them remembering what an impact one enthusiastic and generous individual had made on their own lives at a similar age. I saw them happily – no sense of obligation – posing for pictures with fans at the end of every day's play, even when those days had brought bitter disappointment on the field. At Chelmsford, I was approached by a father who had heard me talking about this book on the radio and wanted to make sure I knew that his cricket-mad ten-year-old daughter had written to Jenny Gunn to request a signed photo and received back in the post Jenny's personalised Test match shirt signed by every member of the team.

I was struck by the unencumbered joy the girls derived from each other, their respect and gratitude towards the people who supported them, from friends and family to sponsors, supporters and employers. They were funny, friendly and forthcoming and made an outsider feel most welcome. I didn't ever pursue the issue of the effects of periods on performance – a topic that was being raised by tennis player Heather Watson around the time I embarked on the book – but I did get to know more about sports bras than I ever envisaged. When my time with the team ended, the overriding feeling of relief that usually accompanies the completion of writing a book was absent. I would miss them.

Inevitably I spoke more to some than others, a natural function of the different personalities within the squad, which will come across in the pages that follow. But my sincere thanks are due to every single one of the Girls of Summer. This book is their story and any failure to do them justice is entirely mine.

1

Back to School

'We manage everything for our players, but it's important that we create an environment where they assume responsibility for themselves. There is only so much you can do and when they cross the white line they are on their own' – Paul Shaw

OUTSIDE the row of fancy cosmetics stores on the St Pancras shopping colonnade there's an escalator that carries you up towards a stark choice of travel options. Turn back on yourself after being deposited on the station's upper level and you join the lawyers and lovers heading for Eurostar's hourly departures to Brussels and Paris, with their whiff of sophistication, romance and Agatha Christie-style intrigue. If it's too early in the day for a visit to the champagne bar before departure there are any number of tastefully furnished coffee shops, with their siren calls of rich roast and elegant patisserie, in which to await your boarding call. On this particular January morning, I left such delights to the businessmen checking their tablets and smartphones. Instead, I headed straight ahead to the more prosaic charms of the East Midlands Line, which serves Leicester, Nottingham and Sheffield and where, with any luck, I might be visited at my seat by a tea trolley and a shortbread biscuit.

The sky below which we journeyed north offered a singular graphite shade of grey and was hardly the kind of landscape to inspire thoughts of summer sport. Yet, having disembarked at Loughborough and taken advantage of the returning university students' burden of oversized luggage to arrive first at the taxi rank, I was soon being dropped outside the doors of the National Cricket Performance Centre.

Three stories of unimposing glass and steel, but with an immaculate full-sized playing field spread out alongside it, this north-east corner of the Loughborough University campus had been the educational home of English cricket since 2003. Officially opened by the Queen, its doors had welcomed all the national squads; men and women, boys and girls, from the professional level to the disabled sides. Tour preparation, training camps, rehabilitation, science and research all fell under the centre's remit. Ashes victories, global tournament triumphs and the ascension to the top of the world rankings – in both the men's and women's game – offered justification for the £4.5 million invested in its creation.

On this day it was staging a reunion of sorts; the England women's team's first training session of 2015 – a year which, for the first time, they had seen in as full-time professional players.

It was just before ten in the morning and in the entrance lobby, situated on the structure's middle tier, I was greeted by Beth Wild, the team's engagingly cheery media manager. Fair-haired and smiley, and a decent player herself, she broke off regularly from our conversation to exchange greetings with players, the early arrivals among whom were emerging from the lower level changing rooms. Others I watched lug bulging equipment holdalls through the front doors. Professional, yes. Mollycoddled, clearly not.

'Beth Wild!' called one of the girls, clad in the team's blue and white training uniform.

'Kate Cross!' was the response, delivered on cue.

As similar ritualistic welcomes continued, the mood appeared to be less first-day-of-term than start-of-school-trip, in this case an adventure that would soon find the girls heading to New Zealand before returning home for an Ashes summer.

Heather Knight, vice-captain of the team, pulled up in a taxi; those enrolled as students at the university had merely had to walk from their rooms. 'A few of the others have homes in Loughborough,' Beth explained.

And then: 'Here she is.'

'She' could mean only one person: Charlotte Edwards, team captain. The leading run-scorer and dominant player in women's cricket; the most recognisable face in the game. Right now, that face – bronzed from her three months in Australia with Western Fury – was stuck on the wrong side of the glass, waiting for someone to buzz her in.

While most of the eighteen players given professional contracts by England the previous May had been getting together at Loughborough two days per week during the autumn, the return of Edwards and Knight, who had been playing for the Tasmanian Roar, meant that the team was more or less back together, although a third Australian opportunist, wicketkeeper-batsman Sarah Taylor, was remaining a few weeks longer with the South Australian Scorpions before joining the squad in New Zealand. 'We could have stayed out there as well,' said Heather, 'but the domestic season is winding down and we were missing our families. And it's good to be back with the girls.'

Edwards had barely been back in the country long enough to wash off the sun screen and post on Twitter how happy she was to see her two-year-old niece again. When we spoke five days later at Lord's, she would admit that her return to England had been 'a whirlwind'. 'Out there all I had to do was get up and think about playing cricket. They thought I was a workaholic, but I just loved being able to train every day. Now I'm back I have to remember where I have to be each day and what I'm doing. And I had a pile of post that high,' she added, indicating the approximate size of a cricket stump.

The girls gathered round someone who had become as much mentor and big sister as teammate and captain. 'It will be interesting to see how the dynamic changes now that Lottie and Heather are back,' Beth noted. 'When they are away it is a chance for some of the other personalities to come to the fore a bit more.' It is easy to see why. Seam bowler Tash Farrant was six weeks old when Edwards, her county captain, made her England debut in 1996.

While the players prepared, I took the opportunity for a walk around the university campus, making my way initially to the Bastard Gates, presented by an eponymous former chairman of governors in the thirties. As well as serving as the university's northernmost entrance, the landmark's name continues to amuse many of the institution's 18,000 students. Elsewhere, the architecture is evidence of Loughborough's century of growth. Alongside the 1930s structures that surround the picturesque fountains are the harsh square legacies of sixties and seventies planning and the smooth modern curves of its School of Business and Economics.

Starting out as a technical college early in the twentieth century and reaching university status in 1966, Loughborough achieved its popular reputation through sporting achievement. The Paula Radcliffe Stadium and the Seb Coe Building are a reminder of that heritage. Among the arresting pink- and purple-lettered hoardings that decorated much of the campus, lamp posts bore signs reminding everyone that Loughborough had been 'inspiring winners since 1909'. The relaxed yet purposeful air of the place gives you an idea of why it has been such a productive environment; why it has consistently been credited as 'Best Student Experience' in the land; and why the England and Wales Cricket Board chose it as home.

Before heading back to join the team, I stopped for a cup of tea in the Student Union, where I overheard a young blonde lamenting that her boyfriend had left her to become a professional rugby player in New Zealand, 'after all the support you gave him,' according to her sympathetic companion. The hazards of dating at an institution that churns out elite sportsmen.

Back at cricket headquarters, the sound of Aerosmith signalled that the girls' warm-up session had begun in the main sports hall. Muscles were being stretched and loosened, football and rugby passes exchanged in carefully controlled drills, and sprints undertaken over a variety of distances – all under the direction of strength and conditioning coach Ian Durrant, whose previous role had been with Great Britain's synchronised swimmers. 'Three more minutes,' he yelled at his tiring charges as Coldplay took over from Lenny Kravitz.

Along with the seventeen contracted players present, the four additional girls who completed the Performance Squad meant that the team could be conveniently split into three groups of seven. On either side of the net bisecting the hall, one group was designated for 'scenario batting' while another prepared to bowl at Edwards and Knight, who would be batting in partnership. Former Leicestershire player Carl Crowe, one of the team's assistant coaches, explained the imaginary set-up to his group: 50 for 2 after fifteen overs, with fourteen overs now to be bowled by those not batting and wickets and runs judged by an 'umpire'. Laura Marsh, a spin bowler fighting her way back from injury, drew the first stint as adjudicator, noting Carl's underscored notice on the whiteboard that her 'decision is final'. There would be, Carl warned, a five-minute 'fitness and fielding intervention' after eight overs. It would be 'short and sharp; and there will be the opportunity to take some catches'.

To the backing of the Rolling Stones' 'Gimme Shelter', Anya Shrubsole, the Somerset seamer, began proceedings on the other side of the net by delivering a ball outside off stump. Lottie cut calmly and then trotted a pigeon-toed, hypothetical single to send Heather to the striker's end. A few minutes in, the sound of *Frozen* favourite 'Let It Go' filled the building and brought instant smiles on both sides of the dividing net. Spin bowler Becky Grundy mimed and acted, Dani Hazell sang out the first line of the chorus and her efforts were taken up by Katherine Brunt as the music built to crescendo. It was the first time I had heard a Yorkshire fast bowler singing Disney in the nets, but you never knew what Fred Trueman used to get up to. Suitably inspired, Brunt – no evidence of the back problems that had plagued her career – hurried Knight into popping the ball up to where square leg would have been. Bleached blonde and athletically built, Katherine could frequently be heard emitting grunts of effort and later she shrieked in approval after getting county teammate Lauren Winfield to glove one.

Well-timed shots and good deliveries were greeted all around the hall by approving noises from players and coaches.

'Yes, Grundy.'

'Well played, Nat.'

'Bowling, Anya.'

Another of the coaches, former England all-rounder David Capel, approached Anya and told her that he'd instructed the new batsmen to go after her bowling. 'What are you going to do to combat them?' he challenged. I noticed at some point the music had stopped, which made for an even more focused, intense atmosphere in the hall. Light-hearted comment receded as tiredness advanced.

After an hour in which she'd gone from facing her teammates in one net to batting against the bowling machine in another, and then back again, Lottie was finally able to pull off her helmet and strip the pads from her legs, only to be told that the BBC had a film crew waiting for an interview.

'Hat or no hat?' she asked.

'Probably no hat,' Beth replied.

'That means I'd better go and do my hair.'

'At least you can show off your tan.'

Also free of batting duties, Heather selected a white ball from the pile at the end of the net. Over the previous year, following a hamstring injury, she'd been converted from a seamer to an off-spinner and was still considered something of a novice in her new craft.

'How much bowling did you get over there?' asked Capel, referring to her Australian excursion.

'A lot,' she answered, to the nodding satisfaction of the coach.

During my stroll around campus, I'd crossed the Hazlerigg-Rutland Hall fountain courtyard. Embedded in the paving stones circling the water feature, the university's motto is spelt out in Latin and English: 'Veritate. Scienta. Labore' – 'Truth, Wisdom and Labour'. The man responsible for ensuring that English women's cricket lived up to such lofty values – he who was charged with 'inspiring winners' among the national women's team – was Paul Shaw, who assumed the role of Head of Women's Performance in 2013, five years after arriving at the ECB as Academy head coach. After a couple of years in his original role, he'd progressed to the position of High Performance Manager, so it was a natural succession to put him in charge of the whole kit and caboodle when Mark Lane moved on after five years as head coach, a title that had been made redundant.

Formerly head coach at his hometown club of Barnsley and aged forty when he took up his latest position, 'Shawsy', as those around the team called him, is short in stature and with a cheerful demeanour accentuated by the dimples that appear in his cheeks whenever he smiles, which he does a lot. Moving quietly from net to net, he encouraged and advised, never chided or criticised – at least not on this day – and rarely lost the look of a man deeply in love with what he was doing.

When I asked him for an assessment of his winter months with the girls he answered, 'Things have been going very well. It is nice to have four months with the players, to work with them, not just from a strength point of view but from development as players. Now we'll have four weeks of preparation for New Zealand, going into a fair amount of detail in readiness for their batters and bowlers.'

The thinking behind the 'scenario net' – where Lydia Greenway was helping the batters take their score to a theoretical 112 for 2 in the prescribed time – was obvious. I asked about the logic of having two batsmen on the go in the other one rather than giving them twice as many deliveries in individual nets. 'We want people batting in partnership so they can start reading each other,' Paul explained, his accent soft but clearly indicative of his geographical roots. 'We will also have individual nets, but the closer we get to New Zealand the more we will do to replicate match situations. We might have a fatigue session where we get them running hard between the wickets, or take out the running and just focus on shot selection.'

He continued, 'We manage everything for our players, but it's important that we create an environment where they assume responsibility for themselves. There is only so much you can do and when they cross the white line they are on their own. Carl and Capes are great at facilitating that. They will ask them the right questions at the right time.'

I picked up with Paul the notion of the senior players' return changing the personality of these training sessions. 'We have spent two years creating an environment of high performance and protecting that. When a number of the senior players are away and then come back it does have an effect. The players Lottie, Heather and Sarah left in October might not be the same as when they meet them again. It is important to maintain contact by email, phone and text, to update them on what we have been doing and how the players are growing as cricketers and people. Those three are strong players and personalities, so when they are not here it creates a void. We have encouraged players to grow and fill that void, to grow as people. It is not just about being captain or vice-captain; we want leaders all over the field, players who are going to contribute.'

Lottie would confirm later that she had indeed noticed a change on her return. 'There was much more focus in what they were doing,' she said. 'Everyone seemed to know what they were trying to do and I thought something had clicked. Some of the younger girls used to just come along and wander around net sessions not really knowing what they were trying to do or get out of it. The way it is structured now, Paul's attention to detail, is really good.'

Approximately two hours after they had entered the hall, the team was allowed to break for lunch, although Heather and Lauren's stomachs had to wait until the BBC cameras had finished with them. Like disciplined factory workers, everyone clocked back on at 2pm. No lunchtime finish and off to the snooker hall for these players.

The afternoon would feature two further sessions like those staged in the morning. In the scenario net, the skiddy seam bowling of Kate Cross and Sonia Odedra was being handled expertly by Fran Wilson, trying to fight her way back into the team after a four-year absence. One of the non-contract players, she was driving fluently until ruled to have clipped to imaginary mid-wicket. Such judgements were eagerly sought by the bowlers. Kate looked aggrieved to have been denied a caught behind against Danni Wyatt by the non-decision of Beth Langston, one of the Academy players. When Dani Hazell's off spin was twice edged just wide of the notional wicketkeeper she looked as wounded as if it had happened against the Aussies. Even with the music back on, this was clearly more work than play.

And so it continued until the traditional down-tools time of 5pm, after which it was my turn at the crease, so to speak. I'd been offered the chance to outline to the girls the plan for this book and duly took my place at one end of a large rectangular arrangement of tables in an upstairs meeting room. With everyone spread about me and free of headwear, I sensed the dominating force of Charlotte Edwards, almost six years older than the teammate closest to her in age. I fought against the urge to speak mostly to the skipper, to seek in her facial muscles a twitch or tick that might indicate the level of cooperation I could expect. Wishing to be as inclusive as possible, I endeavoured to share out the eye contact, but couldn't avoid the sense that teammates were similarly watching her body language, taking their cues from their leader.

When Clare Connor, the ECB's Director of Women's Cricket, asked the room, 'Any questions? Lottie?' and the captain offered a good-natured, if somewhat non-committal 'no', I felt like the batsman who had survived a tricky final over of the day. I was off the mark.

* * * * *

Thoughts of New Zealand had already occupied plenty of Paul Shaw's waking hours, but the snow that was wrapping itself round his home in Barnsley a couple of weeks later, a few days before the squad's departure, served to sharpen his anticipation of spending February in the southern hemisphere summer. 'It will be nice to get there and get working,' he said. 'We'll have a little transitional period after we arrive, adapting physically, mentally and emotionally, getting used to the environment, and then we'll step up the preparation for the first ODI.'

Around the time that the men's World Cup would be getting underway on either side of the Tasman Sea, England's women would embark on a series that encompassed five one-day internationals, the first three comprising part of the ICC Women's World Championship, and three Twenty20s. Paul saw the schedule as preparation for the Ashes and for the T20 World Cup in India a year hence, but stressed that those were secondary considerations behind 'winning those games'.

At Lord's a couple of days earlier, Charlotte Edwards had been the face of the announcement of England's fifteen-strong touring party. Admitting she couldn't remember ever losing to New Zealand and acknowledging England's status as favourites, she was diplomatic enough to state that it would be no easy contest and highlighted opponents such as home captain Suzie Bates, who sits alongside her at the top table of excellence in the sport. Much was made of the fact that England had been able to pick from a fully fit squad of players, meaning all those I had met at Loughborough were considered. 'The girls have had the last six to eight months just concentrating on their fitness, preparing themselves and having the support from our medical team,' Lottie had said. 'It makes a huge difference.'

The benefits of that difference might have been lost somewhat on the three players among the contracted eighteen who had been told they were not making the journey. For Tammy Beaumont, who represented England in all formats in 2014, back-up all-rounder Georgia Elwiss and the youngster among the full-time pros, Tash Farrant, it was not the start they had hoped to make to such a big year.

Back in the party were Laura Marsh, who had not played international cricket since 2013 because of a shoulder injury, and another spinner, Becky Grundy, recovered from the groin injury that sidelined her the previous summer.

Coach and captain had been aided in their decisions by fellow selectors Sarah Pickford (chair of the panel), Errol Simms and former Australian international Lisa Keightley, head coach of the England Women's Academy. A full complement of healthy players had made their deliberations more satisfying, yet also more challenging.

'Let me explain the process,' Paul offered. 'Between us all we discuss all the twenty-two players in the Performance Squad and any other players coming through the Academy who might be an outside bet, plus any from outside the system who have shown high potential. We have lots of chats and deliberations and there are a number of things we look for when we select a tour squad of fifteen. One is the players who at this point in time give us the best chance of winning. Then we look at the performance history of the players and we'll consider each player's development plan. Within that there are a number of goals a player has and we look at how they have progressed in line with those goals. The form of the player is important and also the injury history. Are they a high risk? And importantly, one which I am really keen on, is the character, the individual and how that person comes to the fore when they are under pressure.'

Factored into that was the balance between needing to win games now and the desire to look ahead to World Cups at differing formats in 2016 and 2017. 'We consider those time frames,' Paul added, 'but most important is looking to win with the players we have got now.' The potential for the players to adapt to different pitches and conditions, the various tactics and strategies of the opposition formed the basis of further debate. 'A number of those conversations are actually started about five weeks before the selection and then we sit down and formalise those discussions and come up with the best fifteen.'

And then perhaps the more difficult part began: informing, supporting and, in some cases, consoling those who had been omitted. Of course, team selection is a far more compassionate procedure these days; a far cry from the days when England's men would tune in for a radio announcement or check Teletext to discover whether they had been discarded. And if they waited for an explanation, well, they would still be waiting.

The first task belonged to Pickford, a long-time stalwart of England and Yorkshire cricket, who phoned every one of the twenty-two squad players to let them know if they had been selected or left out. The unlucky ones received a further call from Shaw, but only once he had waited forty-eight hours. 'We give them that time to think about it and get their emotions in check. It allows them to think about any questions they want to ask me or any pointers they need. I ask them how they are, offer some feedback and go through the rationale as to why we have left them out. I talk to them about the developmental plans we'll put in place while we are away and then the players get the opportunity to sit down with me another week later and go through it in person to make sure they have clarity in what they need to do next. We are there to develop cricketers, but we also look to develop them as people. In this instance that means understanding the individual, being able to deliver the appropriate message in a really individualised way. That is how you get the best out of them.'

According to Paul, the notion of a 'good tourist' was becoming outdated in the professional era and not something that weighed too heavily on the selectors. 'When you go anywhere for four or five weeks some people adapt quicker than others. Some players, if they are not selected while on tour might find it tough, so we do consider that. But, in essence, if we are picking a home squad or a touring squad we feel confident that the environment we have created is one where the players should be able to cope with any challenge.'

On this occasion, twenty-three-year-old Beaumont, who had been one of the leading scorers in county cricket in 2014 and played in England's summer Test and ODIs, was the most notable omission. 'We had two or three tough decisions and Tammy was certainly one of those,' Paul continued. 'We just felt that we had got a batter ahead of her at this time and wanted to give that batter the opportunity. When you have a squad as fully fit and competitive as ours then it is pleasing to be able to make those decisions in the way that we have.'

A tour such as that to New Zealand, which would be followed by a twelve-month period featuring an Ashes series and a global tournament, posed an interesting challenge in the balance of priorities. 'All the games are important,' said Paul. 'Winning creates winning habits and so on. The games up front with the points on it are the most important and we'll be doing all we can to win. If the latter stages of the tour give us a chance to give younger players more development opportunity then we will do that. But we look at it as a tour that stands alone and our first focus is definitely on winning those games, with the preparation for the Ashes coming on the back of that.'

But there would not merely be conflict between the need for immediate success and the desire for preparation for greater battles ahead. Paul understood his team's role in carrying its sport beyond the current boundaries of comprehension and acceptance, and had mentioned the imperative of playing 'the right kind of cricket'. I asked him to elaborate. 'We always set our sights on playing a really positive and exciting brand of cricket that takes the women's game to the next level and works closely to our vision of inspiring the nation. We're always looking to go that extra yard to be more dynamic, a more powerful type of game.'

That correct 'brand' of cricket was considered so important that, upon return from New Zealand, the girls would
have several meetings at which they were invited, or rather
instructed, to create their own definitions of what it meant.
Paul saw such responsibility as 'a great opportunity' for him
and his team rather than any kind of burden. 'We can create
something really special here and lead the global women's
game. I see it as a chance to really excite people around the
world.'

When I mentioned those comments to Shaw's immediate
boss, Clare Connor, she looked pleased. 'I feel that really
strongly and it is interesting that Paul does as a coach,' she
said. 'I chair the ICC women's committee so I do feel our
wider responsibility. I am so well supported here at the ECB
and the women's game is so well supported that I do feel we
have a responsibility to try to take things forward.'

2

Home and Away

'Before, when you were out of the team,
you were left to your own devices to a large
extent. Now we have a lot more support in
place' – Tammy Beaumont

ENGLAND'S first women's touring team had left home
eighty years earlier, bound for Australia, where they
won two Tests and drew a third, and New Zealand,
whom they beat by an innings. The squad had included four
Marys and a trio of Bettys, and had taken four weeks to get
there by boat. The 2015 tourists – with a couple of Danielles,
a Katherine and a Kathryn – arrived in New Zealand's Bay
of Plenty within forty hours, after three flights and a three-
hour coach journey.

Their first few days on the north-east coast of New
Zealand's north island were a mix of intense practice sessions,
walks up nearby Mount Maunganui – the landmark that
gives the beach resort its name – a trip to the movie set of

The Lord of the Rings and a one-sided warm-up match against the Northern Spirit. Practice at the pretty Bay Oval ground, site of the first three one-day internationals, had allowed the girls to enjoy the feel of grass below their feet again after several months stuck indoors, a gift received most gratefully by those whose job it was to run in and bowl. Mind you, the wind did make it feel like Scarborough at times.

Net sessions and that one low-key game offered only a few clues to the first team selection of the year. The top five in the order appeared set: Charlotte Edwards, Heather Knight, Lauren Winfield, Sarah Taylor and Lydia Greenway. The new ball would be shared by the established pairing of Katherine Brunt and Anya Shrubsole, who would receive support from seam bowling all-rounder Jenny Gunn and possibly Nat Sciver, if deemed ready to bowl while work progressed on remodelling her action. The final two places boiled down to a question of whether to play one or two specialist spinners and, if the singular option was preferred, whether the additional spot would go to Amy Jones as a batter or Kate Cross as a third fast bowler. When the players gathered on the outfield to award slow left-armer Becky Grundy her first ODI cap it emerged that her three wickets in the warm-up match had secured her a place. At the toss, won by Edwards, it was revealed that off-spinner Dani Hazell had edged out Cross and Jones.

A strong hint of green on a flat-looking wicket persuaded Edwards to put New Zealand in, but then England proceeded to play like a team that had not seen action for five months. A succession of bowlers were unable to prevent New Zealand reaching 157 before the fall of a wicket. Analysing for BBC Radio, former teammate Ebony Rainsford-Brent offered particular concern that Brunt's bowling lacked 'that sort of oomph' of a couple of years earlier. Knight eventually took four wickets as the home side were pegged back to 240 for 8, which included a sixth ODI century for Bates, dropped in the

40s by Lydia Greenway, generally considered the best fielder in the women's game. England's batting was no less disjointed and disappointing, particularly the loss of both openers, Knight and Edwards, to careless run-outs. Only a ninth-wicket partnership of 47 between Hazell and Shrubsole lifted them to 173 all out in the forty-fifth over. It had been easy to mistake which was the fully professional team.

Professional. In the case of England's female cricketers it is a word that brings with it great opportunity. Yet it also comes burdened with accountability: to employers, of course, and also – especially in the eyes of those quick to jump online to criticise – to the wider cricket public. When, after England's loss, BBC Radio's Henry Moeran posted on Twitter a picture of himself with reserve batter Danni Wyatt, whom he'd bumped into on the evening of the game, it received this reply from one user: 'Yay, more selfies. England women just get demolished by part-time minows *(sic)* and we get selfies. Professional.'

'Being professional allows us more time to work on our skills,' said Laura Marsh, 'but there is more pressure from the outside. We put a lot of pressure on ourselves because we have been quite successful and we expect to win most games we play, but especially with things like Twitter and social media we get asked more questions if we don't perform. There is more of a backlash.'

When some of the girls tweeted pictures of the view after a gruelling and fully-authorised trek up the mountain after the third game, team management had to remind them, 'You are losing. Don't make it look like you are on holiday.'

Lottie often warned players not to leave themselves exposed on social media. 'One thing I have learned is that when you are winning you can do what you want, but when you are losing there are lines you can't cross,' she explained. 'It's something I have tried to get across to the girls. We are not saying that you can't go out, but you don't need to tweet everything and you don't have to tell everyone on Facebook what you are doing. There is more scrutiny on us.'

Welcome to the modern world.

The day after England's loss, Tammy Beaumont told me, 'I had never really experienced too much trolling [on Twitter], then last summer after we became professional I noticed more unpleasant comments sent my way or to the girls. It is not very nice, but we have to take that. If I was working in an office I'd have an annual review, so I am just being judged for my job – just slightly differently.'

We were seated in the MCC Cricket Academy's canteen at Lord's, where she was about to join former England batsmen Owais Shah and Ali Brown to test cricket equipment for *All Out Cricket* magazine. That Tammy – short, dark-haired, wearing a Jack Wills hoodie and surprisingly bright-eyed after an early morning drive down the M1 from Loughborough – was in London rather than New Zealand was a subject she approached as philosophically as she did the antics of Twitter critics.

There are few more potentially destructive places than the periphery of a sports team; the space occupied by the reserve. It's a neighbourhood where, if you're not careful, self-doubt and paranoia can gang up with resentment and frustration and turn the occupant into a mess of contradiction and confusion, especially if that person has previously known life within the comfortable inner circle of the team.

Beaumont was there right now. But, in a testament to the closeness of the England team and her own level-headedness, she showed little sign of succumbing to the perils of such a place – or to the voices that try to get inside your head and make you root against players whose spot should be yours. 'I was very disappointed not to go to New Zealand. It is weird not being there, but at least I am heading off to Dubai in two days' time. I am doing my Level 3 coaching course and coaching the Loughborough University ladies' team out there. It is obviously difficult from a personal point of view but I am someone who is team first, self second. Lauren Winfield, who has taken my place in the team, is my best friend. I sent her a message saying, "Go on, mate, go well." A few years ago I might have been a bit more out for me.'

Still without an England half-century to her name in two Tests, twenty-three ODIs and thirty-three T20s, Beaumont admitted that the situation for players omitted from the team 'has got a lot better', adding, 'I have been in and out of the team quite a lot so I can speak from experience. Before, when you were out of the team, you were left to your own devices to a large extent. I would work hard but I love training with other people and pushing myself against others. It was particularly tough when I missed the last Ashes in Australia. I lived with four girls and three of them were out there, so we had an empty house. Now we have a lot more support in place. We have a strength and conditioning coaching intern working with us so we're in the gym about four times a week. We have got access to other camps and are getting real support.'

When I spoke to Lottie about her Kent teammate, she admitted that one of the challenges of her position was to deal sympathetically with players who were left out of the squad. 'I have always said this: I have never been dropped in my life. To actually empathise with someone who has been dropped I have to say, "Well I don't know how you feel, I can only imagine it." That is tough for me, to try to support them and let them talk to me. Dropping them is hard because I am always involved in some way. What do you say to someone who is not playing? I hate it actually. It is especially hard with someone like Tammy, who I have played a lot of cricket with. It's a tough part of the job.'

Tammy found her way into cricket – and this will become a recurring theme – by following a course set by her father, Kevin, a good club player at Sandwich Town in Kent, and older brother Michael. 'I was a massive tomboy until I was fifteen or sixteen. Sixth-form shopping was the first time I bought a dress. Even when I was a bridesmaid my mum would have to bribe me to get into the dress.'

The question of whether cricket plants the seed of such tomboyism or merely harvests its crop is one for the anthropologists, but it was within the game's environment that Tammy felt most at home, removed from the disinterest of non-sporty girlfriends and gradually earning the respect of the boys with and against whom she played. 'My brother went to a summer cricket camp when he was about nine and I was six. They were low on numbers and the guy running it said, "Do you want to stay, Tammy?" Mum let me off shopping with her and after those four days I was completely hooked. I carried on practising with my brother, who was so good with me. He'd let me get out about five times before he made me swap over. The first hard-ball game I played was when my dad was trying to get a team up and ringing around all these people. I was saying, "Dad, I can bat better than that boy, why can't I play?"'

Tammy is what her England teammates call a 'badger' – 'completely cricket mad. I used to sit there and score the Test matches off the telly.' Although right-handed, it was Graham Thorpe who made the biggest impression on her. 'My dad and brother are left-handers so I have always had a thing for left-handers.'

Success in boys' cricket saw her representing Kent girls' under-11s at the age of ten. At age twelve she joined a women's club, The Moat CC, and was in the first team within a year. 'You learned the hard way in boys' cricket. They wouldn't take it easy. You'd hear comments like "you can't come to nets" and "they have got a girl playing". It makes you think, "I will show you."'

Hers was a steady and mostly smooth progression through county age group cricket, including her first century for the county as a twelve-year-old. She looked pained, though, when recalling that 'for some reason the under-15s coach didn't really like me; I was batting at seven and not doing anything'. She scored particularly heavily as an under-17 player, by which time she had already had her first encounter with the county's greatest player. 'When I first went to Kent training when I was about fifteen I got put in a net with Charlotte and Lydia. I was so star-struck. I hung on every word she said. Still do, to be fair.'

Elevation through the England Academy to the full national team came in a rush, with her England ambition fulfilled at the age of eighteen in the West Indies. 'I always knew I wanted to play for England. There is a story that my mum tells everyone about when my dad's team was playing against Lashings and I went to watch straight from training. I was about eight and was walking around with my bat in my hand. This old West Indian guy who used to play for them' – quaintly, she has no idea who it was – 'said to me, "What you doing with a bat, girl?" and I told him, "I am going to play for England one day." He said, "Come on, I will throw you some," and after that he said, "You might do actually."'

Tammy bats with the kind of flamboyant back-lift that served Brian Lara so well but which, when dismissed cheaply, can look unnecessarily showy. With her friends on the other side of the world and magazine photographers waiting for her in the Lord's nets, she knew it had yet to take her as far as she wanted. Being sent home to her shared flat in Loughborough without a plane ticket to New Zealand was a miserable feeling and my mention of Paul Shaw's empathy with players left out of England's team prompted a smile and a reply that began with a chuckle. 'I love Shawsy to bits. He is a real people person so the last thing he wants to do is just say you are rubbish or you're not good enough. He will tell you why you have been left out, but he will also try and protect your feelings a little bit, which isn't a bad thing. But sometimes you might want things to be a little bit more clear-cut: "These people are better than you are at this moment in time and this is why." But I sat with Shawsy before they left to make sure I was working on what he felt I need to work on, not just what I thought. We have come together and agreed on some areas to work on.

'For me it is trying to up my fitness levels; I am quick but can't do it over and over again. Then it's my mindset going into bat and getting relaxed at the crease. My technique is pretty much there. It is about giving myself a chance to build a score. My one-to-one coach, Carl Crowe, and I talk about what I need to do to cement a place in the team. I just need to get a fifty. He'll ask, "Well, how are you going to do that if you have never done it? Why can't you just go out as if you have scored one, and then it will happen." In my mind, it is pretty much one innings away. It has happened at Kent and the same with the England Academy. It takes a little while longer than I would like, but when it comes the next one is never far away.'

Lottie would confess, 'Tammy is a tough one – she has been in and out. It's good that she thinks that she is close because once you get that score you do feel you belong at that level. That sense of belonging is the hardest thing to crack with a lot of them.'

'It is about trying to be patient,' Tammy concluded, unaware of how much the months ahead would test that patience. 'I honestly feel more confident than I ever have.'

* * * * *

In New Zealand, England's confidence, and competence, emerged from its hiding place in the second ODI. Having won the toss, Edwards (65) and Taylor (45) took the tourists to 129 for 2 and, even though an ugly collapse restricted them to 194 all out, the foundation had been laid for victory. Looking sharper than forty-eight hours earlier, Brunt and

Shrubsole helped dismiss New Zealand for 104, the former picking up two wickets and the latter effectively settling the game with a four-wicket spell in the middle overs. 'I haven't bowled brilliantly on this trip, I'll be the first to admit that,' said Anya. 'I owed the girls a little bit in terms of wickets. I just bowled straight with a lot of cutters.'

Two days later, Edwards and Knight had England sitting at 71 without loss in the seventeenth over until the skipper feathered one to the keeper for 40. When Winfield went for a never-convincing 29 it was 133 for 2, but then followed another clatter of middle-order wickets and the eventual loss of Knight for her ODI-best score of 79. 'I was quite scratchy to start with and I had to fight through,' she admitted. 'It was one of the toughest fifties I have had to get for England.' The insertion of Jones for Greenway had done little to change the familiar pattern and it needed some more thumps by Brunt and Shrubsole to achieve 217 for 9. England's bowlers were tidy and economical enough to keep the game alive until only eight balls were left, but penetrating enough to take only one wicket, the prized one of Bates. For the second time in three games they allowed a partnership of more than 150 as Priest ended unbeaten on 96 and Amy Satterthwaite hit the winning runs to reach 76.

The manner of the New Zealand team's celebrations – they posted on YouTube a video of them standing in a circle singing and chanting in the dressing room – demonstrated the unexpected nature of England's failure to launch. And, despite an ECB story pointing out that their one victory had moved them into joint second in the ICC Women's Championship and the reminder by many that there were still two ODIs to play, there was no disguising the disappointment of being 2-1 down in the section of the series that mattered most.

Despite the widening knowledge and understanding of women's cricket it was still, it appeared, possible to take opponents a little by surprise; every new series a potential journey into the unknown. If Australia, for example, wanted a full insight into England's latest personnel and playing patterns prior to the Ashes they'd have to have someone in New Zealand with a notebook and laptop inputting their own data, rather than relying on full broadcast coverage and statistical breakdown. The videos England had watched of New Zealand prior to the tour proved to have been overtaken by developments in their hosts' team and tactics.

'It is a bit of an eye-opener,' Lauren told the ECB website. 'They have played some really good cricket and we have got to improve.' Perhaps remembering the pre-tour insistence of so many, she added, 'I don't think there was an under-estimation.'

What was widely debated was whether the team had needed more than one warm-up match before being pitched into real action. Certainly, the only meaningful contributions from the batters had been from those who'd been playing in the Australian summer. Paul would argue, 'We could have done with an extra warm-up game and the one we had wasn't challenging enough.'

What seemed to be generally accepted, though, was that England had played sloppily and tentatively. The perfect antidote to that, it was suggested, was the timely arrival of the three-game Twenty20 series, beginning four days hence at the Cobham Oval in Whangerei, the country's northernmost city. Forced by the format to free themselves with the bat, the real England would emerge after a six-hour bus ride from Mount Maunganui, it was anticipated. It was a general theme returned to by the various blogs written by the players, Cross for Sky Sports, Gunn for the ECB's website and Knight for the BBC. 'We just haven't batted well enough,' said the latter. 'In all three matches we looked well set to make a decent score, but clusters of wickets in the middle overs have really cost us.'

In the opening T20 game, New Zealand never recovered from losing their first five wickets for 11 runs and their final score of 60 all out meant they had only just limped past the previous lowest women's international score – 57 by Sri Lanka. As she had done in the previous two 50-over games, Knight had opened the bowling with her off spin, picking up 3 for 6 in four overs. Hazell took two wickets in the middle and Shrubsole took care of the tail. Along the way Greenway re-established her reputation with one of those catch-it, toss-it-up, catch-it-again boundary dismissals that she performs too regularly to be of any great surprise. Edwards guided England unfussily to an eight-wicket victory in the twelfth over.

Batting first twenty-four hours later, Edwards fell without scoring before Winfield anchored the innings with 48 off 59 balls, her most accomplished performance of the tour. Knight's 30 off 15 balls, including a six over mid-wicket – only England's second in the format since January 2014 – saw them to a score of 122 for 5. To defend it they would need to get off to a good start, which was exactly what they didn't do, Bates and Priest sharing an opening partnership of 64. Marsh and Cross, the final member of the squad to be picked for an international, took a couple of wickets each, but the damage had been done and the home side won by six wickets with four balls in hand. Just in time to watch the humiliation inflicted by their male counterparts on England in the World Cup.

The deciding game of the T20 series came five days later at the Bert Sutcliffe Oval in Lincoln – about fifteen miles south-west of Canterbury – where most of the pre-game attention centred on Edwards's remarkable achievement of leading England for the 200th time since taking over from Clare Connor late in 2005. The team she led out had more or less picked itself. Brunt returned after being rested for the previous game, although illness to Shrubsole made it somewhat surprising that Cross was the one healthy player to be left out. A quad muscle injury, meanwhile, sidelined Winfield, replaced by Jones, and Gunn was back in.

Edwards sent the opposition in and watched her bowlers limit New Zealand to 97 for 9, Knight, Marsh, Gunn and Hazell taking two wickets each, the latter's first giving her an England record 64 in the format. Edwards fell early in reply but, as she insisted, 'Today was not about me, it was about winning the series,' and she was happy enough to see the job completed in the penultimate over by Brunt's leg-side six after Knight, Taylor, Sciver and Greenway had all chipped in.

The resumption of the ODI series brought forth England's most complete performance of the tour, spearheaded by the bowling of Cross and the discovery of form by Taylor. Having removed the dangerous pairing of Bates and Priest in her first spell, Cross, upright of action and determined of spirit, returned to achieve her first five-wicket haul for England (5 for 24). Grundy, back from injury, weighed in with 3 for 36 as New Zealand were dismissed for 168 off the final ball of their fifty overs. Gunn, still struggling to make an impact with the ball, equalled a world record with four outfield catches, while Sciver added two and a run-out. The early loss of Knight was soon forgotten as Edwards (64 not out) and Taylor (89 not out) calmly accumulated their runs before the latter's flurry of fours – seven in the final eleven balls she faced – hastened their team to victory in the thirty-third over.

It had been a strange old tour. Not only had results, until this latest England victory, alternated back and forth, but every game in either format had been one-sided. The teams appeared incapable of playing at a similar level on the same day. At various points it appeared as though the ODI series decider, the third contest at Lincoln Oval in five days, would at last provide a nail-biter, but in the end England's elevated form of the latter stages of the tour took them to another comfortable victory.

Having elected to field once more, England saw their hosts breeze to 34 off five overs before the openers both gifted catches off the effervescent Grundy. Sophie Devine and Katie Perkins each responded with half-centuries as New Zealand closed on 230 for 8, Grundy having added a third wicket and Cross and Marsh capturing a pair apiece.

The score appeared competitive, even more so when Knight was trapped in the first over, but Edwards and Taylor offered another calming partnership of 59 before the skipper fell. By this stage of the tour, though, Taylor was in irresistible form, firm drives and well-balanced leg-side clips flowing from her bat. Greenway offered her support and another partnership with Sciver had taken the score to 167 when Taylor took on a throw from the outfield and was run out for 93 off 99 balls, including ten fours. Sciver took up the baton and had moved briskly to 65 off only 63 balls by the time England completed a five-wicket victory with five overs remaining.

By the end of the tour England were playing in the manner and with the command expected of them and most of the key players in the squad could look back with some satisfaction. Edwards had been her usual consistent presence at the top of the order, while Knight, despite some disappointments in the later games, had performed well as an all-rounder. Winfield had been finding form when she got injured and Greenway chipped in at important moments later on after a slow start. Sciver's final innings, her highest for England, was reward for some handy earlier contributions, while Taylor's storming end to the tour erased memories of some eccentric earlier dismissals, saw her named as best player of the ODI series and reaffirmed her reputation as one of the most devastating and inventive run-scorers in the world. Seam bowlers Brunt, Shrubsole and Cross all had excellent performances to take away with them, as did spinners Grundy, Marsh and Hazell. England ended the tour with plenty of options for the make-up of their attack.

As on any tour, some would go home frustrated on a personal level, even if they took pride and satisfaction from the collective achievement. Young batters like Jones and Wyatt had few opportunities and failed to capitalise on those that did come their way, while veteran Gunn saw her role diminishing with bat and ball as her wicketless ODI series progressed, not even being called upon to bowl in the final game. After more than 200 England appearances, her continued presence appeared to be one of the issues facing the management in the coming months.

Paul Shaw's assessment upon his return home was that 'the players learned a lot about themselves and we learned a lot about the players. From that perspective, and the resilience the players had to show, it will hold us in good stead as we go into the summer.'

He continued, 'It was a challenging start to the tour. New Zealand have a new coaching team in Hamish Barton and Jacob Oram, who have been working with their players for quite a while now, and they have certainly moved forward. That presented a challenge in itself. What was pleasing was the way we came back from 2-1 down to win four of five games with some pretty good cricket. And to get results at the end of the tour when we were continually rotating players because of injury was pleasing.'

Yet those injuries had been worrying, especially in a squad that Paul insisted was 'much fitter than they have been'. One of the immediate tasks would be to 'review the players' programmes to see if there is anything that we need to change'. From a form perspective, the areas of concern were clear when, in the days after returning from New Zealand, the England Academy squad was announced for a series of games against their Australian counterparts in Dubai.

Beaumont, as she'd expected, was included – as captain – but so were Winfield and Jones from the senior squad. It appeared the three could find themselves competing for one available place in the Ashes batting order. Danni Wyatt, meanwhile, would instead attend a forthcoming spin camp in Sri Lanka.

'We are closer to the line-up we want,' Lottie ventured. 'I could probably tell you the Test team and the ODI team but in terms of what we have learned in New Zealand I wanted to be clearer on who was our number four batter. We have not established that.'

Explaining the Academy squad selection, Paul said, 'With Lauren and Amy it is really important that we give them as much exposure as we can against tough opposition in tough conditions. It puts them in a good place for the Ashes. For Tammy, she can develop from a leadership perspective and it is an opportunity to get more experience in a tough environment and work her way back into the England squad. We considered Danni strongly, but we think it is really important she spends time at a spin camp, batting against spin and getting her back to her best form from a spin bowling perspective.'

So was I speaking to a happy coach four months out from the beginning of the Ashes series? 'Everyone will tell you I am never 100 per cent happy with anything and I think that is a good thing. What I would say is that we have learned a lot in New Zealand and over the last few months. From that point of view we are in a good position. It gives us every opportunity in the coming months to work in the areas we feel will move us forward. We are in a decent place, but we could be in a better place.'

The winter's cricket, then, was over and even though Britain had not yet welcomed spring, the girls now had a clear view of summer. The Aussies would be here before they knew it.

3

The First Lady

'At my age I constantly want to be challenged in what I am doing and I feel like my game has gone to another level. The work we are doing and the commitment we have has reignited something in me' – Charlotte Edwards

A S she chatted over a latte almost as big as her head, she played absent-mindedly with one of those long stirring sticks, pointing it at certain times for emphasis before eventually it snapped between her fingers. Two decades in the England team, more than 200 games as captain, almost 10,000 international runs, yet Charlotte Edwards, it appeared, still couldn't bear not to be wielding a piece of wood in her hands.

'We have three weeks off after the New Zealand tour,' she said, with almost two-thirds of that sabbatical still to go. 'It has been quite a challenge. I am just bored now. It is really weird; you think you want a break but I struggle with it sometimes, switching off from it all. I am just working on my fitness at the moment.'

This is someone who explains that, away from playing cricket, 'I watch a lot of cricket.' Someone whose face, with her brown hair pulled back, reveals the beginnings of lines around the eyes that, as well as adding extra warmth to an omnipresent smile, bear witness to hour after hour of squinting down the wicket as bowler after bowler has tried to prise her away from the crease. Which makes it all the more surprising when she speaks of the times when she was terrified of showing up to play the sport she loves and which she has served so loyally that she has earned both MBE and CBE.

'I captained all the [Huntingdonshire] county boys' teams I played in and it was incredible. But it was so tough. I would arrive at games and the parents would look at me and snigger. I used to dread turning up for county boys' fixtures. I would walk in with my bag and think, "I have got to find a women's changing room here. They are not going to realise I am playing." Going up to Leicestershire and Nottinghamshire – big counties, mining counties – these lads sniggering at me; it was horrible. I am quite shy and I won't push myself forward unless I have to. I really hated it. But it made me so tough. I had to prove myself every time I played cricket. These boys would bowl beamers at my head and I would go out there without a helmet because I can't let these boys know in any way I am worried – and there were some quick bowlers. My dad was working on the farm and my mum didn't drive, so I had to deal with it on my own. In a way it was the best thing that happened; I couldn't run to anyone. My dad said, "You go off and sort them out," but it used to churn me up. Now, playing for England is a doddle, I tell you.'

New Zealand, as it transpired, had been anything but 'a doddle'. The home team's winning of two of the three

ODIs that counted for the ICC Women's Championship offered evidence of resurgence in the women's game in that country and an antidote to fears that England and Australia were coming to dominate too much. It also meant that Lottie became the latest England captain to be 'looking for positives' from disappointing results.

'It was tough actually,' she said. 'We looked a bit rusty early on so I was pleased with how we bounced back. We didn't win the ICC Championship part of the series, but there was a lot more to come out of it than that for us as a group as we move into the Ashes. It seems like we need to get our backs to the wall to show that kind of determination and that is something we have got to look at. How we start a series has been a little bit of a problem. We can't keep going through it every series – in an Ashes series it can potentially all happen too late. We have got a bit to work on, but we are still winning series and that is the important thing.'

The most trumpeted aspect of the New Zealand series was the celebration of Lottie's 200th game as England captain. The host nation's most illustrious cricketer, Sir Richard Hadlee, managed to offer his congratulations to Kate Cross by mistake and you got the impression that Lottie would have been happy to let her young teammate deal with all the fuss while she got on with the business of actually skippering the team. It was, after all, a job she'd done pretty well, as four Ashes successes and the dual World Cup and World T20 successes of 2009 bore out.

'She is a fantastic person and was always a potential captain,' said Clare Connor, her predecessor as team leader. 'She and I roomed together a lot. It was as though we were programmed to wake up in the early hours of the morning chatting about who was going to bat where or what would your boundary fielders be if so-and-so was bowling. For a number of years we were the only two badgers in the team like that. The others loved cricket, but in terms of stats and fielding positions, and talking about it endlessly, they had to put us together otherwise we would have just driven everyone else mad. I don't think I have ever seen hunger like hers in anyone else, especially now towards what may be the latter years of her career. She has got more enthusiastic and hungry and watching her journey as a captain has been lovely.'

Lottie was quick to point out that her progress as captain since taking over in 2005/06 had featured its share of challenges. 'You think you are ready but it takes time to handle all the things that come with the job. At the start you are trying to find your feet and find out what works. It was only in 2008 I really felt I was getting to grips with it. My form was coming into its own and the team was playing well, and then 2009 speaks for itself. But then we went into a bit of a lean spell after that. Losing in the 2013 World Cup – not even making the final – was really tough to take. I really considered retiring, but there was this feeling that I hadn't achieved everything I wanted to.'

What followed was further consistent run-scoring and the honour of being named as one of the Five Cricketers of the Year in the 2014 *Wisden Cricketers' Almanack*, making her only the second woman – after Claire Taylor – to receive that accolade. As captain, she achieved victories in the first two multi-format Ashes series, at home in 2013 and in Australia in the following winter, where her highest T20 score, 92 not out, earned the series-settling victory. Even though there was the disappointment of defeat to the same opponents in the final of the 2014 World Twenty20, just as there had been two years earlier, she concluded, 'Sat here now it is probably a good decision that I didn't retire. I really wanted to take the team forward.'

Balancing the burdens of leadership and scoring runs had never appeared to be much of a problem, even though she insisted, 'When I first took over the captaincy I put too much pressure on myself. I just wanted to win all the games myself and lead from the front and all that. I realised quite quickly that you have got to separate the two roles.'

Nowadays, the fact that captaincy dominates her thoughts – it is still field placements and bowling changes that wake her up in the early hours – has added an additional element of freedom to her own performance. 'Captaincy helps my batting. You don't get so fixated on yourself. If you are worried about fourteen other people, that kind of takes the pressure off me in a strange way. When I am batting I am Charlotte and when I am fielding I am the England captain. I really love the time I am batting. I don't have to worry about anyone else and when I train I am really strict with myself; no thoughts about anyone else. If someone tries to talk to me I'll say, "This is my training session and I will come and talk to you later about what field you want to have." I am quite selfish about my batting time.'

The respect, affection, even love, that Lottie inspires in her teammates is obvious. In a video released by the ECB to celebrate her captaincy landmark, the girls took obvious delight in recalling moments of greatness on the field and high comedy off it, including karaoke performances of Bonnie Tyler's 'Total Eclipse of the Heart' and some questionable dance moves.

'The fact that they can take the piss is brilliant,' said Clare. 'Even though a lot of the younger players say she has been their hero, she doesn't take herself too seriously, which maybe someone after playing international sport for so long could have done. She has great banter with the girls and, although she doesn't really drink, when she drinks after a big series win it is hilarious. The dance moves come out and the girls just think it is the best thing ever. They think the world of her.'

Those post-series celebrations even acquired some notoriety when, after the Ashes victory in Australia, she tweeted her intention to 'get completely smashed'. Cue indignation from keyboard warriors reminding her of her duties as a role model and the evils of alcohol. While unapologetic about her right to go out and celebrate success, she admitted that the episode had made her more aware of the scrutiny attached to her every comment. 'In the last two years I've learned that everything I say like that becomes a media problem. Sometimes you have got to learn the hard way.'

As sad as it was that someone who had led her country to such a triumph could not express her intention to enjoy the moment in the manner of sports people down the ages, it is even more bizarre to believe that anyone could ever accuse Lottie of being anything other than the ideal person to hold up as an example before any youngster, whatever their sport, whatever their gender.

Lauren Winfield is one of those who grew up idolising her. 'What a fantastic opportunity to be picked with one of those people who has been your hero, to walk out alongside her opening the batting,' she said. But when Lauren arrived in the England squad as a star-struck hopeful she found it was Lottie the person rather than the cricketing icon who was on hand to ease her nerves.

'Lot was a real big part of my integration. Obviously as captain she feels it is her role to look after the new players, to help them find their feet and fit in. I spent quite a bit of time rooming with her. She felt it was important to get to know me and vice-versa. I felt at home straight away. Her passion for the game is phenomenal. She watches and talks cricket all hours. You have a lot of conversations around the game, sometimes about the opposition or the men's game. If we have played a game we will come back to the hotel and sit and chat about what has gone on. She likes to make sure we are moving forward.'

Katherine Brunt explained, 'I go to the nets and bowl my allocation and that will do me. Lottie will go in the nets and bat and bat and bat, and never get bored. Sometimes when I see her go into an international match it is like she is going into a net and she is just going to stand there and hit as many balls as she can. The pressure is there, but when you watch her it is so effortless. She absolutely loves the game more than anyone. She is Mrs Cricket. She has a hard core passion for the game and I don't think she will leave it until somebody shoves her out the door. I have nothing but respect for her.'

Lydia Greenway's entire cricketing career, for Kent and England, had been played in Lottie's company. 'She is very self-motivated and always wants to get better,' she said. 'She never thinks she has done it all. Tactically, she knows the game inside out and she has been in so many different situations and has the skills to adapt. She is a very outgoing and bubbly character, and always wants to be involved in things going on. She has always been good at developing relationships with people coming into the team and made them feel part of it very quickly.'

'We've got this,' has become a featured catchphrase of Lottie's team talks, but there appeared to be no danger of familiarity eroding her influence. 'People know where the line is with her,' Lydia added. 'They have that much respect for her that Lottie can afford to be that outgoing person without fear of any misunderstandings.'

According to another county teammate, Laura Marsh, 'She sets the example. She has such a big passion for the game, which is growing, which is brilliant for everyone else and is quite infectious. She has been a brilliant person to learn from.'

And Tammy Beaumont said, 'Off the pitch she is one of the girls, one of the jokers. She is really bubbly and energetic, doesn't stand out or go off on her own. She doesn't give us mother talks but on the pitch she is definitely the leader, a really strong authoritative figure.'

Lottie summed it up like this: 'I am a lot of things to the girls. That is why I enjoy the role, it is very varied. Sometimes I have got to be very hard on them, use my authority and experience. I don't shout and bawl too often but when I do I think it becomes more powerful. I try to pass on my cricketing knowledge and free them up as much as possible. They can put too much pressure on themselves. With my experience of times when I was struggling I can tell them it's fine, that I have been through it and come out the other end.

'I try to have as much fun with them as possible and help them relax because when I took on the role I wanted to be myself and be part of the team. I think that is one of my strengths. I think I am one of the girls, but they know where the line is. They know I have extra responsibilities and I think they all respect that. But if there is a night out I will go and be part of that. I think that is important. They love to see me let my hair down and they love to take the mickey. I don't do it loads and I don't really drink, but I always tell them if we win a series, they will see me let my hair down. Equally, they respect that I need time on my own. I have my own room on tour. There is a lot that comes with the job and they respect my quiet time, as they call it.'

Experience and achievement had afforded her that esteem, along with age of course. Thirty-five when the team departed for New Zealand, no other member of the squad was at that time out of their twenties, something Lottie admitted she had 'really struggled with at times'.

'One of my really good friends, Arran Brindle, stepped down last year and she was often the person I turned to when we were away. I missed that person to go to and bounce things off. But I have got her on the end of a phone and there is Clare, who is a good friend. There are still people I can turn to when I am having a difficult moment. Anyway, the girls don't need to see that. I don't want to burden them. Some of my thoughts I want to keep private; you don't want them talking about it within the group and it becoming an issue. You really need to trust the people you are telling things and I haven't built that kind of relationship with some of them. Obviously I am very close with Paul and I can go to him, but sometimes I don't want to burden him either.'

Lottie was conscious that it was she from whom the team would take their cue, mirroring her reactions and her disposition. It was another load she had come to accept. 'If I am moody then sometimes I put on an act, my poker face. I have got to be very consistent. I walk into breakfast every morning and I am the same. I walk into a team meeting and I am the same. There will be certain days when I am not quite on it but it is never too dramatic and that is really important among a young group. They think I am the most confident person in the world and I always portray that, but there are times when I am short of runs and I am feeling down.'

Like *Monty Python*'s Brian telling the crowd underneath his window to think for themselves – only for them to reply as one that they will – Lottie was looking forward to more of the team developing their own voices. 'It is not just my view that counts,' she insisted. 'That is what I tell them. Sometimes you have got to have your own idea.' This is my thought, she tells them, but you are entitled to your opinion. Whether Lottie follows their suggestion doesn't matter. The fact that they have thought for themselves is the important thing. Paul used the analogy of a car's satnav. There was little value, he said, in blindly following instructions if you were going to be lost the moment it wasn't available and you had to find your own way.

But, Lottie shrugged, 'They are a young group and don't want to say the wrong thing. But I don't know everything. I want to be challenged. I will quite happily talk things through. You have got to be able to listen and take stuff on board and I think I am pretty approachable.'

According to Clare, one of the keys to the longevity of Lottie's leadership had been her ability to 'reinvent herself' as captain. 'I don't think that is easy because not everybody wants to keep learning and being challenged and keep finding new ways to develop,' she said. 'There are only so many times you can say, "Right, come on, girls, let's up and at 'em." How you instil belief and talk to players, she has found a way of keeping that fresh. She has kept getting results out of herself and the team. She has worked with a lot of different coaches and management teams and she has endured and got better.'

When Lottie became captain in Sri Lanka in the winter of 2005/06, Richard Bates was in his third year as coach of the team. Two years later Mark Lane began a tenure that lasted until Shaw took charge of the team prior to the 2013 Ashes. The changes, she believed, had helped maintain her enthusiasm for captaining the side. 'When Laney came in we formed a really strong relationship early on and it was just what I needed. Then he stepped down and I think you want to impress a new coach. Laney and me were very similar, but me and Paul are very different, we complement each other quite well. He is very thoughtful, a lot quieter than me, reflects a bit more than me. I have learned a lot from him about how to deal with certain situations and moving forward into my coaching that is really going to help me.

'Paul has challenged me in different ways and I like that. At my age now I constantly want to be challenged in what I am doing and I feel like my game has gone to another level. The work we are doing and the commitment we have has reignited something in me. A lot more planning goes into stuff and I am constantly thinking about the tactics. As players we are challenged on our game much more.'

The challenges, Lottie explained, included 'analysis', a dirty word in the aftermath of the men's World Cup failure in Australia and New Zealand, where Peter Moores was accused of relying more on 'data' than the talent of his players. As an example she remembered being called out by Paul in a team meeting for not getting the team off to a quick enough start in a game against Pakistan, prompting her to work in the nets the next day on increasing her strike rate. The data, however, can only be put to use if accompanied by candid self-appraisal. 'You have to be honest and unafraid to criticise people in a team environment,' she added. 'That is the hardest part. Players are not always that honest with themselves, but one thing we have done really well is being very honest in our reviews. That is helping us get better.'

And on the field she always trusted instinct ahead of data. 'It is very much all led by me,' she insisted. 'Paul says my job is to take them on the pitch. I will run stuff past him but a lot of it is completely unplanned. In New Zealand I was making bowling changes because I got a feel for it. That is years of experience and I have learned that you have got to go with your gut instinct. When you think of something just do it. They are the kind of things I wake up at three in the morning thinking about. I am always trying to out-think the opposition.'

* * * * *

Such instincts for the game were born out of summers playing cricket with older brother Daniel on her family's potato farm in Pidley, Cambridgeshire, and tagging along with her father, Clive, and uncle, Hugh, at Ramsey Cricket Club. 'All I wanted to do was play cricket. I always knew I was half-decent because I would play with the lads on the boundary and had good contests with my brother. At primary school I played in a Kwik Cricket tournament and I was the best by a country mile. We got to our regional finals at Chelmsford and I was belting it everywhere. This guy came up to me and asked me to go to county trials. From that moment on, the rest is history. I got fast tracked in everything and I kept being in the right place at the right time. At my first county game for Huntingdonshire Under-12s, this guy called Micky Dunn saw me play and was very good friends with an England Under-19 selector called Elaine Walker. He called her and I was chosen to play in an East Anglia Under-19s game, and by the end of that summer I was playing for England Under-19s. It was incredible how it all happened.'

A batter and leg-spinner, it would have been easy to become a precocious prodigy, but Lottie credits her family with keeping her grounded, even while they were doing all they could to support and encourage her cricket. Even now she says spending time with her family is her favourite thing to do away from the sport and her greatest sadness is that her dad, a minor counties player for Huntingdon, died too early – in 2006, from cancer – to see the full fruition of her career. 'Since I was a child I have been used to being talked about and everyone always expected me to play for England. But my family have been brilliant. At home I wasn't Charlotte the cricketer, I had to do everything I was told. They were really strict, which was really good for me.'

An England Under-19 debut when she was twelve was just the start. Her first game for the full national team was in 1996 at the age of sixteen in a Test against New Zealand, for which she took the field in culottes and had to pay £60 for her own blazer. She made 34 and 31 and a year later, mercifully in long trousers, she scored her first England century against South Africa in only her second one-day international. Before the end of that same year she'd hit an unbeaten 173 against Ireland in the World Cup in India – which remains her highest innings for her country.

It is impossible when reading author Pete Davies's account of that tournament not to be struck by how unfazed this young Spice Girls fan appeared to be by the somewhat chaotic nature of the environment. 'She has the potential to be the best we've ever seen,' England captain Jan Brittin told Davies.

A first Test century arrived in 1999 against India, but only after a score of 15 and two ducks in ODIs had triggered the first 'crisis' of her career. 'It was the first time I had got three low scores,' Lottie recalled. 'It was "oh my God, shock horror, what do I do?" I couldn't deal with it. I was meant to score runs every time I went out to the middle. I had a complete meltdown. But then you kind of learn to deal with it and I responded with a hundred.'

The real setback, however, came in 2001, when she blew out her right knee in a collision on the hockey field. 'I'd been through a little lean period and couldn't really work out what I wanted. The injury came at a good time, even though I was devastated. Honestly, I cried for two days when they told me I needed the operation [to repair the cruciate ligament] and I would have twelve months out of the game. But it made me refocus on what I wanted to do. I'd been maybe taking it a bit for granted and didn't work as hard as I should have. After the injury I got myself really fit and threw myself into it. I thought that if my career was just going to end like that I wanted to have given it everything. It really was a blessing in disguise for me. It made me realise how much I loved the game and from there onwards I have left no stone unturned.'

But even someone as besotted with cricket as the England captain, a player so driven to maximise their talent and remaining time, needs a break every now and again. Lottie is an obsessive, not an automaton. 'I wouldn't say I love every day of training. Towards the end of a trip training does become a little bit of a chore for me. At the start of a tour I love it because I am preparing myself. Once you are playing, training becomes less important for me. It is about recharging my mind and my body. As I have got older I have got better at knowing that and not just going to the nets every day. The staff are really good at saying, "Right, you are not coming to training." I used to think, "I have got to come, I am captain," but they tell me to get away from the whole thing. Sometimes you can waste energy at cricket grounds. In this Ashes series it will be important that I do that. I need to be strict with myself. If the coaches make training optional the girls will want to be there because they think if they don't people will think they are being lazy.

'I don't do it [skip training] very often. I did it once on this last trip. Sometimes I like to go down to the ground and just sit there drinking cups of tea. Depending on where we are in the country sometimes I want to get out of the hotel and do something. I think that is where the girls are quite mature; they realise that everyone has different needs – as long as we are there the next day at half past nine ready to warm up. They know I work as hard as anyone and I know what is best for me. The challenge for young players is working out what is best for them.'

The three months Edwards spent in Australia captaining the Western Fury was, she said, a good opportunity to put the England team out of her mind for a while, even if it did bring a different kind of challenge: that of playing for a losing team, not something she had ever done much of. 'It was good for me to have a break from the girls and not worry about what they were doing. Previously, if I was training remotely, I'd worry about them. That used to work me up. I wanted everyone else to work at the same intensity as me, but now I know everyone is working really hard and I don't have that worry.'

Even though she scored heavily – averaging 48.6 in 50-over cricket and being the country's second-highest T20 run-getter, including three fifties – it was not enough to make her young team contenders for honours. There was also the matter of becoming used to a different type of coach in Steve Jenkin, previously a World Cup winner with the Australian women. 'He is quite a forthright character and shouts at them,' she laughed. 'I was putting my arm around them saying, "Everything is fine." They were inexperienced so there was lower expectation for the team, which was hard for me because I wanted to win.

'I realised that this was a young group and it was a question of trying to get the best out of them, seeing a slight improvement every week. I was very mellow and it was a really good learning experience. You are not going to win the competition so how do you get the best out of the group? I was tough off the field with some of them and told them what I expected. Working with them one-to-one and seeing improvement was the most pleasing thing. I came down like a ton of bricks once when we were bowled out for 50 and I said, "This is really poor, not acceptable," but the rest of the time I was trying to coax them round and telling them the good things they had done.'

Lottie paused and concluded, 'It's been a tough winter, going straight on to New Zealand and not getting the results we wanted there. I have really been challenged this winter, but I kind of like that. I don't want things too easy.'

There would be no danger of the Australians making it easy in the summer, even with the news emerging that Cathryn Fitzpatrick was stepping down as coach after three years and three ICC world trophies and that someone new would be in charge for the Ashes. Such news seemed only to heighten Lottie's anticipation of the coming contests.

'Previously it has always been World Cups we are judged on,' she said, 'but since the change of format in the Ashes for me, personally, it is the greater achievement to win the Ashes. You are playing against the number one team in the world over three different formats and those wins in 2013 and 2014 were just incredible. The feeling of playing that intense cricket over that period of time was unbelievable. We got more media coverage for winning the Ashes at home in 2013 than we did for winning the World Cup in 2009. It was incredible, even in the winter when we won it. It was just ridiculous. I couldn't believe we were front page and back page.'

With Sky Sports and BBC Radio covering every ball, with the tornado of hype around the men's series likely to sweep up the girls with it, the summer promised to be a frenzied one. Prioritising and juggling commitments would be the key to Lottie's continued success and sanity. Time management had already become an increasingly complex challenge. In the early days in the England team she worked as a sales person and PR representative for Hunts County bats, before combining her role as a semi-professional player with coaching and ambassadorial work for the Chance to Shine cricket charity. Now, as a full-time professional, she had fewer moments to herself and more demands upon her diary.

'She is very giving,' said Clare. 'It is probably a little failing, the amount she takes on. She struggles to say no to anyone or anything. One day she will be doing something on TV with Clare Balding and next day she's driven three hours to a cricket club to talk to the under-10 girls for free because she said she would. She is an amazing servant to the game and I think that goes a long way with people.'

On hearing her friend's comments, Lottie conceded, 'I am very lucky to do what I do and I take real pride in it. Whether I am going to a school or captaining England I hope I am the same person. I walk into a school and I am proud to be there promoting women's cricket. It goes hand in hand with playing for England. I do probably give people too much of my time. If someone asks me to do a prize-giving I usually say yes. I don't want to change that because that is me. I have had to be more careful in the last year, don't get me wrong, and I have to say no to a few more things, but usually I will try to help someone out. Sometimes people take advantage, but I am not doing this for long and I wouldn't do the job justice if I didn't do what I do. I live and breathe this. I wouldn't want it any different. I have no regrets. I never feel like I am sacrificing anything. All I have ever wanted to do is play cricket for England and I will give it my all.'

But for how much longer? It was something she was bracing herself to be asked in many, many interviews as the summer unfolded. Even she could not deny, though, that the clock was ticking. 'I am conscious of it. I keep getting asked about it!' she said with a resigned chuckle. 'I will play for as long as I want to. They all think I am packing up after the 2017 World Cup in England, but I have never said that. I could have two years left, I could have more, but I am going to make the most of all of it and get as much enjoyment from it as I can. You look at [Kumar] Sangakkara and the runs he is scoring, I think if I am hitting the ball as well as he is at thirty-seven I will play. Graham Gooch said, "You want to play until there is someone better to replace you." You know what? I am as fit as I have ever been. I am as motivated as I have ever been. People look at me and say that you clearly can't be after eighteen years, but look how things have changed in that time. How couldn't I be?'

4

Another Chance to Shine

'I want the women's team to be seen as good role models: humble, focused, hard-working cricketers and good people' – Clare Connor

THE early spring sunshine that lit up the Nursery Ground before breaking into Clare Connor's office and catching her blonde highlights could not have been timelier. It was the day after England's men had been dumped out of the World Cup by defeat to Bangladesh and Lord's needed all the cheering up it could get. In the ECB offices' reception area, while waiting for the Director of Women's Cricket to finish a meeting with Paul Shaw, I'd sat next to a glass cabinet displaying the Women's World Cup trophy won by England in 2009. See, it *was* possible.

'Yesterday I had a request from Radio 4 asking if they could have an interview with me telling the men how it should be done,' Clare explained as we discussed the previous day's events in Adelaide. 'No, of course not, because that is not how we do things. You understand why the media are looking for that route in, but that would be completely disrespectful.'

While the women's results could sometimes be a stick with which to beat their male counterparts in troubled times, the fortunes of the men's team were more of a double-edged sword for those charged with promoting the women. 'We've really only sat side by side from the early 2000s,' Clare continued, referring to the moment when the women's game became an integrated part of the sport's governing body rather than administering itself. 'It has been a fifteen-year process of aligning everything to do with England women under the umbrella of England cricket. When we've been in a really good place we've seen the positive spin-offs of being part of the same set-up; having the same kit, team sponsorship, being identifiable as part of a strong national brand in terms of Team England. I can recall when the men retained the Ashes in 2013 up at Durham, ours were just getting going and the whole Ashes narrative was fantastic as attention turned to the women's game. The men retained and the media jumped on to supporting us in the first multi-format Ashes. That would be an example of when things have worked nicely.'

And while no one benefits if the failures of the men's national team causes the country to fall out of love with the sport, a successful women's squad could at least take advantage of the need for the cricket public to find an outlet for its patriotism. 'I can remember, for example, the World Twenty20 in 2009, the first ICC joint event, where the men crashed out of the tournament early and we went on to play an unbelievable semi-final against Australia, and then won the final here at Lord's. I think we got a great following behind us because we were the England team left in a global tournament that people could get behind. That worked in our favour. I am not saying we would ever want that, but we were on the front and back of the papers.'

As a cricket-loving twelve-year-old, I'd remembered the publicity surrounding Rachael Heyhoe Flint's England team winning the inaugural World Cup in 1973, two years before the men's game saw its first global tournament. Enid Bakewell scored two centuries; one in the opening game against an International XI, now recognised as the first official women's ODI, and another in the decisive final match against Australia. Three years later Heyhoe Flint, the Charlotte Edwards of her era, led England's women on to the Lord's turf for the first time in a game against Australia.

For me, like many, women's cricket largely disappeared from my ongoing consciousness for three decades – resurfacing every four years around the World Cup, which England won again at Lord's in 1993. That was until the sport's memorable summer of 2005. While the nation was entranced and energised by the men's team winning its first Ashes series for eighteen years, the glare of interest also illuminated the achievement of England's women beating the old enemy for the first time since 1963, taking the two-Test series 1-0. When England's dishevelled, hungover men stood with crooked ties and wobbly legs in front of tens of thousands in Trafalgar Square the day after their triumph, the ladies, somewhat neater and more composed, were alongside them.

Clare, in the last of her eleven years in the side, five of them as captain, had led that triumph. 'I think playing at home in the Ashes is... well, who knows what this summer will bring? But it was amazing in my last series to be part of that and the national celebration. Including us in Trafalgar Square was a really good PR move.'

So having to go out and bang the drum for the England women's team the day after ignominy for the men in Australia was not necessarily a daunting prospect? 'I'd actually say the opposite. An early exit is heart-wrenching and you feel torn because I would say, in general, when the men don't do very well we probably benefit. It seems to put a spotlight on us as being consistent. Yes, I want the women's team to be seen as good role models and humble, focused, hard-working cricketers and good people, but you don't want that at the expense of the England men having some tough times.'

Ultimately, the women can only benefit from events in the men's game – good or bad – if they themselves are winning, which, by and large, they had continued to do since that day in Trafalgar Square. In 2009 they followed up their third World Cup victory in Australia with an English summer in which they achieved a World Twenty20 triumph and another Ashes win. Frustratingly, further global tournaments had eluded them – despite successive T20 final appearances – but victories in the multi-format Ashes series of 2013 and 2013/14 kept the girls permanently in the consciousness of the cricket public.

'Success allows you to put more news stories out there, to be more celebratory,' said Connor. 'Sustained success allowed me to have conversations with the board about professional contracts and the growth in the international playing calendar.' Kia had been signed as the first stand-alone partner of England women's cricket, while the ECB's primary sponsor, Waitrose, 'love that they have a successful women's England team to work with because in their market that suits them well.'

On-field success had nourished the relationship with the Chance to Shine charity, which had introduced 2.5 million children – a million of them girls – to the sport in its first ten years. Its use of leading women players as ambassadors had allowed several of them to work wholly within cricket even before becoming full-time England professionals. 'The wins in 2009 really gave that partnership greater profile,' said Clare. 'Players could go into schools and clubs with World Cups and a real confidence about who they were as cricketers, and that has led to a real relationship in terms of growing the game.'

A few weeks after this conversation *The Guardian* described cricket as 'one of the fastest growing team sports for girls in Britain', stating that the number of clubs offering cricket to females had increased six-fold to 600 over the previous fifteen years. It was an obvious step forward for the women's game in general but, conversely, all the England players I spoke to cited the importance of playing boys' cricket – whether through design or circumstance – in their development into internationals. It seemed important that the growth of girls' teams did not deny the better players the opportunity for that on-field education.

Anya Shrubsole called boys' cricket 'a huge learning curve; you learn things faster'. She continued, 'The attitude of some of the boys' parents toughens you up. You go out of your way to prove that you are more than good enough to be there, not because people are feeling sorry for you. I wouldn't have it any other way.'

Lydia Greenway argued that being made captain of a boys' teams 'gave me a boost in self-esteem to believe I was quite good', while Danni Wyatt was one of the squad members who had continued to play male cricket into adulthood. 'It is really great for improving my game,' she said. 'The men bowl a lot faster and hit the ball a lot harder so it is good for my all-round skills and when you come to play against women hopefully it will be easier.'

Lottie insisted, 'I would encourage any girl to play in boys' and men's cricket as long as you can. Playing that intense cricket makes you tough, a better player, gets you out of your comfort zone and prepares you for international cricket. You still have to play girls' cricket. I used to go back and play like I was the king of the castle. I would whack it around, so it is important to get that element. But I played a lot of cricket. Girls these days don't play anywhere near as much as I did. I was batting two or three times a week under that kind of extreme pressure.'

The ECB's own figures cited 59,000 women aged fourteen or over playing the game in 2014. 'But that figure already feels out of date to those involved in the game,' *The Guardian* said confidently.

'The fact that the team has been successful consistently during my tenure in this role means you have a good case behind you when you ask for greater budget,' Clare added. 'For the organisation, we have been a consistent success story, whether it is around growing the game or international results, and it is absolutely my responsibility to capitalise on everything I can.'

Clare entered her current role in 2008, a couple of years after her playing career as a left-arm spinning all-rounder came to an end at the age of twenty-nine through a combination of injury and the desire to throw herself back into teaching, which had been taking second place to cricket. As you might expect from an English teacher, when she discusses the challenges of her new job she does so in a considered manner yet with an easy delivery; comfortable without appearing rehearsed. If she comes across as someone who spends a lot of time thinking about this stuff then she readily owns up to it. She was exactly the same as a player, as her dawn strategy meetings with Edwards testify.

She is three years older than her great friend, but a realisation that they were 'kindred spirits' quickly transcended any age difference. The one subject they never discussed, however, was any remote possibility that England's leading women cricketers would ever be full-time professionals. Even the Sport England funding that she received in the latter years of her career never earned Clare more than £600 per month. The fact that she was able to focus so single-mindedly on cricket in that period was down to the support of her headmaster at Brighton College, Anthony Seldon. 'I didn't teach in my last two years of playing for England. I had sat there in the headmaster's office not knowing where to turn because I knew I was not teaching to the best of my ability, struggling to fit in all my training and he said, "Have a two-year sabbatical. Get to the World Cup and the Ashes in 2005." That support and mentoring from him meant I had a great place to go back to after cricket. I really couldn't see professionalism myself then. I probably would have said that by 2015 the England team would be, at best, semi-professional.'

Which makes it all the more surprising that the final step from part-time players to fully-contracted England professionals was such a 'straightforward and painless' one. 'I could have stood there and done a handstand and they would have said yes,' Clare recalled of her final presentation to the ECB board. 'It wasn't as though I had to convince hearts and minds; the board were 100 per cent behind the agenda item. Many of my senior colleagues realised that the status quo of a semi-professional England squad wasn't sustainable anymore, and wasn't rewarding the players correctly for their effort and commitment. It needed to happen for us to go to the next level, to be able to ask even more of them and have central control of them as a team. It wasn't some huge masterplan I worked on for two years and had to deliver the world's greatest pitch to make happen. Culturally, within the organisation, there was a sense that this was one of the next big things we needed. Then it was just a case of working out what it looked like. It is not a massive outlay in relation to the overall ECB coffers, but it is certainly a game-changer for the players.'

Lottie was convinced that many people believed she must have been the shop steward in the background, agitating for professional status. Yet she had played no part and her friend had given her no hint of what was afoot. 'I still remember getting this email,' she explained. 'I looked at it and I couldn't believe it. I had to read it again. It was unreal. And then we got a bonus for winning the Ashes as well. It was one of those moments I will never forget because I never thought it was going to happen.'

In a 2009 interview, she had said, 'I spend twenty-five hours a week coaching in the Chance to Shine scheme. I am as much of a cricket professional as a woman's ever going to get.' How wrong she was. 'We had no inkling,' she said. 'It just happened. Wow.'

She refused to believe, however, that it was quite as simple as Clare made out. 'She is very modest and what she has done for the game since she has been involved is incredible. I hope the players appreciate it. It would be very easy for an ex-player to think, "I didn't get it so they are certainly not getting it."'

The inaugural eighteen professional contracts consisted of a 'captain's contract' for Edwards with three tiers of player deals below. A system where everyone was given a points ranking and paid accordingly was disregarded in favour of simpler banding – based, according to Clare, on 'the value and potential of the player to the team'. The media landed on a figure of upwards of £50,000 as the annual value of a contract, but inevitably Clare was not inclined to shed any light on the accuracy of that estimate. In order to quickly fall in line with the rest of the ECB's contract calendar, the deals were structured to run from May 2014 to the end of September 2015, the men's annual renewal date. Before the Ashes series began, however, a review was due to take place to consider any changes to the system.[1]

* * * * *

---

1   A decision was made at the end of the summer to extend the current
    contracts through to the spring of 2016.

Clare is keen for England cricket to be acknowledged as a leader in women's sport, from an organisational and infrastructure perspective to high achievement and the projection of the right image for females in sport. Her own role, which as well as encompassing the chair of the ICC women's committee and membership of the ICC executive and cricket committees saw her sit on the board of Sport England, had her well placed to elevate the standing of her game. 'Crikey, the pace of change in women's sport is pretty rapid at the moment,' she said, 'so my view is that we must jump in and try to lead as much as possible, which is not easy when you are not a sport like netball, athletics, tennis – sports that are more naturally perceived as female sports. I think we have become more mainstream and we have started to "normalise" cricket for women and girls.'

Much can be understood about the perception of a women's sport by the comparisons it provokes with the male equivalent, and whether those constant measurements and justifications ever cease to be applied. A sign of progress will be when women's cricket is acknowledged as being different from the men's game, yet – in the manner of, say, tennis or athletics – it ceases to be a constant frame of reference. 'You don't want to hear the conversation any more that the girls don't hit as many sixes or bowl as fast,' said Clare. 'You want the differences in the game to be celebrated. Whether you can have both I don't know.'

Which ties in with the question of whether the England team are cricketers who happen to be women, or women who play cricket. 'When I was a player I just saw myself as a cricketer. I was playing in boys' teams from the age of eight and in my head I was going to play for England men. There was nothing in my head saying "there is no way". Being in this role and doing the things I do in women's sport I do see it differently now. There is something remarkable about the power of women's sport; it shouldn't be that we are all aspiring to be male cricketers. Let's celebrate women's sport.'

Before heading to New Zealand, seven of the England team – Edwards, Wyatt, Katherine Brunt, Becky Grundy, Kate Cross, Heather Knight and Lauren Winfield – had been invited by Waitrose to undergo a makeover in the Lord's dressing room before being photographed in glamorous evening wear in the Long Room. The girls had an enjoyable day of pampering and received valuable exposure in national media. I wondered whether it had just been a question of keeping the sponsor happy or whether there was real value in the projection of a more 'feminine' image than the usual playing and training gear.

Clare ventured, 'Look at them. Whether they are attractive or unattractive isn't important, but what is important is that they are proud young women who are doing something they love and it is giving them confidence. They are part of a team and there is something really powerful about that; there are not that many things in life that can give you that. That should be celebrated and shared in whatever ways are possible with young girls and it should be a message around confidence, believing you can do whatever you want to do and breaking new ground. Being in an amazing dress in the Long Room is just one way of depicting it.'

Lottie had no doubt that 'those sorts of things are really important'. She continued, 'We want to get across that we are women who play cricket. We can dress up and we can look nice. We are not going to wear make-up on the field, but I think that it is good that some of the kit we have had in recent years has been more feminine. We look like athletes because of what we wear.'

Recalling the sleeveless and somewhat revealing number the team had to squeeze into a few years ago prompted her to point out that 'there is a fine line', but she insisted, 'We want to look like girls. It was great to show another side in the

Waitrose photo shoot and everyone was surprised by what they saw – even us!'

Lauren, another of the makeover girls, argued, 'That shoot was important for people to see a different side to us. If you are looking to develop and grow the game it is about inspiring the next generation and it is important for girls coming through that they look at us and see us not only in cricket whites all the time; they see that "these are girls just like us".'

That ability to inspire is one of the most immediate differences the England players had experienced since they had turned professional. Lauren continued, 'When I am in schools, girls say, "Really? That is your job?" We are benefitting hugely from the changes within the sport but I say to the girls, "You are the ones who have the world at your feet." Another five or ten years down the line, some of these girls coming through can have even more exciting opportunities.'

What exactly the sport would look like in that time was anyone's guess. Clare, architect of the modern women's Ashes format, had frequently gone on record calling for an increase in the amount of Test cricket. The ECB would like to see all women's series follow the Ashes template, which would help reinstate Test cricket as an integral part of the international programme. England are the only country who regularly schedule the longer game, with India's Test at Wormsley in 2014, for example, being that nation's first for eight years.

'It's the most fun cricket, the most challenging,' vice-captain Heather Knight said, voicing a majority view. 'I would love to play a little bit more. Having two Tests in the Ashes series in future would be great, but you'd need to ask Clare Connor about that!'

Clare had spoken a lot about the support she received for professionalising the women's game from within the ECB. Just as great an asset, it seemed to me, was the appetite for the project that the players themselves exhibited. 'We have a bit more free time and balance in our lives,' Heather continued. 'Cricket is our main focus rather than having to fit in sessions after work or in the morning. We do probably feel that extra pressure, like when we lost our first game as pros, but it is a good thing and it adds more status to us as players. We see it more as an opportunity to improve. You enjoy some ambassadorial stuff more than others but a lot of us still do work with Chance to Shine and it is important that we do it because I remember the experience of having sports people visit my school. We are all passionate about growing women's cricket in this country. Telling a young girl in school that it's a career now is a good place to be.'

Kate Cross explained, 'I was at a family wedding and I met my second cousin, Jemima. Her mum, my cousin, introduced me to her and she said, "Kate plays cricket for England. You remember when I said girls can do anything now, well, there you go." She was telling a seven-year-old that girls can do anything and that is amazing.'

The challenge for many of the England players now would be to ensure that their cricket did not become weighed down by the increased pressure and expectation of professionalism. 'You try not to think about it,' said Georgia Elwiss. 'We are not playing for the money, we are playing for the shirt. You just want the win. There will be extra pressure, but I have not heard any of the girls talking about it.'

Kate recalled the formal discussions the squad had held after their elevated status had been confirmed. 'We sat down and had a big chat, asking what turning professional meant to us. We all said that nothing had really changed in terms of our mentality. We always strived to be the world's best, we always strived to be professional in how we went about things, whether it was in our warm-ups or nutrition or whatever. Now we get offered a lot more support and for me it is now everything I do. I wake up and cricket comes first. There are days when you don't have the motivation to go the gym – that is natural with anyone in any job. You have to go like people have to go to the office.

'You can see how the sport has developed in the last twelve months, different attitudes towards it, greater participation levels. For girls, it is on the radar now. They can see it as a career. It is a strange era at the minute because everything is so new and sparkly and brilliant. But just because we have been given money doesn't mean we have the right to win every game.'

5

Contenders

'You do worry that [injury] gives other
people a chance. I can't do a great deal about
what other players are doing. I'll just focus
on getting fit and scoring runs' – Lauren
Winfield

S HE had been the recipient of good wishes from her
friend when Tammy Beaumont was left at home for the
New Zealand tour. Now it was Lauren Winfield's turn
to make the magnanimous gesture. 'Absolutely gutted not
to be fit for the up and coming tour to Dubai,' the Yorkshire
player posted on Twitter, 'but wish Tammy and the girls the
very best of luck out there.'

The quadriceps muscle injury that Lauren had suffered in
New Zealand was still not healed sufficiently to allow her to
join the England Academy team on a trip that, according to
team management, could have been an important part of her
Ashes preparation. Instead she would be at home watching

the online scorecards to see how batters Beaumont, Amy Jones and her replacement for the tour, Nat Sciver, were performing against Australia's second team.

'When it first went we knew it was always going to be a bit of a push to make the Dubai tour,' she explained the day before her withdrawal was announced. There were still ten days before departure, but she admitted, 'It is just too much of a risk considering the summer ahead. I am obviously disappointed because it is another opportunity to be putting your name forward and scoring runs. I know I am not quite where I need to be so I have to accept it and work on my rehab as hard as I possibly can. Naturally, when I first found out I was definitely not going you do worry that it gives other people a chance. If a couple of players get big hundreds they are putting their name ahead of yours. But I spoke to Shawsy this morning and he has been really good in terms of reassuring me. I can't do a great deal about what other players are doing so I'll just focus on getting fit and, when I can play, worry about scoring runs.'

The injury had been a constant presence during her time in New Zealand, the result of 'going from training indoors to running on hard grass outside'. Having hoped the tightness in her left leg would gradually ease, she became increasingly aware of it during her innings of 48 in the third T20 international. 'I felt it go while I was running between the wickets and there was a lot of swelling. The scan revealed it [a tear]. When it is under the stretch and tension it is worse. Fortunately I have not lost much strength.'

At the age of twenty-four, Lauren was experiencing the first real injury of a career that had seen her spend the previous two years in the England squad. 'Having never torn a muscle, I just thought I was in a bit of pain and if I did the right things it would ease off. I just thought my body was in a bit of shock after getting outside again. You know, you do sprint training at home, but it is different to properly legging it after a ball or sprinting between the wickets. I never had anything to benchmark myself against. Now I will know.'

Lauren, captain of Yorkshire, sometime wicketkeeper, possessor of penetrating blue-grey eyes and wearer of a nose ring, would now be prevented by injury from participating in a series that could have offered more valuable time at the crease in an international environment. Still with only twenty-five international innings in all formats to her name since her England debut in an ODI against Pakistan in 2013, she felt that the development of her batting depended more on the kind of mental and strategic elements that can only be learned in the middle than it did on technical tweaking in the nets.

'If you look at the way cricket is played now it has shied away from these perfect technical models, playing all through the V,' she ventured. 'It is more tactical and game awareness, playing different situations and different roles. It is massively mental in terms of the game you are going to play and how you go about your business. Playing Test cricket is a bit different; you have got to be technically sound or you will be found out. It is more a case of time at the crease, more consistency and with that comes confidence. If you are confident then generally you won't worry about what is happening technically and you'll be hitting the ball in the areas you want to.'

All of that would have to wait until her leg was healed, at which point her journey from boys' cricket around York to the top of the women's game could continue. 'My first memory of cricket is a little picture of me when I was about three years old,' she recalled. 'I have got a little tartan dress on and my dad's massive cricket helmet, and a little tiny cricket bat. I think that was the first time I picked up a bat and I pretty much have never put it down since.'

Her typical start in the sport – games on the boundary while her dad Andy, a business manager, played club cricket

– gained momentum after she began training with the boys at Stamford Bridge. 'I went down there on a Friday night, mucked about, got stuck in and found I loved it.' And discovered that everyone thought she was pretty good.

'I was fortunate enough to captain all my boys' teams in the local league and some representative teams. When my coach at my club named me captain of the boys' team, I thought, "I am probably quite good." I never really had any issues with the boys. They always responded well. I was captain, wicketkeeper and opening batter, and I always seemed to score a few runs so I guess they thought, "She can actually play, we are going to listen to her."'

Representative cricket at district level saw her playing alongside future Yorkshire and England wicketkeeper-batsman Jonny Bairstow and, having also played netball, football and rounders, Lauren was known within her group of friends as 'the sporty one'. Inevitably, teenage years brought the pressure of a spurned social life. 'I was always well supported by my friends but the further down the line you go the more dedicated you have to become. There was more, "I can't come out tonight, I have got training." It was not an issue for me but sometimes friends don't understand and found it weird I was choosing to train rather than going out. Naturally there are times when you think you'd rather be out and about but I trained and played cricket because I wanted to. I wasn't doing it for anybody else. I did it because that is what I loved.'

Representative cricket in both boys' and girls' teams led to an inevitable call-up for the full Yorkshire women's team, where her first game in 2007 saw her run out without facing a ball against Somerset. 'Sarah Taylor had a big impact in getting me into the first team because she was doing a wicketkeeping session with Yorkshire and the girl who was keeper before me was kind of on her way out, although no one wanted to do anything about it. It was actually Sarah who said to them, "This girl is a lot better than the one who currently has the gloves," and from then on people started looking at me. I got my foot in the door with my keeping and then people saw me bat a little bit more. It is different, though, opening the batting for the age groups, to coming in a bit lower down and getting fewer opportunities in the first team. I had a year or two when I was in the team but not really playing a huge role.'

Arrival at Loughborough University, where she would graduate in sports and exercise science, was another important milestone, accelerating her progress 'massively' – her favourite adverb. 'Training as a full-time athlete just develops you so much quicker. Instead of one net in the week and playing on Sunday, you are training four or five days a week.' Putting her in position, as it turned out, for a breakthrough season in 2013.

The search engine on the Cricket Archive website reveals the stark, impressive, statistics: scores of 73, 136, 53, 54 and 96 in the first five innings it lists for her that season; 1,223 runs at an average of 64 in domestic games, including one century and thirteen fifties. 'Loughborough helped in that, even though university cricket is a lower standard. The learning for me was batting long periods of time. I was always a classic get-a-nice-30-and-then-get-yourself-out. I went into university cricket thinking, "I am going to bat fifty overs every game." I got 200 in one game and generally you are scoring 100 or 50-plus as often as possible. Knowing what it feels like to be out there for three hours and construct an innings, and go through the gears, was a massive learning for me. It enabled me to kick on in other stuff, in county, Super 4s and the Academy.'

The transition to international cricket had been, as for so many, a tougher proposition. It was not until her twenty-first England innings, in the final T20 of 2014 against South Africa, that she made her first half-century, a 60-ball knock of 74.

That innings ensured that she went to New Zealand as a first-choice selection. The timing of the eventual diagnosis of her injury left her torn between frustration at being ruled out immediately after her first substantial score of the tour and relief that she had soldiered on long enough to put some runs in the bank. 'It's disappointing because I have been given the opportunity to bat in key positions. You start to find your feet, have a bit more role clarity in what positions they want you to play in – and then start scoring runs in those positions. I felt I was just starting to do that and then obviously this injury has come about. But I do feel I am contributing more often and being more consistent.'

* * * * *

Consistency was not the first adjective that would be applied to the England Academy's subsequent performances in Dubai, although few would complain if the Ashes series was as closely fought as the four 50-over games contested by the protagonists' second strings. After the first was delayed a day by a Dubai sandstorm, Beaumont proceeded to win the toss and bat in all four, with England posting 252, 268, 260 and 177. Australia's Shooting Stars reached their target in the first and third games, but in games two and four, England created middle-order collapses to win by 28 and 4 runs respectively. 'We stayed calm under a lot of pressure,' said Beaumont after the final match. 'It was very nerve-wracking, but perhaps worse for the coaches and the girls on the sideline.'

As enthusiastically as those wins were greeted by the team and the senior colleagues who offered support from afar via social media, it was always the individual performances that would have greater significance for the summer ahead. In that respect, it was Fran Wilson who appeared to have put the cat among the middle-order pigeons with scores of 57, 50 and 45 from number four in the first three games. 'Fran was pretty consistent throughout that trip,' Paul Shaw acknowledged. 'She has gone on to the next level and is developing nicely.'

Beaumont, who had filled time between the Loughborough University and England Academy trips to Dubai by attending the Darren Lehmann Academy in Adelaide, reached 59 in one knock, but made no other major contributions, although she did go on to score 41 in each of the two Twenty20 defeats that followed. Nat Sciver never got going and scored only 59 across the entire 50-over series.

Among the bowlers, Tash Farrant was tidy and economical – the only one to concede fewer than four runs per over – and deserved more than two wickets. Jodie Dibble's spell of four wickets was the turning point in the final game, while fellow slow left-armer Alex Hartley took four in each of the final two games and was leading wicket-taker with ten.

Only twenty-one, Hartley had already managed to spend six years in the international wilderness since her first selection for the Academy at age fifteen, at which point she was told her batting and fielding needed to improve. Since then she had faded from the scene and only forced her way back in after opting to join Middlesex in 2013.

With her tiny stature, bright golden hair and habit of elevating both arms towards her head on her run-up, she approaches the wicket with the look of a young chick attempting to fly. It proved an effective enough method to earn fourteen wickets at 14.45 in her second season of 50-over cricket for Middlesex and made the long drives from Clitheroe in Lancashire worthwhile. 'To give myself the best chance of playing for England I thought I had best be playing Division One cricket,' she explained. 'I basically picked Middlesex out of a hat. I'm looking to move down there this summer. I had a pretty good county season last year, but being selected for the Academy was a complete shock. When I got the call I couldn't believe it. I just want to play for England. It would be a big step to get into the

Ashes squad, but as long as I get my name out there, who knows?'

The real winner on the Academy tour was Sussex's Georgia Elwiss. Turning twenty-four early in the Ashes summer, she had ten ODI and eight T20 appearances for England behind her as a right-arm seamer but had got to the crease only twice in her senior international career. It was hardly a reflection of her potential as a batter. That had been proved over the course of her career, including a century for Staffordshire Under-17s, and some big innings at club level for Brighton and Hove Women. Over the previous two seasons she had scored consistently at the top of the order for Sussex, including a first hundred for her county in 2013.

Given the opportunity to bat at six for the Academy in Dubai, she slammed 100 exactly off 80 balls in the opening game, including fifteen fours and a pair of sixes. To prove it was no fluke she followed up with 65, 50 and 47 in the subsequent games and added 43 as an opener in the first T20 contest. She also took three wickets in England's first win of the tour. 'Georgia went exceptionally well batting in that position,' was Paul's verdict. 'She scored runs consistently well in really high temperatures. That links to both fitness and concentration, and she played very positively, which is what we are looking at in the middle order.'

Elwiss is a good-looking cricketer. By that I don't mean in a women's magazine type way – although her dark looks and healthy, outdoor complexion would give her a full dance card on most nights out – but from a sporting aesthetic. Short sleeves sit snugly around her biceps and she strikes you as someone who is no stranger to the gym. You'd pick her out in a crowd as a professional sportswoman.

When I watched her at the crease for the first time she made only 20, but she looked physically imposing, full of intent and confidence, and quick to take advantage of anything wide of the stumps. 'I have always been seen as a bowler who can bat a bit so to change people's opinion you have to put in a lot of hard work and then put in the performances as well,' she said, absent-mindedly adjusting her hair for the first of umpteen times. 'Hopefully I am getting there, showing them that I like batting at that number five or six spot. If I can keep scoring runs this summer then good things will happen from there.'

Elwiss acknowledged that the continued form and fitness of Katherine Brunt, Anya Shrubsole and Kate Cross meant that an all-rounder's position offered the more likely route into the England team. 'I have not got the pace that they have, so I've always had to have something a bit different in my game. I have been fortunate that my batting has come off and the way I play is, I think, the way the game is going.'

She credited her success in Sri Lanka to a thorough winter of preparation after recovering from the broken hand that kept her out of the latter half of the previous season. 'My method was strong,' she said. 'I went out being really clear about whatever ball was bowled at me. I knew where I was going to hit it. I did a lot of work with Saliann Briggs, my one-to-one coach. I messaged her after games and told her our sessions were so much harder than it was out in the middle. You have to replicate the hard situations in training so that out in the middle I was really clear what I was trying to do, what my options were. It was just one of those tours where everything came off. Not getting picked for New Zealand may have been a blessing because I got to go to Dubai and play the role I want to play.'

Born in Wolverhampton, Georgia got into cricket through bowling at her brother, Luke, in the garden and being taken to Warwickshire by her grandparents. Another who put up with sledging from opposition boys' teams, she didn't play girls' club cricket until her early teenage years, by which time she had already been faced with an important sporting decision. 'I had to make a choice when I was eleven between rugby and cricket. I was getting to the stage at rugby where I couldn't play with the lads any more. I think I just enjoyed cricket more. I'd had representative honours at cricket by that time so I went that way. Everything in my life was cricket. I had cricket heroes: Allan Donald, who was at Warwickshire at the time, and female-wise it was always Lucy Pearson. She used to play at Staffordshire, where I grew up playing, and she taught my brother at school as well.'

By 2007, she was achieving success with the England Development squad and in 2009 she took the decision to spend two winters in Canberra, where she played for the Australian Capital Territory second eleven. 'It was pretty smooth up to the end of high school and then I went out to Australia for a couple of winters and I fell off the pathway with England. The management felt others had progressed more than I did in that time. I was playing a good standard out there but they weren't feeling it. I felt like my cricket was improving – although I probably didn't feel like my fitness was – and I came back and was on the [MCC] Young Cricketers programme for the summer, where you are basically a professional. I made the choice I wanted to do it for me rather than anyone else and got fit and my cricket kicked on from there. Then I got to [Loughborough] university and all the support we got there was amazing.'

In 2011, Elwiss changed counties from Staffordshire to Sussex, although her accent still frequently gives away her origins. She called it 'probably the best decision I have made', citing the bad balls she was previously able to get away with. 'It wasn't challenging enough. If I wanted to get into the England squad I needed to be bowling at England players and being seen.'

Call-up for England came later that year. 'It was a little bit scary at first,' she admitted. 'I had grown up playing with all the girls but then had a few years out of the Academy system.

Then you have got to prove yourself. In the early days I was only ever getting into the team if there was an injury, not breaking in on my own performances. That was something that has made me want to turn myself into an all-rounder and get in on merit. Now I am completely at ease.'

That journey towards comfort was aided in 2012 when she was named Player of the Series as England beat India. 'It's my favourite series ever,' she smiled, 'a time when I was really in control of my bowling and my game.' Back injuries had prevented her from achieving the same level of success since – and now she was reinventing herself in a new role.

'I have always felt I have been getting better but it has been weird because I have been transitioning from opening bowler into an all-rounder and then I have had injury issues that have held me back a bit,' she continued. 'I was plagued by my back; never had any consistency of overs or rhythm. It is nice to have had a long winter to be really able to practise and hone my skills. I have done loads of core work in the gym and a little bit of remodelling of my action, making sure that I am really strong and doing all my conditioning stuff, logging all my overs.'

Injuries to others meant that Elwiss was barely back from Dubai before she was packing her bags for England's spin and batting camp in Sri Lanka; she, Katherine Brunt and Gloucestershire's Alex McDonald having taken the places of Laura Marsh, Jodie Dibble and Amy Jones.

Danni Wyatt seized her opportunity in the first 50-over game against Sri Lanka A with 69 off 74 balls in a total of 151, which proved enough when Hartley took three wickets in a collapse of eight for 48 runs, leaving the hosts 141 all out. In the second game, Knight (47) and Winfield (45) put on 84 for the first wicket before Wyatt added 59 as England totalled 240 for 7. That was 82 too many for Sri Lanka as Hartley, continuing her great run of form, and Dani Hazell took three wickets each.

Wyatt's success continued in the third game, with the ball this time. Her 3 for 27 helped restrict Sri Lanka to 183, a total England passed with six wickets in hand. Elwiss, who had earlier picked up a couple of wickets, hit an unbeaten 66, while Brunt weighed in with 45.

Assessing the two tours, Paul concluded, 'A number of the players had the opportunity to play certain roles for us that they could potentially play for England as they develop. So from that perspective I was delighted with the majority of the players and how they went. A couple had a few challenges and weren't as prolific as they would have liked, but there was a lot of learning that they were able to take on board. So we have a number of players who are developing nicely under the England team, which is obviously very important.'

April was proving to be a momentous month for the English women's game. Within the space of a few days *Wisden* was published with a new section devoted purely to women's cricket and a Women's International Cricketer of the Year (Australia's Meg Lanning); most of the bigger county teams included their women in their season launch media days; the *Cricketer's Who's Who* featured Heather Knight on its cover alongside three men's England internationals; and Charlotte Edwards received her CBE from the Queen at Windsor Castle.

Such landmarks provided further evidence of the potential rewards in front of Elwiss and the other England hopefuls in such an important, historic summer. 'The Ashes are what I have my sights on,' she said. 'There is a lot of cricket to be played before then, but I know if I put in performances week in, week out, the rest should take care of itself.'

6

A Career at the Crossroads

'Everything had all just built up and I really struggled. I was battling on my own. I only had to be in university four hours a week for my course, but I just didn't want to get up' – Kate Cross

KATE Cross had read enough books as part of her psychology degree studies to realise what was happening. She understood why she was feeling so low, why all she wanted to do was spend the day in bed, even though she knew that going to the gym was exactly what she needed to break the cycle of lethargy and fatigue. She knew why she wanted to split up with the boyfriend who was doing his best to get her through such difficult times because she didn't feel she was worthy of him; why, when she looks back now at her second year at Leeds University, all she can think of is a dark room. The self-diagnosis was easy.

Depression.

It's an illness that, partly through the honest and brave revelations of the likes of Marcus Trescothick and Michael Yardy in recent years, has achieved greater levels of understanding and care within cricket, a sport whose unforgiving characteristics of individual exposure and constant measurement appear designed to seek out and magnify any vulnerabilities. Like those men, who both had to return home from England trips, one of the women's game's most promising fast bowlers was forced to acknowledge that her salvation lay in time away from her sport.

'It was a really big decision to make because I was in the England Academy at the time and you think, "Am I ruining my chances?" But I wasn't handling university and being away from home, with the added pressure of all the training and looking after myself. Then, when I had made this decision, I realised I had to tell my mum and dad, and they are the ones who have driven me up and down the country all these years, spent all the money on kit. But I wasn't enjoying cricket any more. It was a chore. I remember sitting down and thinking, "Am I doing this for me or am I doing it for all the people who think I should be playing for England?" I just had to take a break.'

If they'd known that their little Kate, the girl they had seen grow up before their eyes, was considering giving up the sport for good, the people of Heywood Cricket Club would scarcely have believed it.

Occupying the south-eastern corner of the Grade 2 listed Queen's Park, the club's ground, Crimble, is approached via the narrow terraced streets of one of Greater Manchester's northern suburbs and sits down a dirt track that appears at first to be leading nowhere. I had arrived on a misty and chilly Sunday morning during one of club cricket's annual rites. Once the clocks have gone forward every player and supporter knows it is time to get down to the ground, grab a paintbrush or hammer, and spruce everything up for the new season. This day has become such an integral part of the calendar that one of the sport's major sponsors, NatWest, had even successfully formalised it into an annual event with its Cricket Force programme, designed to maximise the number of volunteers giving up their time.

Crimble had been home to Heywood for ninety-four of its 150 years. Stretches of blue or white seats border parts of the playing area, a variety of small local businesses deemed the crowds for a Central Lancashire League match worthy of an advertising board and the slate-roofed pavilion bore the logo of a sports shop and had vacancies for match-day sponsors. It's unlikely ever to win any prizes for the most picturesque setting for the sport, but its members are welcoming and hospitable – and fiercely proud of Kate Cross.

'Do you want to grab something and lend a hand,' ventured one formidable-looking lady who was attacking weeds at the foot of the pavilion with the gusto of Brian Lara pouncing on a long hop.

Sporting one of the Cricket Force T-shirts he'd been distributing to volunteers, Bobby Cross spared me from manual duties by greeting me with, 'You must be here to see Kate. Come inside and get a drink.' I took an ECB-logoed mug of tea and resisted the mounting pile of hot buttered toast while Bobby explained how young Kate and his other sister, Jenny – who would grow up to become a Super League netballer – had fulfilled the roles of bowler and fielder while he practised in the garden.

That the family would turn into a local sporting dynasty was hardly a surprise given that their father was David Cross, who, as a bearded, bruising centre-forward of my youth, played around 700 games for a variety of teams, most notably Norwich, Coventry and West Ham, with whom he scored ninety-nine League goals and won the FA Cup in 1980.

While Bobby and I chatted, a space was being cleared for the sale of kit and equipment that Kate was donating to the club to raise money for the youth section. When she arrived, tracksuited, pony-tailed and straight from the gym – 'we get rest days but I find that your body switches off and when you train again the next day you are knackered' – six large cricket bags emerged from her car. Doing her bit to help the club was no big deal; as natural an act as bowling to her brother. After all, Heywood is her extended family.

'If I didn't have Heywood I don't know what I would be doing,' she said, pulling her knees up and hugging them close with hands that she'd neatly decorated with green nail varnish for a family wedding the previous day. 'Hopefully I am going to play first-team cricket here this season. I don't think there has ever been a girl in the Central Lancashire League. Bobby was captain for ten years and he would never pick me; he couldn't justify picking his little sister. But there is a new captain now and he said in winter they are a bowler short and would I be willing to play? I would absolutely love it. One reason would be to play in the same team as my brother. And it sounds daft when you play international cricket, but one of my goals has always been to play first-team cricket for the club I have grown up at.'

Kate was eight when she began playing at the club for her uncle, Bob, who was the under-11s coach. But the economical and easy bowling action that would become a feature of the England squad and which had allowed her to remain largely injury free – the most vital of all achievements for a fast bowler – had already been honed in the garden by then.

'My dad came home from work one day and Bobby said to him, "I have taught Kate how to bowl and she has got a natural action." I was about six at the time so I had no idea what a natural action was, but Dad had a look and said, "Yes, you've picked it up quite easily." So when I was eight I was about ready to start playing with the guys around here. I have spent my life down here and if I was here watching Bobby I would actually be over by the scorebox playing cricket.'

Yet there were some, even at Heywood, who were not convinced by her achievements in the Lancashire girls' age groups, where she played for the under-15s at age twelve, and in boys' club cricket. 'My stats in boys' cricket were always quite good because they would either never try to score runs against me because they were afraid of being out to a girl or they'd try to hit me and it would go wrong. You have people who are set in their ways and there was a lot of talk about me playing senior cricket when I was about fourteen. But we had one particular coach who would just not pick me. He didn't say, "You are a girl, you are not playing," but I would always look at the team sheet and see I wasn't on it. I don't know whether he thought it was because I was a girl or because I wasn't good enough, but I probably didn't play for the third eleven until I was fifteen or sixteen.'

By that time, Kate had already achieved a degree of local notoriety by being the first girl named as part of Lancashire's cricket academy. She sighed at the memory and explained, 'I was fifteen and I didn't realise what a big deal it was. I just thought it was brilliant and I'd get to train more. There was a lot of media attention around me being the first girl and a lot of people were saying I was taking the place of a boy. I remember reading some not nice comments underneath an article in the *Bolton Evening News*, where someone had said that women should be in the kitchen. But John Stanworth, who picked me and made me realise I could go far in my career, did an interview with Sky and said I had got there on merit and they could have had any number in the academy.'

It was hard to argue against her inclusion on cricketing grounds. She had played her first game for Lancashire women aged only fourteen, bowling at Charlotte Edwards.

Two days earlier she had taken 5 for 13 for the county under-17s against Yorkshire. The highlight of her 2007 season was a return of 7 for 7 for the under-15s against Northumberland.

By 2008 Cross was playing for the England Academy, but it would be another five years before she made the full team in the West Indies, where she took four wickets on her ODI debut. It was the kind of day she'd wondered if she would ever see, especially during the battle with depression that had so nearly derailed her career in the meantime.

'Everything had all just built up and I really struggled,' she explained, recalling the pressure of course work, exams, training and homesickness. 'My boyfriend at the time, Liam, was the only person who knew about it, so I was battling on my own other than him. I only had to be in university four hours a week for my course, but I just didn't want to get up. I think university just wasn't for me. I'd purposely made sure I wasn't too far away from home, but I was still away and not eating the food you should be. I think I lived off Super Noodles for two years. I didn't have the money for nice food. When I eventually told my mum she said she had known for weeks. I told my dad about taking a break from cricket and he just said, "If you are not enjoying it, don't do it." My mum was worried about throwing away something I had worked so hard for. I ended up having the start of the 2011 summer off and didn't play any county cricket.

'The frustrating thing for me was that there were no triggers, no reason why I had this depression. If I'd had financial troubles it would have been something that could have been fixed; my mum and dad would have helped me out. There was never anything specific that was a problem so that is why I got so frustrated. I thought once uni was over it would just disappear. After I finished my final exam I remember feeling quite cheerful and thinking, "Right, I am going to turn over a new leaf. I can start things again." It didn't go. I had moved back home and it got worse. I couldn't understand why. I didn't know what was wrong. Then eventually I just started to notice some difference. I saw some counsellors and that was a real big help.'

The worst had passed. Kate said it had now been eighteen months since her last episode. But those around her remained watchful and cautious. 'We have a personal welfare officer at the ECB [Purdy Miller] and she knows everything that went on and Paul Shaw knows everything because he was the guy I had to speak to about getting some time off from cricket. They are wary of the fact that I could fall back into it, but they keep an eye on me. Every time we go on tour Purdy gives me a call to see how I am and we do some [mental health] number scales to make sure everything is OK. The only thing that occasionally happens is I get fatigue. That's not really linked with depression; I just do too much sometimes. I remember when I came back from the last Ashes I was absolutely wiped out and just couldn't get back into training and the ECB told me to just stop and rest. We write goals every three months and one of my goals is making sure I'm not falling back into that fatigue that could lead to a state of depression.'

The support of her employers is indicative of the enlightened approach that the ECB, in particular, and the sporting community in general has begun to take towards mental health issues in recent years. 'It's a natural and intended consequence of spending more time and money on the [women's] programme that we are able to support the players in a broader range of ways,' Clare Connor explained. 'I hasten to add that we don't spend money recklessly and we have to be accountable for the inclusion of more support staff. In recent years, some players have needed additional support from a nutrition perspective and some have needed a deeper level of psychological support. Through our strong relationship with the PCA we have made real strides on the latter. It's commonly known that cricket has an undesirably strong link to depression, for a range of reasons, and it's vital that we can support the players to cope with such issues.

'Kate is an example of a player we nearly lost. She found life highly stressful when she left home to go to university. It all got on top of her; being away from her loved ones, undertaking a challenging degree and being expected to be a high-performing sportswoman. Through the relationships she had built with our staff she was able to pick a way through those dark days and I think that Paul Shaw probably ensured the development of a future England women's "great" through his sensitive handling of Kate, and through being able to call on an infrastructure to offer her the right level of support.'

Family, too, has continued to provide a firm foundation for her career. Her father, now employed as a scout by Blackburn Rovers, remains as solid a presence in her life as he was in the forward lines that he led with enough force and strength to score more than 200 goals in the top levels of professional football. 'He just understands it and he has been there,' Kate continued. 'My brother was a professional at Lancashire too so I am lucky I have both of them to speak to about things. They see everything that goes on away from the media whereas someone who just follows me on Twitter won't see the hard yards behind getting a five-fer.'

It was from the greatest day of her dad's career, West Ham's 1-0 win against Arsenal at Wembley, that she acquired the superstition of taking the field with a metal pig pendant around her neck. Her dad, convinced that seeing that particular animal on match-day was a lucky omen, had been clutching a small porcelain pig in his fist when he'd played a part in the Hammers' winning goal.

On a more practical level, Kate added, 'My dad always knows what to say in any situation. When I wasn't selected for the third one-day game in New Zealand he sent me this text message saying, "Don't sulk. Make sure you are there for everyone in the dressing room. That is the type of character you need. It is not about you." It makes you realise it is better to be twelfth man over there than being at home watching. Whenever I hear him do interviews he always just says he is really pleased for me because of all the hard work I have put in. Whatever I had chosen to do, whether it was music – it would never have been music because I am hopeless at that – he would have supported me. And the best advice he has given me was after we won the Test in Australia. I was absolutely buzzing and he sent me a message saying, "Never get too high when you have done well or too low when you have not done well." That was it. No congratulations.'

It was that dramatic victory in Perth, the launch pad for the 2013/14 Ashes success, that marked Kate's arrival as a force in international cricket, taking three wickets in each innings on her Test debut. 'People were saying that match saved women's Test cricket and it was one of the best ever, but we were just in a bubble so you don't see it in that respect,' she recalled. 'We were emotionally, physically and mentally up and down,because the game ebbed and flowed so much. I have never experienced anything so emotionally draining. I didn't sleep for four days, mostly through adrenalin. We finished the game at lunchtime [on day four] and we had a few beers in the changing room and went down to a pub on the waterfront. [Then chief executive] David Collier came down and had the ECB credit card and was buying us drinks. I was there for an hour, ordered a pizza because I was starving and then Anya had to take me home because I was just asleep. I had completely gone.'

Even though England lost their next Test, at home to India, she repeated her success with three more wickets in each innings. 'I really like Crossy; she takes her chances,' was the simple summary that Charlotte Edwards gave me of her teammate.

It is Test cricket that Kate believes most suits her bowling, which owes more to reliability than a revelatory concoction of deliveries. 'At the moment I don't think they see me as a Twenty20 player. I have been pushing all winter to prove that I can play it. My style of bowling is that I consistently hit the top of off stump, whereas in T20 you are meant to change things every single ball. My argument is that if people can't play my best delivery then why not bowl six of that? In one-day cricket and certainly Test matches you have got time to get yourself into a spell. You know it is not just going to be one or two overs. In the India Test I bowled seventeen overs in one afternoon. You have time to get into a rhythm and if I am in a groove I don't really have to think about anything, I just run in and bowl. I think the five-fer I took in New Zealand was all about pressure. I was bowling in the right areas, cramping the batters up and then they were doing things differently. That is why I enjoy Test matches and have been more successful.'

The recent tour of New Zealand, where she was the last squad member to get a game, proved that Brunt and Shrubsole remained the first-choice pairing with the new ball. Cross, who would eventually take 5 for 24 in the fourth ODI, had to be content to wait for her chance and follow her dad's advice in being the perfect team player.

'I did a lot of drinks carrying,' she laughed. 'Your first instinct is that you want the team to win and you want everyone to do well, but then you also want to be in the team so it is difficult. I have to bide my time. I know Katherine and Anya are the main strike bowlers and if anything happens to them that is my opportunity to come in. This is where my dad is quite good. He always says to me, "You are a team out there. You are a bowling unit. Back your bowlers." I have always tried to be supportive. I always think about what I would want someone to do for me if I was on the pitch and they were twelfth man. Everyone says I do the twelfth really well. If getting someone that extra drink means we are going to win the game, I would rather put the yards in off the pitch. And you know personally how frustrating it is when you don't do well so I would never ever wish that upon anybody, I would always want to do better and be better than somebody but not want them to fail.'

As the do-it-yourself work going on outside the Heywood pavilion served to make the new season appear imminent, Kate explained that another of her priorities was to find a greater voice within the England dressing room. Agreeing that she had been one of those players Paul and Lottie had hoped would benefit from the absence of senior players at winter training, she identified herself as 'a bit of a newbie in the squad' who had the chance to 'come out of my shell a bit more'.

It is easy to raise sceptical eyebrows when you hear that the girls went for a bonding and leadership day at RAF Cranwell in Lincolnshire before departure for New Zealand, having previously had a similar outing to the National Space Centre in Leicester and even taken part in a *Come Dine With Me* challenge. But Kate felt it proved to her, and others, that she was enjoying important growth among her peers. 'We did a lot of team building this winter, purely because we were doing a five-month stint indoors and that would drive anyone crazy. You just get forced into situations you would never get into. There was an obstacle course and you had some equipment and you had to get your girls from one side of the room to the other. You were in charge. It was just you, with four of your teammates looking at you waiting for you to make a decision. God knows what Lot does on the pitch when she has the whole world watching her. Things like that put you on the spot and you find out you can cope better than you would ever think. I feel I am a bigger part of the squad now.

'When you get on to an England pitch you are not just going to say, "Hang on, Lottie, can you just do this?" You have to find the balance of integrating into the squad and not coming across as arrogant. It is the challenge of having confidence to know your decisions are the right ones. Lottie always says whatever you choose she will back you 100 per cent. Obviously, if you get hit out of the park, you get your head down and go back to your mark. But she is brilliant. She always seems to be at mid-on or mid-off when you are bowling so she is always in your ear. I remember in New Zealand, my first game for five months, she was saying, "Crossy, just breathe." I was a bit nervous.'

Cricket had dominated so much of Kate's life that I wondered if there was room for anything, or anyone, that was unconnected to it. 'There is a line,' she insisted. 'I have school friends who are very different to my cricket friends, but I have my life down at Heywood and in the summer this is my second home. When I am with my school friends it is food and drink and going out, but obviously I am a bit more disciplined when I am with the cricket girls. My job is cricket so my life is ninety per cent cricket at the moment. It makes it equally special when I get to see my other friends and have a bit of a break.

'Sacrifice is the wrong word because at the end of the day I am representing my country, but there were a lot of things I had to say no to. My school prom, I missed that because I had a game in Loughborough the following day. I miss birthday parties, family gatherings, especially in the summer. But I always saw it as what I did and I have a good group of friends who understood that. There are a few younger girls coming through the system at Lancs who say, "I am going to miss going out with my mates if I play in this game." Well, what do you want to do? Do you want to play at the highest level? I don't think they have realised yet that they might have to sacrifice to achieve something.'

As we left the committee room we'd been talking in and walked back through the main hall of the pavilion Kate spoke of the anticipation that was building ahead of the summer months. 'I try not to put too much pressure on myself, but I do get nerves,' she admitted. 'When you are in an England shirt everything gets seen; you are so desperate to do well. You do enjoy it, I can't say that I don't, but it is such a different game to playing for Lancashire. This summer is going to be one of the biggest women's cricket has ever had. Sky and BBC doing every game; everything at home; using all the county grounds. There is always a buzz around an Ashes summer and if we can recreate that excitement from Australia and produce something and get the crowds in, it will be massive.'

For now, though, the Australians could wait. There were fences to be painted.[2]

---

2   Two weeks later, Cross made her historic Central Lancashire League debut, taking 3 for 19 in a seven-over spell as Heywood won their opening game against Clifton by eight wickets. 'I was more nervous than I was before my England debut,' she said. 'Everyone that I've ever known or grown up with was watching. I am pleased I was able to hold my own and not make a complete fool of myself.' Brother Bobby made an unbeaten half-century to secure the victory, but only after he had dropped a sitter off his little sister's bowling.

It proved to be just the warm-up: on 10 May, Kate returned figures of 8 for 47 to bowl her team to victory against Unsworth. According to the club's website, 'Crimble has witnessed many magic moments in its 94-year history, but it's hard to see how anything can have topped what the venerable old ground saw on Sunday.' It was the thirty-fifth anniversary of her dad's FA Cup victory.

'For Crossy it is fantastic,' said Paul Shaw. 'We felt for her development it was really good for her to play good standard men's cricket, so that she is challenged. The wickets are great for her confidence but, equally, in tough pressure situations, the guys hit the ball more powerfully and more consistently. Dealing with those situations and understanding the lengths, lines, adaptations and variations you have to bowl in those situations; these are less publicised perhaps, but are of equal importance.'

7

County Court

'When the girls score runs in county cricket, what value is that? Sometimes we are playing poor opposition. Sometimes it is quite difficult to select our team based on county cricket' – Charlotte Edwards

'YOU'RE the light, you're the light,' chorused the girls of the Sussex team. 'When I close my eyes, I'm colour blind.' After a couple of decades working around American football teams I was used to hearing rap or heavy metal blaring out across dressing rooms. The sound of female voices singing along to former *Pop Idol* contestant Darius as they prepared for action was rather endearing. Along the balcony of the Beckenham County Ground pavilion, Kent had selected Calvin Harris's 'Acceptable in the '80s' as their soundtrack.

Inevitably, it was the only participant in this game whose birth pre-dated that particular decade who was first down the steps ready for warm-ups. 'I'm a bit tired,' Charlotte Edwards laughed, looking anything but. She had scored 88 unbeaten runs here the previous day to help her team beat Yorkshire. 'They have brought the boundaries in today,' she added, looking across a field with a bank of functional green seating at one end and pleasant-looking apartments with plant-festooned balconies at the other. 'They were right out yesterday and it was bloody hard. We had to run everything.'

It was quite possible that the champion county, the title afforded to the winners of the 50-over Royal London One-Day Cup, could be decided on this first weekend in May. No team other than Kent or Sussex had prevailed for ten years. With almost half the contracted England professionals and a couple of decent overseas players between them, few people expected that pattern to be broken in 2015, although Sussex had got off to a losing start against Surrey a day earlier.

The two skippers, Edwards and Sarah Taylor, had been the cornerstones of much of the national team's success in recent years and they chatted amiably as they walked out for the toss. Within two minutes of seeing her opposite number call correctly, Edwards had hurried back to the pavilion and re-emerged padded up for some throw-downs by the boundary rope. Yet it was Taylor who was the more buoyant of the two leaders after the first few overs, with England batters Tammy Beaumont and Lydia Greenway both dismissed cheaply.

As Kent placed their hopes in the hands of their skipper, I took the chance to catch up with the injured Laura Marsh, who'd been hitting ground balls to the fielders before the game and was now sitting alongside those yet to bat, her attention divided between the game and her phone. 'I wish I was out there,' she sighed as we relocated to the pavilion. 'I missed a lot of games last year with my shoulder, so I have got used to watching.'

It was a hamstring that was keeping the twenty-eight-year-old out on this occasion, an injury suffered during a gym session. It had forced her to miss the trip to Sri Lanka with England's other spinners and now meant a delayed start to such an important summer. 'It's frustrating I guess because my shoulder was back to normal,' she continued, more shy and self-conscious than many of her England colleagues. 'I suppose I still have quite a lot of time so hopefully I can get back in the next couple of weeks.'

Her return to the England team in New Zealand had ended an absence of more than a year after shoulder surgery. 'I had played for quite a few years with pain and had injections. It got to the point where I had used my quota of injections and they went in and found a tear at the back of the socket. They repaired that and stabilised the joint and I did quite a bit of rehab to get the muscles strong again. Then unfortunately I did the same thing again so did all the rehab again. It is fine now, it held up really well in New Zealand. I understand the importance of looking after it. It is never going to be back to how it was before so I have to adapt my throwing and make sure I use the rest of my body and not just the shoulder.'

The fact that her rehabilitation came within the new professional era ensured that Laura was never made to feel as though she was completely outside the team. 'We train together two days a week and, even though I wasn't doing everything, I was around the group and doing all the gym sessions,' she explained. 'I suppose the hardest part was being sat at home when everyone else was off on tour or playing games. I went to the grounds as much as I could, but when I was not there I was following it on Cricinfo, which was quite hard. After seven or eight years in the squad, to not be part of it was quite alien.'

Laura developed her cricketing skills in Sussex, for whom she played until a switch to Kent, the county of her birth, in

2011. It was somewhat ironic that she had developed shoulder problems after changing from bowling seam to spin, a switch unrelated to her health. 'I got into the England team bowling seam when I was nineteen but never cemented my place. It wasn't really my idea to bowl spin. I was experimenting in the England nets and one of the coaches said he thought I had the talent for it. So I worked on it through the winter of 2007/08 and then went out to Australia and bowled spin for the first time in international games. I ended up being better at it so I am glad I made the transition.'

That series marked the first of four Ashes successes in which she had been involved, including a crucial half-century in the 2013 Test at Wormsley in support of centurion Heather Knight. She had also played a key role in the 2009 World Cup triumph, taking sixteen wickets in the tournament, including a career-best 5 for 15 against Pakistan. It meant that a lot of experience would be left on the bench if fitness or form prevented her lining up for yet another crack at Australia later in the year. 'The new Ashes format is a massive step forward for the women's game. It makes it a lot more exciting for the public. I hope I can get some matches in and get back to the form I have shown in the past. I suppose any runs and wickets in county cricket are going to help and give players the confidence to perform in an England shirt. But also the training in an England environment is very important as well.'

As Marsh was leaving the pavilion to rejoin her teammates, Edwards appeared, having been out during our conversation – stumped by Taylor off a leg-side wide bowled by Georgia Elwiss. 'A freak dismissal,' Lottie sighed, grabbing a cup of tea. 'Anyone else, it would have been four byes.' That Kent rallied from the loss of their England trio to post 187 for 5 was due mainly to a determined unbeaten 82 by Deanna Cooper, a dual sportswoman who also plays football for Brighton and Hove Albion. It was a below-par score but, after being 64 for 5 at the halfway point, was at least a defendable total.

* * * * *

This Bank Holiday Monday represented the second day of games on the opening weekend of the women's premier county tournament, one level down from the international contests that would dominate the summer, the feeder for the professional England squad. For the first time the competition was being played in coloured kit with a white ball, but such cosmetics could not conceal the complications of the opening day.

For a start, many of the country's top players had missed the first action because they had only just landed back from the England spin camp in Sri Lanka. It was easy to conclude that more effective scheduling could have avoided such a situation, although the ECB had been forced to push back their original tour dates when local religious New Year celebrations made opposition and facilities unavailable. Even so, it meant that some counties were without important team members for the first of only eight games in the tournament.

Then there was the cancellation of Middlesex's game against Berkshire at Edmonton Cricket Club because the hosts' covers had been vandalised some weeks before and the replacements had yet to arrive. The tarpaulins that were meant to do the job proved ineffective and a sunny afternoon was wasted while the wicket dried out. Raf Nicholson, a renowned observer of the women's game, wrote on the CricketHer website, 'This isn't an isolated incident. It happens every year and the ECB never seem to do anything about it.' At Beckenham, spectators and players would have to contend with a rickety scoreboard incapable of offering the totals of individual batters. This was the environment in which the England players would be preparing themselves to take on Australia in the Ashes.

As long ago as 1997, England coach Megan Lear had told author Pete Davies, 'Our top thirty [players] are extremely talented. The problem is getting the standard of game to prepare them.' In almost two decades, for all the advances in the women's game, it appeared that not much had changed in that regard.

When I'd sat in Clare Connor's office she had pointed to a blue folder. 'The big challenge now is this piece of work, which is around what women's cricket needs to do next to underpin and sustain having eighteen contracted players and grow that number to sustain success at the top end. It's about what needs to be there to make sure that high-potential players can challenge those players for a contract, otherwise the contracted players will just get further away from the pack.'

Going into the 2015 season, women's county cricket simply did not have a deep enough talent pool to ensure the continued supply of England players capable of remaining ahead of the rest of the world. The tour to New Zealand, which ended with PR manager Beth Wild preparing to take the field as twelfth man, demonstrated the need for reinforcements. There could be times when eighteen players might simply not be enough. 'Without that tier below of fully fit internationally-ready players we are a little fragile if we pick up a few injuries,' said Clare. 'In 2016 we have a tour to South Africa late January/February, the World Twenty20 in India in March, Pakistan at home in early summer and then we go away to the West Indies and Sri Lanka before November. It's as busy as we have ever been. You can't just have these contracted players and then a mix of 400 county players. We have the Academy players, of course, but they are a mix of precocious talent, some of whom are nowhere near ready to play international cricket.'

The danger – of which the ECB was fully aware – was that the elitism of the national team, while helping to take that group forward, contained the potential to undermine standards in the county game. 'We have five England players but since I lived in Loughborough I have not made the effort to go to Kent training,' said Tammy Beaumont. 'It's a three-hour ride for two hours of training. None of us England players will go to that training so the other girls don't have the chance to improve by training with us. We will just turn up and play and get away with it because we have been training with England. If we all have a bad day together we will lose. If the girls below us aren't getting better, that is where the problem is.

'The gap is even more prevalent now. You can see the difference because other countries now are more professional. Some, like Sri Lanka and the West Indies, you could beat easily, but international cricket has jumped up massively, while county cricket has stayed the same. It needs a lot of help from the ECB. I know that at Kent we don't get the kind of support that potentially we deserve. It is the men's set-up that earns them the money to keep them going, so why would you bother with the women?'

Even Edwards, someone who takes a lot of dissuading from the opportunity for a net, had long since ceased making the long round-trip to county training. While she might have been as keen as ever to win everything possible for the county she led, she was realistic enough to understand the relevance of the domestic competitions to her England side. 'When the girls score runs in county cricket, what value is that?' she wondered. 'Sometimes we are playing poor opposition. Sometimes it is quite difficult to select our team based on county cricket. If they score a hundred, well you should score a hundred. If not, why not? It is pretty evident that we need a stronger domestic competition. We are the envy of the world in everything else we do and this would be a real game-changer for us. It would help in getting more girls playing as well; a competition that people want to be part of.'

The answer, according to Clare's blueprint folder, was the insertion of an additional level – 'franchise cricket' if you must – where the better players could be challenged more profitably for their future development. The intention was to have six teams, either centrally controlled or contracted out to interested cities, counties or universities. Clare's hope was that a new Twenty20 competition would be in place by 2016, with a 50-over version to follow a year later. 'Even in Division One the players think they only play two or three competitive games of 50-over cricket a year. That is not going to take the England players on or stretch the players below that. We have pockets of brilliant work going on in a lot of counties, but we have some counties where they have only two women's club teams. We have got to try to unpick some of that if we want a strong development model.'

Clare, who had discussed similar structures with the Football Association and England Netball, continued, 'This is the biggie for me. This will take a lot of persuasion, influence and selling, and a lot more money if we are to do this how I would like to do it. We'd probably be doubling what we invest into the England women central contracts. We need to work out how best this can operate and what appetite is out there from people who think it is commercially viable, or has the potential to become so.'[3]

Of course, the big difference in these conversations to the debate over the desirability of a franchised Twenty20 competition in the men's game, was that women's county cricket did not need to worry about protecting its own

---

3   On 18 June, Clare was able to share her vision publicly, announcing plans for the Women's Cricket Super League, into which the ECB would invest £3 million worth of prize money and running costs over a four-year period. She described it as an even more important development for the women's game than professional contracts.

television money, its own attendance figures – because there wasn't any. On a sunny, if a little brisk, holiday Monday the best two women's county teams, including the two biggest names in the English game, drew a crowd that might just have crept into three figures. Yet even some of the women's counties had their reservations.

On the Beckenham boundary I chatted with Don Miles, who, as well as being a regular photographer on the women's circuit, is chairman of the Sussex Women's Cricket Association. Prefacing his remarks by stating that he was a big fan of Sussex old girl Clare Connor – 'the shrewdest captain I have ever known' – he informed me that he was a traditionalist and protective of his county's status as the highest level of domestic cricket. Besides, he argued, how much difference would it make to the standard of cricket if a nine-county Division One was reduced to a six-team competition?

A couple of weeks later I would be at The Oval, where several hundred – mostly schoolgirls – had taken advantage of free admission to see Surrey play Middlesex in a special Twenty20 challenge for the Pemberton Greenish Cup[4] on what was being billed as 'Women and Girls Day'. Watching from the viewing area outside the main pavilion's committee room, my eye was caught by pink advertising boards at the opposite end of the ground bearing the '#ThisGirlCan' hashtag of Sport England's female participation campaign. Ebony Rainford-Brent sat down alongside me, clutching a glass of white wine and cheering loudly when Surrey picked up a wicket in the first over. She had just about regained her voice after getting 300 excited children to remain quiet long enough to conduct a question-and-answer session with England player Nat Sciver. As a former England Ashes winner, a BBC Radio commentator and the new Director

---

4 Won by Middlesex, thanks largely to a top score of 48 by England candidate Fran Wilson in her first game for her new county.

of Women's Cricket at Surrey – a county that had visions of being one of the women's franchise owners – she was well placed to see all sides of the ongoing debate.

'The problem,' she ventured, 'is that women's cricket has been built backwards.' Whereas the men's game developed through its clubs, she explained, the female version was going top down, attempting to gain leverage from the strength of the national team to bolster the various levels below it. Rainford-Brent, who puts her own cricketing career down to the 'pot luck' of picking up a bat when she was ten, had taken her role with Surrey on a part-time basis. Its remit covered awareness, player development and elite performance, although she saw herself as someone who was providing 'checks and challenges' more than being responsible for every little detail.

She agreed that a tier between county and international was desirable, but far from running scared of it, saw Surrey as playing a key role within it. 'I am so competitive that I want our bid to be the best,' she said, referring to the proposed method of determining who controls any teams at the new level. 'But the counties will always play an important part as the connection with the clubs,' she added, looking across a pavilion full of youngsters dancing and singing along to the music between overs.

* * * * *

Back at Beckenham, Sussex seemed poised for victory until they lost Taylor, who had scored 77 the day before, at 104 for 3; revenge for Edwards with a sharp catch at slip. With progress having slowed considerably, despite a spirited half-century by Izzy Collis, they arrived at the final over in need of a further five to win. Edwards had brought herself on late in the innings, proving hard to get away, and by the time she prepared to deliver the last ball, Sussex, seven wickets down, still needed two runs. Ellen Burt took a big swing and missed, wicketkeeper Lauren Griffiths removed the bails, and the Kent players became a shrieking, whooping mass, thrilled that they had pulled off an unlikely victory and maintained their record of not dropping a point in the competition since 2013.

Yet, as they reached the boundary edge and turned back to shake hands with their opponents, they noticed that the Sussex team were crowded around the umpires. The stumping appeal, Sussex pointed out, had been turned down and while Kent's players had been busy celebrating, Collis had raced to the stumps to complete a bye, tying the game. The home team were having none of it. The ball was dead, they argued. Edwards stomped back out to the middle and the final action on the field was the remarkable sight of her and England teammate Taylor shouting and gesticulating angrily at each other.

As I headed to my car the debate had reached the point where a website videographer's camera was being commandeered so that umpires could figure out in peace exactly what had happened. Say what you like about the suitability of women's county cricket as a development platform for the international game, but no one could argue that the players didn't care about it. I doubted I'd see a game more intensely disputed all summer.[5]

---

5   Sussex, it was subsequently ruled, had legally run a bye and therefore tied the game. A day later, Kent lodged an appeal, invoking the 'spirit of cricket' and claiming that the umpires had changed their minds under pressure from the visiting team after congratulating Kent on their win. 'Sussex knew full well they would not have been able to score a run,' argued coach Stuart Eddicott. Yet the ECB said there was no reason to change the result upon which the umpires had finally settled.

8

Man on a Mission

'You look at self-esteem, confidence and belief. They are tremendously important attributes in the woman athlete. Understanding that and how to forge a relationship based on that is really important' – Paul Shaw

TWO months to go before the Ashes would begin with the first one-day international at Taunton. Paul Shaw stood overlooking the nets at the ECB's base in Loughborough and glanced through his printed schedule for the next two days of team activity. 'We have just come off about five weeks' general preparation,' he explained, 'focusing on how the team is developing and making any technical modifications. Now we are going into specific preparation, the likely roles of the players in game situations. We go into the competition phase in about three or four weeks' time, building towards Australia. We will gradually feed in two or three opposition batters and bowlers per week and we'll identify specific plans.'

The 'performance suite' at Loughborough would become the strategic nerve centre, analysing the tendencies, targets and statistics of the Australian players. 'On a weekly basis we will sit down with the players and go through the footage, start formalising the plans and getting everyone's insights. Obviously we had a few players in Australia recently playing against their players.'

Charlotte Edwards explained, 'You get video analysis of everyone now. It can be a good thing and sometimes a bad thing. We try to keep it as simple as possible, we try not to look too much into the opposition because you have to focus on yourselves and what you are doing. Unless there is a glaring technical glitch in their team, we tend to focus on ourselves.'

And, expressing sentiments that critics would find themselves challenging later in the year, she added, 'We try not to be predictable, to be brave at times and to do things that people don't think you are going to do.'

Once plans were formulated, batters and bowlers would be recruited to replicate key opponents in the nets. 'Where that's not possible we will still have our bowlers running in and bowling in the areas they would against the Australian batters,' Paul explained. 'Then we gradually refine that the closer we get to the Ashes.' Like his skipper, he stressed that the intention was not to get too hung up on the opposition. 'Within the next month the plans will be pretty clear for Australia. We will be focusing on our strengths and we have warm-up games to put plans in place.'

As he spoke, Paul illustrated his vision by drawing what he called 'pillars', indicating the calendar moments at which the team would transition into each stage of preparation. But, he laughed, 'I've told you before; we're never as far along as I want to be.'

A couple of hundred miles away, Paul Farbrace was about to begin his term as interim head coach of the England men's team against New Zealand at Lord's. While Farbrace, one of the assistants to Peter Moores, was taking over from someone who had never achieved the level of success desired by his bosses, it was now two years since Shaw had succeeded – in Mark Lane – a coach who had inked Ashes victories and global tournament triumphs into his résumé. Anya Shrubsole, one of the players who had served under both Lane and Shaw, said, 'They have a different way of going about things, but I think you get that with anyone. Mark was a hugely successful coach and did a lot for this team, driving us forward and making us a dominant force from 2008 onwards, and Paul is looking to continue that in a different era. There is potentially more pressure on him, more eyes on him with how the game has gone into the professional era.'

'I have never felt pressure from that perspective,' Paul insisted. 'I worked closely with Mark and enjoyed it so I could see first-hand the fantastic job he had done. When I came in professionalism was around the corner so I was already looking at how to manage that transition, developing an England programme for the professional age, how we would structure and staff it. It is about results ultimately and there is that expectation on any coach.'

Laura Marsh had said that while Lane 'wore his heart on his sleeve, Shawsy is much more measured'. But, Paul pointed out, 'I do get excited. There is no getting away from the fact that it will be a terrific Ashes series and the staff and players are starting to get excited. But I am pretty level in the build-up to a big series, and – win, lose or draw – I try to stay focused on what we need to do. There are always ups and downs along the way so it is absolutely crucial that as a management team we are able to deal with that. It is important for me to have everyone really focused on the task in hand.'

Today's first priority was to run his coaching and support staff through the day's programme. As they gathered in an upper floor meeting room, Lydia Greenway and Sarah Taylor were in there putting the finishing touches, in red and green capital letters, to a flip chart presentation of fielding drills. One page was headed, 'How to get a dot ball for your team,' and included bullet points relating to: diving stops in the ring; anticipation in the ring; diving stops on the boundary; and saving twos on the boundary.

Once the players had departed, Paul stood off to one side of the room and reminded everyone, 'We are at the end of the general preparation phase, so in terms of fitness this is a chance to see if we have made significant gains.' The fitness testing session would be staged in the morning so that the girls could 'get it off their minds'. Then the players would work in three groups, rotating through different disciplines. One would focus on batting against swing and spin bowling, another would feature power hitting against bowling machines, a third would be working on fielding drills.

Chris Guest, who would take charge of fielding, explained his intentions. 'Same theme as the last few weeks; throwing to hit the stumps,' he said. Having reviewed video of previous practices he had found a big variance in the players' speed. 'Some are standing up and then throwing, while the better ones are starting to throw before they even get up. In some there are ten frames difference in when they throw.'

Carl Crowe was next up, outlining the need to create greater context when the girls were hitting against machinery. 'We need to make it match specific,' he said. 'Not just have them going for it for the sake of it.'

Paul continued, 'I am conscious that in the last two weeks we have done no reviews, so I have asked for a summary after tomorrow's activity and we'll let the players feed back on where we are and what we need to do.'

Having checked if there was anything he needed to be aware of in terms of injuries – there wasn't – Paul concluded the meeting with a word of warning. 'I have been speaking to the PCA and ECB and we have clarified that when girls go abroad to play it won't affect the money they receive. But I plan to have individual chats with players over the next two days about when they are able to play overseas. Be aware of that; some players might be up, some might be down.'

With that, the eight staff members moved to the room next door, from where good-hearted chatter had been audible during their meeting. The contract issue was the first thing Shaw addressed with his players. 'We didn't want contracts to be adjusted if you go overseas. There will be no reduction in money,' he reiterated, before clarifying that it would be the ECB's decision about who went abroad and when. With the Women's Big Bash League in Australia having just announced plans for teams to field up to three overseas players, it was obviously a pertinent subject. 'I will be fair and consistent,' Paul declared. 'That said, it will be an individual decision. We'll discuss how it affects you positively and how it affects Team England.'[6]

Without allowing anyone to dwell too long on that, Paul spoke of the impending fitness session. 'Really push yourselves,' he urged, his words carrying a quiet pointedness rather than representing a marines-style rallying cry. 'On the back of the training block we have done it will give us a good insight into your progress.' The players filed out quietly, many with heads bowed in thought. It appeared that the next couple of hours were weighing heavily on them.

---

6   By the autumn, nine of the England squad had been confirmed as participants in the Women's Big Bash in Australia: Charlotte Edwards and Katherine Brunt (Perth Scorchers); Kate Cross and Lauren Winfield (Brisbane Heat); Heather Knight (Hobart Hurricanes); Sarah Taylor (Adelaide Strikers); Danni Wyatt (Melbourne Renegades); Nat Sciver (Melbourne Stars) and Laura Marsh (Sydney Sixers).

Paul, meanwhile, could not have looked more at ease. This job, he'd said, was the culmination of fifteen years of coaching. 'There are transferable skills from every role I have ever had. And it is fantastic to be working with such a group of players, good people who are working harder and harder.'

His working week had begun two days earlier, at 5.30 on Monday morning, the time for which he'd set his alarm so he could answer emails before his phone started ringing. Monday and part of Tuesday had been spent travelling round to meetings, or with a mobile stuck to his ear talking to players and staff, before he had driven down to his ECB housing in Loughborough. There, he would typically refine the training programme for the following two days. He would be back home in Yorkshire by 11pm on Thursday and would use Friday for further meetings and to finalise the following week's training plan, which he would email to all involved that day. Most Sundays found him watching women's cricket somewhere. 'I try to have a family day on Saturday,' he said, family in his case being Jackie – 'a very understanding wife who has got her hands full' – and sons Matthew and Adam, ten and eight respectively at this time.

A wicketkeeper-batsman for Barnsley in the Yorkshire League and Holmfirth in the Huddersfield League, Shaw's own playing career had been curtailed by back problems at the age of twenty-seven. 'At that stage I was heavily into coaching anyway, so it enabled me to focus more on that and planning out my career. I wanted to be connected to the game.'

Head coach at Barnsley and regional under-19s coach with the ECB, he became a support coach for the England team and worked as one-on-one coach for a small group of England players, most notably fast bowler Katherine Brunt, a product of his own home club. That led him to become England Academy head coach for three years, responsible for 'identifying players with potential and transitioning them into players who would perform'. He held the role of director of cricket for Yorkshire women and had also served ICC Europe as an elite coach for boys and girls. Elevation to the ECB's High Performance Manager was the final step before taking up his current position.

Clare Connor had no doubts that she and her ECB colleagues had placed the right man into the right position. 'Paul is seriously hard working, a really good thinker, unbelievable with people and developing relationships,' she said. 'He creates trust and rapport, he invests in people and has got vision.' His title as Head of England Women's Performance rather than head coach was not simply a matter of semantics, but a real reflection of his abilities and the demands of a new professional era.

'Rather than a conventional head coach, the skills that were needed at the time were around strategy and vision and bringing people together,' Clare said, 'creating a high-performing management team, which we didn't necessarily have quite how we wanted it at the time. Someone to oversee the specialist coaches, the strategy, clarifying the roles of the players. Those are his skills. I spoke to him about how it wasn't going to be a conventional head coach's role, more of an overarching strategic leader.'

Paul described himself as possessing 'a fairly broad background' but, he believed, there was one common denominator: people. It was that, you sensed, that drove him more than cricket. The sport happened to be the vehicle he had chosen because of his own interest in it. If he'd hated cricket he would have found a different outlet for the same professional principles of 'teaching, coaching, management and leadership'.

'I have done lots of research and my background is very much on understanding personality types and going into some detail on that,' he continued. 'I have always been interested in how people look to get the best out of others. My style is creating an environment where you allow people to fulfil their potential. I have really enjoyed that from being really young and I have had some good teachers work with me. Ultimately it is about getting the best out of people.'

Achieving that with women cricketers was, Paul accepted, a different challenge to working with men, but one that still benefitted from his basic ideology of human psychology. 'Understanding the physics of [women's cricket], challenging it and working to push the boundaries is important. But, ultimately, I am a huge believer that you are coaching individuals. Every man is different, every woman is different. My coaching and education background is based on what makes people tick and how to work with people. Then it is a case of refining that and working with female athletes.'

Clare suggested, 'What guys say they notice is that women want more information and want to talk more. They don't let things go as easily. They want a lot more structure. If they have a training weekend they want itineraries. It is about understanding people. Paul is excellent. He is a big Myers-Briggs thinker and that guides a lot of his behaviour with people.'

Georgia Elwiss told me, 'Paul has come into the set-up and he is a very people person. He makes you feel valued and really wanted. He knows it is important to have those conversations with you so that you know why you are in or not in, what you can get better at. He has been really good.'

Paul continued, 'I have found there is a real emphasis on creating the best possible relationship between female athletes and once that is in place you can work fantastically together. While that is important in the men's game it is perhaps emphasised more in the women's game. Knowing female psychology definitely enables you to do that. You look at self-esteem, confidence and belief. They are tremendously important attributes in the woman athlete. Understanding that and how to forge a relationship based on that is really important.'

Observing the squad at close quarters, or even just following the daily back-and-forth between the girls on Twitter, a clear vision emerged of the closeness between the players; those relationships of which Paul had spoken. It was difficult not to juxtapose that against all the discussion of unrest in and around the England men's dressing room over the previous eighteen months.

'I certainly encourage us to enjoy ourselves,' Lottie said. 'I think if you are happy off the field you will play better on it. The girls do have some very close friends and when it gets tough that really helps. We don't allow egos; you would be pretty much shot down. They are just a lovely bunch of girls. Sometimes I wish they would have a bit more about them and be more cocky and arrogant when they walk out there. But that doesn't need to spill over into team time.'

Kate Cross suggested with a chuckle that 'we spend so much time together we have not got much of a choice but to get on'. She also suggested that the many days of home-based training were where bonds could be forged in a more relaxed environment, giving them an advantage over their male counterparts. 'The men don't train together so much, they just tour. Touring can really take it out of you; seeing the same people day in, day out. Even when we get back from a tour after a month you are ready to get away from people and see your other friends.'

According to Jenny Gunn, 'I think that closeness has just got stronger over the years.' With eleven years of England service to her name, she added, 'When I first came in we all got on, but you had maybe four little groups who hung around with each other. Now you can happily go for a drink with anyone in the team; you don't just stick with your little group. We have worked hard at being open and honest. When you are close you can give and take criticism of each other.'

Lauren Winfield said that the celebrations of Lottie's 200th game as captain in New Zealand were an example of the team seizing an opportunity for a collective laugh. 'We did all those videos and montages, which were obviously fun, and it was good reflecting on little funny stories that had happened over the years, for some of them longer than others. We really enjoy each other's company. We are a very close-knit unit and we enjoy playing together and spending time off the field. That is especially important when you are away from home for four or five weeks. You know when people need down time and people need someone around or to just go out for a coffee. It is important that we have that insight into each other's lives and how the different personalities fit within the group. The last thing you want is to be on tour and not be able to relax and do the type of things you need to be able to do off the pitch.'

The atmosphere of mutual support from which the England women's team drew so much of its breath was about to become apparent as the players faced up to a dreaded couple of hours. As they warmed up in Loughborough's main sports hall, the chatter had returned, although when Paul walked in the girls went silent; the boss arriving on the factory floor. Even I felt the urge to be seen to be paying closer attention and making more notes. 'My legs felt amazing this morning, now I am not so sure,' said Sarah Taylor to no one in particular, before feigning horror when she realised that Paul was right behind her.

'Here we are then,' fitness coach Ian Durrant greeted the girls with. He then split them into two groups, one of which went to the gym for various tests while the other embarked on a series of twenty- and forty-yard sprints. The longer runs were done one at a time, accompanied by screams of encouragement, and were followed by much huddling around a laptop to see how times compared. It was in these scenarios where the senior status of Edwards was most noticeable. In a vest and shorts she lacked the tanned, toned legs or the well-developed upper body muscles of the younger girls. She busted a gut, though, and the shouts of support were at their loudest as she pushed herself past the timing markers.

In the gym, fast bowler Katherine Brunt was setting the standard by pulling herself up on a horizontal bar twenty-seven times, double the amount of many of her teammates. Tash Farrant excelled in the push-ups, just failing to achieve a thirty-fifth attempt despite the presence of Lottie on her knees alongside her and yelling 'Go on Tash!' at aircraft-like volume in her ear. 'They are a great bunch,' Durrant beamed proudly. 'Today is about a line in the sand, a benchmark. But it's not all about the measurements. Sometimes you can tell that they are doing something better even if it doesn't show up in the results.'

Jenny suggested that conditioning represented the biggest change since her arrival in the England team. 'We were fit before, but we are extra fit now,' she said. 'If you want to stay at the top level for as long as possible and keep players on the field for longer you have to be. We are up with the fitness levels of women's football. People think cricket is all about standing around on the field, but it is very harsh on your body, especially if you are bowling.'

The group gathered as one in the main hall for the 'yo-yo' session, a sequence of 20-yard shuttle runs completed at increasing speeds and carried on until each individual in turn became too knackered to go any further. 'Don't run next to me,' spinner Jodie Dibble instructed Danni Wyatt, who set off with the balance and energy of a middle-distance Olympian. 'Danni will be the last one standing,' offered David Capel as he passed through the hall. 'She is so light on her feet.' She was indeed, with Farrant having pushed her hardest, once again to the accompaniment of shrieks and shouts from all.

Sarah added, 'We have all grown up together so there is that bond. Sometimes in training you have to gut it out. Fitness sessions are agony, but we get each other through it. Then the cricket takes care of itself.'

'At the end of the day we have this purpose of playing for England and winning,' said Georgia. 'Going through really tough gruelling sessions brings you together. We have had a couple of really horrible sessions and we have come out knowing it has brought us closer. You know everybody out there has got your back and will really fight for you. We drive each other on.'

For all the relationship benefits of the sprints and squats, however, there was no disguising the relief of having bat and ball in hand again after lunch. At the end of the first rotation, Capel, who had been overseeing the swing and spin bowling session, made a point of asking everyone in his group how they felt it had gone. 'It was a bit rushed,' was one of the replies, from Katherine. The coach praised his players on 'good use of feet', but told them it had not gone as well as he had wanted.

'I like to get people's feedback first,' he explained, as the players headed to their next station. 'Some will say, "Oh, that was terrible," and you have to tell them they are being a little harsh on themselves. It depends on the personality of the player.'

His approach, he went on, was to focus where possible on a player's strengths much more than their weaknesses. 'That is the modern way,' he said. 'Using an old player as an example, if David Gower's strength was hitting bowlers on the up through extra cover then you would want him working on that because it knocks the bowlers off their length and line.' He also said he wanted to see 'strong power hitting – and by that I mean hitting hard through extra cover or straight, or just hard at the field. Not everything has to go out of the ground.'

That power was what Carl was urging his next group of players to unleash. Again, asking questions first and instructing later, he challenged players to describe the principles of hitting the ball hard. 'In your own words, not Capes', he added.

After several comments, Kate suggested, 'Everyone is committed in a session like this. But it needs to become part of your batting.'

'Yes, you really need to stop calling it a power session,' Carl agreed. 'It needs to be part of how you bat. So how do you work it into your batting? If it is not quite there to hit, how can I get a two or three? What do we do today to make sure we transition it into your batting?'

He instructed the girls to stand in a different position before each ball to combat the mechanical nature of the deliveries. 'The more you can make it random, the more relevant it is to what happens out there. Keep challenging yourself. Happy? Yes? Cool, let's go.'

Another day of training would soon be done. The Ashes would be that little bit closer. At the end of the following day the girls would disperse and spend the forthcoming weekend playing in the next set of games for their counties. There would be Kent half-centuries over the course of two games for Edwards, Greenway and Marsh, who would also take 5 for 15 in the same match against Lancashire. Taylor and Gunn would post half-centuries, while in Division Two there were centuries for fringe players Dibble (Devon), Evelyn Jones (Staffordshire) and Sophie Luff (Somerset).

As important as those contests were, Shaw would trust the evidence of his own eyes at Loughborough more than reports from around the country when it came to selection. 'We have scouts all over the country watching county and club cricket,' he said. 'But working with the players every week you can see their development and growth and you trust your own instincts. We are fairly clear on the squads.

Then it is looking at giving yourself options up to the end of the day, so there will be two or three places up for grabs in each of the formats. What we look to do is ensure that in certain key positions we have got players in form and playing with confidence. The door is open on a number of places.

'In practice sessions the players are now performing as much as possible in the roles they are likely to be playing. Seeing them adapt to the roles we give them and excel in certain pressure situations is important. County performances are taken into account without doubt, but the challenge is that the standard between county and international is a big difference. It is a balance of all areas, but you have almost got them in game situations at Loughborough, batting and bowling against the best players in the country. From that perspective it gives us a better insight.'

9

Carry On, Matron

'It can be quite a lonely place and there are
so many sacrifices, so many ordeals, you do
wonder whether you should keep doing that
to yourself' – Katherine Brunt

CONSIDERING it was her day off, Katherine Brunt
had been busy. In the morning she had undergone a
session with her physiotherapist and in the afternoon
run some errands in Loughborough town centre before
picking up her niece from the train station so that she could
stay the night. Any other moments had been spent thinking:
about her back; about the Ashes. The two were inseparable
trains of thought. England's senior bowler, she had played a
part in her country's victory in Australia in 2013/14, but only
a truncated one. 'My last Ashes series was cut short by a back
injury, but I did make it through the Test at the beginning.
I got that last wicket to win the match and you just can't
compare that feeling, even though I was in agony the whole

127

time. That was where it finished for me and I thought that might be the end. From that moment until when we start the Ashes here I have just been wanting to get that feeling back.'

With her thirtieth birthday only a few days away and her back having undergone two major surgeries and multiple stress fractures over the previous decade, Barnsley-born Katherine's ability to recapture those emotions depended, initially, on being fit and healthy enough to make it on to the field. 'My back and the history of my injuries dominates my day and rules my life, you might say,' she said, sounding surprisingly upbeat about such a state of affairs. 'If I am not doing something about it I am thinking about it, or having a conversation on how to manage it or having a physio session to deal with it, or having a doctor's appointment or an MRI, or looking at how many overs I am bowling, or doing rehab or strength training. Everything is geared towards looking after my back and my body.'

Hence the importance of not missing her morning physiotherapy session, even though it was 'just a little catch-up because there has been a lot of cricket recently. It is going to be mental so we need to keep ourselves in good shape.'

She continued, 'I try to get myself in really good condition before each tour, but I have to look at each series and think: is this important? Do I sacrifice myself by playing against the lesser teams like Pakistan and Sri Lanka or do I save myself and aim towards the Ashes? I have missed out on easier tours where you can take a lot of wickets.'

The operation she underwent on her lower back in 2014 after suffering a prolapsed disc had been put off for as long as she could stand the pain that grew with every day's delay. 'It became really debilitating and was ruining my life. I had to think about my health and life after cricket. I couldn't walk the dog or wash my face without pain.'

When you have watched Katherine, her dyed blonde hair pulled back, breaking her back to bowl 75 miles per hour;

or seen her face contorted with effort in the gymnasium; or heard her cursing fate when an appeal goes against her, it is initially incongruous that her conversation is frequently punctuated by girlish giggles. When you have spent a bit of time around her you recognise it as indicative of the joy, optimism and energy she puts into each moment, even in the times of pain and struggle. The fact that she was, literally, still standing in the face of physical hardship, not to mention other mental and physical challenges of her teen years, she put down to her upbringing as the youngest of six – three boys, three girls.

'I have always tried to get myself noticed and not blend into the background,' she explained. 'I am the shortest and tiniest out of everyone so I guess that is why I am so strong; to protect myself. I always wanted to stand out more and wanted my parents to be proud of me. My dad, Michael, was a miner for twenty-five years and my mum, Susan, is quite a strict religious type so it was not an upbringing with a lot of [displays of] love. It was a tough-Yorkshire-lass kind of thing.'

The result, Katherine said, was becoming 'one of the most competitive players in the whole squad'. She added, 'I want to be the best at everything. I could be in a cooking competition with the girls, or a strength contest, or who can hit furthest. I want to be the top at everything. If I had not had that mentality I would not have come back from the injuries.'

Her bowling was modelled on brother Daniel, the sibling closest to her in age at three years older and 'pretty much the only one I grew up with. He wanted me to bowl at him and wanted me to bowl fast so he could hit it further. He taught me everything I know about sport and I wanted to be like him. He was a really good role model, really hard on me, and could have played for Yorkshire. He played with Darren Gough at Barnsley. But he would rather go on holidays with his mates and play golf. I used to watch Goughie as well, who was short and stocky like me. My action is pretty similar to him and so is my attitude! I had my first net session with the boys at eight years old. I was shy and timid and just wanted to impress my brother. I got some boys out and they started crying, so I thought that was pretty entertaining.'

Yorkshire age group teams beckoned but at that stage she had no thought of pursuing the sport seriously. It was only a literal long, hard look at herself and another example of her single-mindedness that saw her cricket career take off. 'I only did it as a hobby but I was really quite fat between the ages of thirteen and seventeen, really big. I used to get bullied at school because of it and it was the cause of a lot of self-loathing. When I was sixteen people said I could play, including Paul Shaw, who was my coach at Barnsley, but I really wanted to play football or basketball. When I was seventeen I looked in the mirror one day and decided I didn't want to be like that anymore. I didn't have a clue how to do it but in one week I lost a stone. Next week I put a stone back on. I had no idea what I was doing. I figured it out myself and over three and a half months I lost four stone. I went to the gym every day and I ran with my dad because he used to run marathons. He used to drag me out.'

Within two years Katherine was in the senior Yorkshire team and attracting the attention of the England selectors. Remarkably for someone who became so obviously committed to her country's cause, she was uninterested. 'I originally said no because I really didn't fancy it. Everyone I know has gone through the England Academy and England age groups, but I hadn't done anything like that. I didn't want to be anywhere near it. I was put off by some of the coaches, who were pretty harsh. I didn't like that kind of environment.'

Having made a Test debut at home against New Zealand in 2004, she needed her family to talk her into accepting an invitation to tour South Africa and 'I never looked back'. In fact, the battles she had waged with her teenage self had, she believes, helped prepare her for the challenge of playing for England. 'It needed a lot of willpower to be able to do that on my own as a teenager. I knew after that I could handle anything that was thrown at me. It is not often you get preparation like that, physically or mentally, so that journey set me up nicely for international cricket.'

Returning from South Africa after competing in the World Cup, she was thrown into her first Ashes series, responding with thirteen wickets in two games and taking nine in the second Test at Worcester. Since then, not an Ashes series or global tournament victory had gone by without Brunt playing a part. In the 2009 World Twenty20 final against New Zealand at Lord's she returned match-winning figures of 3 for 6 in her four overs and a few weeks later achieved a Test-best of 6 for 64, again at Worcester, in the Ashes Test. Given the frequency of her injuries, it is an impressive testament to medical management.

'If you were going to label me within cricket it would be as consistent,' she suggested. 'I started out with a bang in the Ashes, getting a nine-fer and maiden fifty. Then I had my first surgery at twenty-one and it seemed that every time I got somewhere, something bad would happen and I would have to try again. With every setback I try to come back stronger and fitter, and each time I have delivered.'

One of the quickest bowlers, when fully fit, to have played women's international cricket, Brunt admits that she looks a different bowler to the one that broke into the England team. While saying she modelled her action partly on Gough, there is a touch of Jacques Kallis in there as well. 'We looked at my action after my first surgery. At twenty-one I had quite a mixed action. You would think it was side-on, but the top half was a little bit straighter and the bottom half very side-on. Moving the top half around to align my hips and shoulders has been key. It has been very little adjustments, though, because my action has always been pretty sound and that is what has allowed me to bowl quickly over the years.

'What they do now in the Academy programme is a lot of core stability and gym work, but I didn't do any of that. You can't expect to run in and bowl 75 miles per hour at that age and not break down if you are not doing the right things. Looking at my discs on the MRI scan they were quite dehydrated so [the damage] might have happened anyway at some point in my life, but not to the extreme it did. You are twisting your vertebrae when you bowl.'

Relieved to have survived the New Zealand tour at the start of the year, Katherine admitted that 'this summer is going to be the real turning point for me' but felt comforted by the additional support she had at her disposal. 'I have wanted to give up a few times, but there is now a lot of help you can get from within the ECB if you reach out. It is not something you are pushed towards, so if you don't go down that path yourself you could find yourself suffering on your own. It can be quite a lonely place and there are so many sacrifices, so many ordeals, you do wonder whether you should keep doing that to yourself. But the good things that come with it just outweigh the bad so you don't want to stop.

'I knew I would benefit massively from seeing a psychologist, whether it was sports or clinical psych, whatever would help the most. I went to a few before I found someone I felt really comfortable with. I have kept in contact with them since the end of 2011; they are just a constant who is there when I need them, need any advice. It is a private individual outside of the ECB, who still pay for it. They are really good with things like that.'

The era of professionalism had clearly made a significant practical impact on someone like Katherine, for whom time management was so important. 'I am an old-school player,' she said. 'When I came into the squad we got about £6,000 a year, less to start with. I played for my country about six months a year and that covered all my expenses, but I never did further education so I totally dedicated my life to playing for England. There wasn't anything else I wanted to do. The new contracts take off the pressure in terms of wondering where you fit in outside of cricket: where is your place in society without being Katherine Brunt the bowler? It takes away a lot of anxiousness and builds a security network after cricket.

'Also it means that instead of going to the gym at six in the morning or nine at night I can have two or three sessions throughout the day and not get so exhausted or feel like I don't want to do it. Managing my body is a hard task and now I can do it freely and properly.'

Katherine and I were talking the day after she had wrapped up a Yorkshire victory over Berkshire by hitting three sixes in an unbeaten 41 from number three. The ability to clear the fence is a valuable commodity in the women's game and she obviously hoped to make an impact as an all-rounder against Australia. Her batting, she shrugged, had been one aspect of the sport that she'd been forced to put aside in the pursuit of health and career longevity.

'I am really loving that I can be looked upon as someone who can come out and change a game by being aggressive with the bat. It is disappointing that I have not been able to dedicate more time to batting, but with having to manage my back so much, it has been something I have sacrificed. When you bat and swing you do put a lot of tension through your spine.

'In the last few months, I have been able to allocate time to my batting because I don't want to be wondering whether I can finish off a game for England because I have not been able to devote time to my batting. I would rather take time away from bowling now and add it to batting. I don't have much time now so I want to be able to show that I can do it.'

Brunt talks a lot about, and is obviously very aware of, the timeline of her career. Like most of her teammates, she said that the home World Cup in 2017 was both a target and a potential milestone for re-evaluation. Charlotte Edwards, she said, was constantly goading her about who would play on for longer. 'I am so competitive that it probably will make me play longer. I will play until my health is at risk or something comes along I can't say no to.'

Eleven years after her England debut, seniority was a cloak she had come to wear with a twinge of regret, but mostly with pride and an appreciation of its benefits. 'Staying within the top three in the squad in fitness and strength is what makes me feel young. Having experience and passing it on makes me feel old. But working more in a leadership role has helped push my game forward and given me more of a cricket brain. I bowl smarter now, which I need to because bowling is harder. In limited-overs cricket you have to have more tools. Being more senior has made me a better player.'

It had not, however, taken away any of the competitive fire burning through every ball Katherine delivered. Nor had working with the quieter figure of Paul Shaw – 'the Barnsley lad' – by whom she had first been coached thirteen years previously. 'I enjoyed working with Mark Lane because I am a massive heart-on-my-sleeve person. When I play it comes across in a bad light sometimes, but everything I do is because I love the game and I want to win. I am quite honest about myself. Mark and I worked well together because I always knew where I stood with him. But Paul and I are more communicative, so it's nice now to have someone like that. Having Paul around is like home away from home. Everybody takes the mickey out of my accent and now I can take the mickey out of his. He was at the club when I joined so I have known him for twenty-one years. He is quite a calming figure. If I ever want someone to bring it back to basics, give me a level head and be there to support me, I can count on him.'

Known to her colleagues as 'Nunny' ever since the day she set off a fire alarm during a residential course at a Benedictine-run college, Katherine's fierce and undisguised will to win was something that could both inspire and amuse her colleagues. 'I am an easy target, always have been,' she conceded. 'I actually hate that about myself. I am so easy to wind up, even now I still bloody do it and it really annoys me. But I am a bit of a joker in the squad and if anyone wants any entertainment they come to me. On the pitch I have been told I give a lot of energy to people. If you are in a bad position in a one-dayer, or if a four-dayer is dragging, come and have a rant at me and I generally find a way to pick them up. I like that.'

Lottie had endured, and enjoyed, her colleague's on-field dramatics for a decade. She declared, 'We have got a funny relationship. I think the world of her, but I am probably the hardest on her and she frustrates me more than anyone. She is just so incredibly passionate about what she does and fired up. Sometimes she sees the red mist. She just wants to get wickets and she doesn't care how she gets them. There was a funny moment in New Zealand when there was a misfield off her bowling and she threw up her arms and screamed, "Why me?" But she gives her all and it is a question of managing her. She comes across as a big fast bowler who is really strong, but she is soft beneath it all really. She is the heartbeat of the team.'

Katherine had also become something of a den mother to younger England players Nat Sciver, Amy Jones and Beth Langston, with whom she shared a house – a role for which she had earned another nickname, 'Matron', courtesy of Jones's dad. 'They have all been at uni for the last three or four years and he looked to me to look after his daughter. Anything they need doing – if their cars are dodgy or something – I am there. Now they all call me Matron. I am not sure if I appreciate it because it makes me feel old.'

'I think she enjoys it secretly,' Nat insisted. 'She makes out like it is a bit of a burden, but I think she likes it. Having that experience in cricket and life is quite useful for us to tap into.'

You suspect that Katherine actually revels in her title, being born out of the affection of people she truly loves in return. 'For the last eleven years the people who have been in the squad with me have become like family. The best people I have ever met and my best friends are through the England team. The friends I have made through cricket hold a place in my heart and always will.'

When Katherine's will or body gives up and playing days lie behind her, it is probable that cricket will retain her services in a coaching capacity. 'I enjoyed being head coach of the women's youth squad at Loughborough, progressing them from being high-skilled players into the England Academy set-up. I loved that and when I do retire working in that kind of age group, taking skilled individuals to the next level, is a real passion of mine. And they need a few more northerners.'

When I asked her about the significance of the script she has tattooed on her tanned right arm, 'Grands Yeux Fermés' – 'eyes wide shut' – Katherine, unusually, became rather coy. 'I can't tell you that,' she smiled. 'It's personal to me.' Indicating her right side she added, 'I have some others. The dates of the first Ashes win, the World Cup, the World Twenty20 and the date I came back from my operation after they said I wouldn't. Maybe I will add the date I retire. I don't know. I want it to be an open book. Maybe if we win the World Cup in England in 2017.'

Talking about the landmarks of her career, all she had been through with those close friends – a journey that was bound to see more twists and turns once the Australians arrived – brought us back to those all-consuming thoughts.

'I can honestly say I am like a little kid and I think about the Ashes every day. The excitement is still there and that is only going to be heightened by the fact that every ball is going to be live on Sky, which is absolutely phenomenal for women's cricket and women's sport in general. I am getting excited now because it is just around the corner and it is going to be brilliant, isn't it?'

Discussion among observers of the England women's team centred on whether Katherine would be considered fit enough to bowl upwards of fifteen overs a day in a four-day Test, or whether she would be saved for the shorter games. England had taken the field for their previous Test, against India in 2014, without her. In a couple of days she would participate in a four-day intra-squad match that, she hoped, would rubber-stamp her fitness for the longer contest that would constitute the centrepiece of the Ashes battle.

'I would really miss Test cricket,' she said. 'Just being able to run in and bowl and bowl; not having everyone attacking you every ball; being able to settle and find rhythm and timing. That is why I love Test matches so much. I am really excited that I am ready for that. My body is in good nick, as good as it is going to get. I am really excited for the summer and in this four-day game I want to prove that I have what it takes to have the ball for longer spells.'

Playing at Loughborough for the team captained by new-ball partner Anya Shrubsole, she would bowl eleven and thirteen overs respectively over two innings. She picked up one wicket in each against a batting line-up that featured a top four of Heather Knight, Lauren Winfield, Sarah Taylor and Edwards – who was batting in the middle-order slot she'd occupied in seven of the last eight Tests, a further clue to England's Ashes intentions.

The details of the game, irrelevant now but significant at the time, were that Knight, Winfield, Edwards, Sophie Luff (twice) and Georgia Elwiss all made half-centuries in the match for Team 1, with Taylor also scoring consistently in both knocks. Amy Jones scored a first-innings 118 for Team 2, supported by a fifty by Evelyn Jones, before Tammy Beaumont (84), Shrubsole (75 not out) and Nat Sciver (47) ensured that their side held on for a draw against the threat of Dani Hazell's spin (3 for 50). Looking at the batting performances, the pattern of the winter months and early summer was continuing, with the established senior trio in consistent form and the rest all registering enough significant innings to be making a case for inclusion without anyone making it an inarguable one.

Katherine had already presented her evidence over the course of a decade in the team. Now it was up to the jury of England selectors to decide how much cricket they felt she could handle. 'I have family and supporters coming to the Ashes games and it will be great,' she said, feeling no need to hide her excitement. 'The next few weeks are either going to crawl or they will fly by and I will feel under-prepared.'

10

These Girls Can

'I got to a point in my career where I had won everything and I was only twenty-one. I needed to go away and find out what else was out there' – Sarah Taylor

IT remains one of the iconic moments of women's cricket in recent years, even being highlighted early in 2015 in *All Out Cricket* magazine's 'Better Than Sex' feature. Dani Hazell bowled, Australian batter Jodie Fields took up position and executed a seemingly perfect reverse paddle sweep to send the ball in the direction of third man. Yet England wicketkeeper Sarah Taylor had seen it coming. By the time the bat made contact, she had hopped to her right and proceeded to thrust out her right arm, the ball settling in her glove as she toppled over on to her right knee. That description doesn't do justice to the speed of it, although the look of delighted amazement on Hazell's face came pretty close. Look it up on YouTube. But you'll need to wait for the slow-motion replay to realise fully what has happened.

Part of England's victory in the third one-day international at Hove during the 2013 Ashes series, it was the kind of brilliance that showed why, earlier that year, there had been talk of Taylor taking a place behind the stumps for the Sussex men's second eleven. It never happened, and was perhaps a distraction to her game for a while, but with one flash of brilliance the discussion had been largely justified.

'I haven't done it again since,' she laughed over a chicken salad lunch one day at Loughborough, 'although I got hit in the face once trying it. I can honestly say I had no real idea about it. I had done it once before but I was literally just trying to get in the way and all of a sudden I just threw my hands at it.'

That earlier debate over a possible appearance for Sussex seconds had centred on the viability of a woman playing such a role in men's cricket. There was little disagreement that if anyone could make it work it was Taylor. As well as establishing herself as one of the most dangerous batsmen in limited-overs cricket – ranked world number one in ODIs as the Ashes approached – she was considered without peer in the female game when it came to glovework.

'I have Laura Marsh's dad, Steve, to thank for becoming a wicketkeeper. He was under-15s coach at Sussex. Our keeper didn't turn up one day and I was probably being annoying like usual, always wanting to be part of the game. He said, "You like fielding, why don't you put the gloves on?" They couldn't get them off me. I loved being in the thick of it. I am not the loudest person behind the stumps, but I would get bored if I wasn't doing it. These days practice-wise I focus probably more on batting. My keeping coach, Jon Batty, is based in Surrey so it is quite hard to see him on a regular basis. But if there is any kind of fielding, then I will muck in; not as a keeper but as a fielder.'

On the tall side for a wicketkeeper, although hardly out of step with the modern norm, Sarah's role models are, unsurprisingly, Brendon McCullum and Kumar Sangakkara – 'for the flair of McCullum and the simplicity of Sangakkara' – but she has never attempted to copy them. 'Growing up, keepers' coaches tend to be quite mechanical,' she said. 'Some of the best coaches are the ones who say that you have a method so just stick to that. [ECB wicketkeeping coach] Bruce French told me, "Work on your strengths. If you can catch the ball brilliantly one-handed and that is how you do it, then keep doing it." I believe that if you have your own style you work with what you have got rather than trying to mimic anyone.'

Sarah's individual way of doing things included the distinctive absence of wicketkeeping pads, which had become something of a trademark. I asked her about it one day in the dressing room as she was pulling on football-style shin pads under red and white hooped socks. 'I felt that pads got in the way while I was trying to take the ball,' she explained, 'so I asked if I could get rid of them. I don't wear knee protection because you rarely get hit on the knees and it makes me use my hands. So it's a win-win.'

On a sunny Sunday in June, the Ashes looming larger on the calendar but still agonisingly distant, Sarah found herself in the role of coach, surrounded by a large group of young girls at an England women's team open day at Hampstead Cricket Club in north London. A bright, chirpy character herself, always happy to take the chance to kid around, she seemed a natural in the environment. 'It's nice to see so many girls enjoying cricket and what we have to offer. It was so much fun. There was some brilliant cricket being played. There were some girls of six or seven and they were hitting the ball better than I was at nine or ten.'

The event was being staged as part of Sport England's Women's Sports Week, an initiative that had allowed the ECB to launch its own '#ThisGirlCan: Play Cricket' campaign. Around 300 showed up to be coached by Sarah and her colleagues and to watch them beat a young Hampstead men's team in a 25-over game. Other similar events would be staged around the country in the ensuing weeks, while Sarah herself had forty-eight girls sign up for an evening coaching session at Hove a couple of weeks later. 'She is an inspiration to any player,' said Charlotte Burton, Director of Women's Cricket at Sussex. 'She is so good with the kids. I don't think she realises how good she is.'

Born in London and remaining a staunch Arsenal fan, Sarah clearly enjoyed giving starry-eyed girls the kind of opportunity she'd never had. 'I was one of those girls who played with the boys. One of the teachers said they were starting cricket after school so I thought, "I have tried everything else, I might as well try that." I absolutely loved it. I kind of enjoyed that I was the only girl in the team and I joined the boys' club because there was no girls' club in our area.'

The Brighton College boys' team she went on to play for also featured future England teammate Holly Colvin – and previously Clare Connor – and opposition based on her sex was minimal. 'To be fair, the only real resistance I got was from parents annoyed that their son got dropped for a girl. I was ahead of someone at school and ended up not playing for the county because he played. But that was the only resistance I got and it didn't do me any harm.'

Eyebrows were raised nationally, however, after Taylor commented in a newspaper interview early in 2013 that she had informally discussed with Sussex the possibility of playing some men's second eleven cricket. The avalanche of reaction, immediately before the 2013 World Cup in India, careered between support, intrigue and downright derision.

She explained that it had been nothing more than a case of 'if we really need you, you are an option' and was taken by surprise at how the story was seized upon. It didn't help quieten the nay-sayers when she made a run of three ducks in the World Cup and only made a face-saving 88 against New Zealand in the next game after being dropped on nought. 'I'd like to say it didn't affect me,' she said. 'But I don't know.'

It might, of course, have been the simple cycle of fortune turning temporarily against her, as it does to all players at some point, even one with the kind of career highlights that Sarah could boast. Selected for Sussex Under-19s as early as age thirteen, she was an England player by seventeen. She made her first international century a year later and the following season, 2008, scored 129 as she and Caroline Atkins mounted a record-breaking partnership of 268 against South Africa. She finished that season by becoming the youngest woman to 1,000 runs in ODIs and in 2009 made 120 at Chelmsford, the highest score by an English woman in an ODI against Australia. She was the women's Twenty20 Cricketer of the Year in 2013. Then, of course, there are all the Ashes wins and tournament successes.

Yet two years before those World Cup ducks, there had been a far more serious roadblock in her career; one created by her own confusion over the direction in which she wished her life to travel. It led her to quit the sport completely, missing out on the 2010/11 Ashes in Australia. 'I got to a point in my career where I had won everything and I was only twenty-one. The novelty had worn off a little bit. Is this what I want to do for the rest of my life? I decided that as a person I needed to go away and find out what else was out there. I went to New Zealand for six months with a friend and became more independent. Being away from cricket made me appreciate it more and I ended up playing out there even though I had not wanted to. I had said, "That is not why I am here." Around Christmas I had missed the Ashes and asked if I could start playing again and ended up playing for Wellington. I was supposed to play one game as cover and it ended up being eleven. It was the best thing I could have done. I came back a better person, really grew up. Then my cricket excelled from there. I realised there was a balance in life.

'You give yourself goals and I had done them and I didn't see what I wanted to do. Then I panicked because all I had known was cricket. What are you going to do now? When my response was "I want to do it again" I knew it was time to come back. All I had achieved I wanted to do again. To say you have done it twice in your career is a massive achievement.'

Any ambivalence that Sarah – twenty-six going into the Ashes – once harboured towards her sport had long since disappeared. As well as the motivation of winning a second World Cup, she added, 'As you get older there are personal goals along with the team aspect. In Test cricket I have kept well but not put the runs on the board.[7] I wouldn't want to walk away from my career with my Test record.'

And far from needing time away from cricket, she had jumped at the chance to spend the previous winter playing for the South Australia Scorpions. Even though she won the team's award as best player across both 50- and 20-over formats, her own assessment was that 'I probably didn't perform as well as I wanted to'. But she added, 'What I got out of it personally is sometimes more valuable; the knowledge of cricket I probably didn't realise I had, which I was able to use to help others. When I come back to England I know not to sit there and say nothing, that what I have to add is valuable. Any coaching I could do I did. I was even spin coach for a couple of sessions because they wanted the knowledge of what batsmen hate. I am also interested in the high performance side of things, looking down and saying that is the area we need to work on; not just the cricket side of things, but the whole.'

---

7   Taylor went into 2015 with a Test batting average of 22.16 and a highest score of 40.

There was also the opportunity to see her Ashes opponents up close. 'Most of the time you are gathering information about the batsmen,' she said. 'If you are around for a while you pick up hints, get to know their shots.'

Her own shots, she believed, were in a good place, especially on the occasions when she could drive through mid-off or hit through the covers off the back foot early in an innings. 'I am at a point in my career when I have built up certain knowledge and I am happy with my technique. I am more driven now by outcomes and looking at every possible situation. Lottie is a very good person for that, not just the way she plays the game but the way she goes about things. Having watched her over the years you learn what to do in certain situations.'

The captain, meanwhile, had been given plenty of opportunity to learn about her precocious teammate. 'She is a very funny girl,' said Lottie, 'so laid back about her cricket that you just want to leave her to it. She doesn't hit as many balls as everyone else, she doesn't catch as many balls as everyone else, but she produces the goods. She is without doubt the most talented player I have played with. As a wicketkeeper she is unbelievable. You don't over-complicate things with her. She has no ego; just goes about her business.'

It was the practicality of Sarah's excellence, as much as her personality, that excited Paul Shaw. 'The bonus of having Sarah as a wicketkeeper who you can class as an all-rounder – bats at three and bats really well, and is probably the best wicketkeeper in the world – is that it gives the squad that crucial balance. That is important when you are talking about a series between the best two teams in the world. You want to ensure you have flexibility and strength in depth within that squad, so the number of all-rounders is absolutely vital. We have three quicks and we will be in the best position to either play all three or rotate them and look at the balance of all-rounders, the balance of spin bowlers. Whatever pitch we come across, we have got the balance and the flexibility to play the team we feel will give us the best chance of winning. Sarah's role is important to that.'

* * * * *

Such is the stature of Charlotte Edwards that she needs two heirs apparent. While Taylor appeared ready to assume the mantle when it came to pure run-scoring, the captain's chain of succession pointed towards Heather Knight, Lottie's opening partner in 50-over cricket. First named vice-captain in 2014, she was still only twenty-four when confirmed in that position for the forthcoming Ashes series; an announcement made in Cardiff a couple of days before the start of the men's competition.

'Heather has obviously been identified as someone who could succeed me as captain,' Lottie said. 'She is fiercely competitive and we are quite similar in many ways. I think for her now it is about learning the job. You think you can probably do it but until you are given it you never know. I talk to her a lot. I always go up to her and tell her what I am thinking, and ask what she thinks. Sometimes I take her a bit by surprise because she has not thought about something. We get on well.'

Heather was being careful not to get too far ahead of herself, warning that 'a lot can happen in a few years' and adding, 'I am pretty sure Lottie has a few years left in her. It is about being a better cricketer and leader and if it happens when Charlotte leaves that will be amazing, but you don't take anything for granted. I try and think about the game, even if I wasn't vice-captain. I always look at what I would potentially do next and if anyone needs a word then I am always thinking about it. I am sure the rest of the girls do.'

Heather, fair-haired, blue-eyed and, according to Lottie, 'good fun around the dressing room', dismissed the notion that she was now serving some kind of apprenticeship for the captaincy. 'When I was made vice-captain I put a bit more pressure on myself than I needed to, but once I had relaxed into the role it was easy to be myself and do nothing too different. I am trying to develop, not thinking that I am going to take over from Lottie. It has given me a little more responsibility. I help Charlotte out when she needs it and I probably have a bit more confidence in giving her ideas. She knows what is going on but she is willing to listen. You don't realise you are playing with one of the legends of the game when you are playing with her. She is just Lottie. Batting with her is great for my development and in getting ready in case I have to step up in the short term because of injury.'

Born in Rochdale and raised in Devon, Heather began playing cricket because she 'was an annoying little sister and copied my brother, Steve'. Even though she enjoyed the pressure of being a girl in a male sporting environment, she was not one of those who grew up with dreams of playing for England. 'I scored my first hundred for Devon Under-15 girls when I was thirteen and thought, "I am not too bad at this cricket lark." I absolutely loved it. I used to watch Michael Atherton – opening batter, the character he played the game with – and Marcus Trescothick, coming from the west country.'

Scoring big hundreds for Devon's senior team, while still representing them at under-17 level, gave her an inkling of her own potential, even if it didn't lead immediately to wider recognition. 'Devon weren't in the best league back then,' she explained, 'so it felt like I was going unnoticed and it took a long time for me to be picked for the Academy. It was a bit of a struggle. I went to play for Reading, which was a better standard and qualified me to play for Berkshire. I proved I could score runs against better players. It was a good move for me.'

Early success for the Academy, including 103 in her third game against an ICC Europe team, meant that a full England debut against Ireland came within barely half a year, in the spring of 2010. Her consistent accumulation of runs for Berkshire began two months later.

Her nickname within the squad, 'Trevor', had come about as the result of a misheard introduction and had stuck fast. So had the memory of the defining innings of her England career to date, a seven-hour 157 in the 2013 Test match at Wormsley, a drawn game that helped England towards regaining the Ashes. 'That was the summer when I proved to myself I was good enough to score a lot of runs at this level. To win the Ashes was special and having that period under my belt really helped me. You go through ups and downs as a batter, everyone has their own little battles in their head. I wouldn't say it was a breakthrough moment but it definitely gave me a bit more confidence and made me more secure in the team, which is a massive thing. If you are not playing for your place every time it takes a hell of a lot of pressure off.'

Most people would consider that the position of opener creates additional stress, but for Heather it had always felt like home; comfortable and reassuring. 'I am not the best watcher of cricket. I like to know when I am going out to bat so that is why I like opening so much. I went out to dinner with Lottie and Laura before that Test match and I just remember saying how relaxed I felt. I am not a nervy player when I am out there, but I had a spell batting in the middle order in the one-dayers and I am not sure whether I did very well with sitting and waiting to bat.'

Secure in her place at the top of the order, Heather had not only progressed to become vice-captain in the previous twelve months, but had elevated her newly-acquired skill of off-spin bowling to the point where she was given the new ball during the New Zealand tour. 'I used to bowl dibbly-dobbly seamers but I ripped my hamstring off the bone,' she explained. 'I started bowling spin in the nets for fun. It started off as a bit of a joke, but Carl Crowe told me I might have something. I kept working at it and it went well.

'I always see myself as a batter, but that has probably helped my bowling, thinking of it as a secondary discipline. If I bowl badly, well, I can still bat. In terms of putting in my time off the pitch, I have done a lot of bowling. I am trying to get overs under my belt and develop a little more. Getting the ball down and having a little bit of dip; things like that and having the confidence in the balls that I have in my armoury. I am always likely to be more of a controlling bowler than a big spinner. It's about learning what my role is in the team, which is more to hold up one end.'

Her early winter with the Tasmanian Roar in Australia had offered further opportunities to develop her new bowling style, although it had been with the bat that she had excelled, named the country's best Twenty20 player after 419 runs at an average of 59.95, including five fifties. 'Probably the biggest change for me is in my Twenty20 game,' she admitted. 'It hasn't really been my format over my England career. It is about developing the right mindset: How am I going to score? What are my strengths? Having to get out of my game and score a bit faster benefitted my whole game. And working with a new set of girls is quite refreshing. Hopefully Paul and others have seen the benefit of that and we will see more players going out to Australia if they get the opportunity. I have always loved one-day cricket and now I have learned to love Twenty20 a lot more. I used to hate it. I am starting to really enjoy it and having a bit of fun and trying some new skills.'

No one could accuse Heather of being afraid of extending herself. At the end of 2014 she had climbed Mount Kilimanjaro as part of a group, including Clare Connor, that staged the highest-altitude game of cricket ever played. She even skippered the winning team against a side led by Ashley

Giles, with a percentage of funds raised by the expedition going to the Rwanda Cricket Association, of which she is a patron.

And the beginning of the 2015 season had seen the launch of the Heather Knight Collection of cricket equipment. 'I had a bit of input into the designs, which probably isn't my forte, but it turned out all right,' she said. 'The bats are a little bit lighter and the pads and gloves slightly smaller. I remember when I was young playing with massive pads and I couldn't run. To have a specialised women's size is ideal. My sponsors, SM, wanted to put a women's range out there and they wanted to use my name. It's something I am not really used to and find a little bit strange – and I got a bit of stick from the girls. But it is exciting.'

* * * * *

It was all a bit of flummery, of course, compared with the important business of trying to beat the Australians. That first group of girls assigned the task – the fourteen names listed by Clare Connor at the Swalec Stadium – featured only Georgia Elwiss from outside the group that had gone to New Zealand. Her first full squad call-up for more than a year was reward for those performances against the Australians' second string in Dubai and had been ordained, on this occasion, by Paul Shaw alone rather than a selection panel.[8]

'She showed she is capable of playing consistently the powerful brand of cricket we are looking for,' Paul explained. 'From an all-rounder's perspective she has the capability to

---

8 The ECB had agreed to hand ultimate selection power for the Ashes series to Shaw, who would pick his squads and then consult with captain Charlotte Edwards on the final elevens. 'Paul would not just write down names,' Clare Connor explained. 'He would want to be challenged and would talk to everyone he needed to in order to make his decision. We wanted to really empower him and strip away the panel.'

bowl consistent lines and lengths and build pressure on the opposition if we need four or five overs from someone.

'You know fairly broadly the balance of the squad you want,' he went on, 'and where you have potentially got 50-50 calls you look at what the player offers from a cricket perspective first – primary skills and secondary skills – but also the other disciplines the player can offer, on and off the field. We have had three or four players we have had to compare and contrast over the last few weeks.'

Among the batsmen, Danni Wyatt was the New Zealand tourist to miss out. Her fast start for Nottinghamshire, including 89 and 102 on the same day in a pair of Twenty20 games, had won her notable support from those blogging on the women's game, but not enough in more significant circles to nudge out Amy Jones, Lauren Winfield or Lydia Greenway in the middle order. She and the other batting candidates, Tammy Beaumont and Fran Wilson, would have to wait.

'Players have performed pretty well in county games or the prep games, but it is about turning those 30s, 40s, 50s into big hundreds,' said Paul. 'That is really what we are looking for from as many players as we can. What is pleasing is that Tammy, Fran and Danni are all playing some positive cricket, are in good frames of mind and are in some form. It is about transitioning those fairly good scores into large scores, which would give them the best chance of finding their way into the squad.'

The second player to lose her place since New Zealand was off-spinner Dani Hazell, who saw the specialist slow bowlers' berths awarded to Laura Marsh and Warwickshire left-armer Becky Grundy, the only selected player never to have played an Ashes match, even though she had featured in England's World T20 final defeat against the same opposition. Marsh's experience and Grundy's ODI performances in February on her return from her groin injury outweighed Hazell's T20 record.

'Some of the conversations have been fairly delicate,' said Shaw coyly when I asked him about the decision. 'For a spin bowler we look at the primary skill of spin bowling, then what they offer with the bat, in the field, and what they offer off the field if we are under the pump – all those areas.'

Becky, who celebrated her twenty-fifth birthday a few days after the squad announcement, suggested, 'I think I've established myself. It went well for me in New Zealand after I made my ODI debut, but I am still quite inexperienced at international level. [The Ashes] is all new to me and I am thrilled. Being the only one not to have been included before makes it really special. I've come through the other side [of fitness problems] so hopefully I, and the rest of the squad, can have an injury-free run this summer.'

Born in Solihull, she had made her Warwickshire debut at the age of sixteen and earned her first call-up to the full England squad at the end of 2013, when the team's established slow left-armer, Holly Colvin – in the team for eight years since the age of fifteen – chose to take a break from the sport. Becky's first international appearances were in the World T20 in Bangladesh at the beginning of 2014, taking six wickets in the tournament at an average of 17.50. Derailed thereafter by a groin injury, the form she had showed on her return in New Zealand had been continuing throughout the county season, evidenced by a return of 5 for 10 against Staffordshire a few weeks before the England squad announcement.

'Grunners is just brilliant,' Lottie had said. 'She is the epitome of what this team is about. She is just a girl who gives her all. It is great to have people like that who have come in a little bit later and she takes every opportunity. She is quite refreshing actually.'

The selection debate offered a storyline to the media and allowed further promotional opportunities for the coming series. I wondered, though, whether there was a practical advantage to the coach of naming a fourteen-player squad, given that there were no tour party practicalities to worry about and he was working with all of the contracted players on a regular basis anyway. Wasn't it just window dressing? 'It allows us to take the players who are going to play a part in the ODI series and work with them on refining our game plans and the roles they are going to play,' Paul countered, although I wasn't convinced.

As it happened, the squad announcement came on the same day as the final of a women's football World Cup tournament in Canada that had seized the attention of the English sporting public. Almost two and a half million people had sat up past midnight to watch England lose in the semi-finals to an injury-time own goal against Japan, and as many again saw them clinch the bronze medal by beating Germany. 'The momentum is massive at the moment, the support in general for women's sport,' said Becky. 'The football girls did extremely well and inspired a nation, and hopefully we can follow that success and go on from there.'

Her views were echoed by Lydia Greenway, who said, 'I love seeing other female sports teams do well. I watched the women's rugby World Cup and it was fantastic and the spirit and fight of the women's football team is so exciting to see. It's something we want to carry on. We want to make people proud of us like that.'

Clare Connor, in whom female sport has its biggest champion, said that the BBC's viewing figures proved that the event had 'gripped the nation'. She added, 'Women's sport is winning over more hearts and minds than ever.' The culmination, she said, was 'the biggest, most-anticipated, highest-profile women's cricket series there has ever been'. Of course, by the time it began, England's men had romanced the cricket public back into their bedroom with an exciting drawn Test series against New Zealand, a scintillating triumph against the same opposition in a for-the-ages ODI series, and a bold and unexpectedly joyful start to the Ashes series against Australia. The dark days of the World Cup seemed like a foolish holiday romance that had been forgiven and forgotten. The public's love for cricket remained; there for the girls to tap into.

'It certainly felt like they did that in the last Ashes here in 2013,' said Paul. 'We got a couple of wins and played positive cricket and from then on we got the media and, more important, the public behind us – and it really is like a twelfth man on your team. If we play the brand of cricket I feel we can, then quite quickly we can get people backing us and enjoying the way this England team plays. They play with a smile on their faces, they play hard and you can see they are enjoying it.'

Lottie admitted that 'there is pressure in being flag bearers, but it is nothing we cannot deal with it and I relish it'. Expressing her pride in such a state of affairs, she added, 'I don't want to put too much pressure on the team, but I am very aware of what we need to do to be successful. We don't want to keep banging on about it all the time – "you are professional this; you should be doing that" – but you have got to remind them every now and again. I think we have worked that well. You have to let them do what they do. They are young players.'

It was time for some of them to come of age.

11

Ashes at Last

'These games are going to be very, very high pressure, but as a group we tend to really rise to it' – Charlotte Edwards

IT was shortly before seven on the first morning of the Women's Ashes series. Jenny Gunn sat alone in the reception area of Taunton's Holiday Inn, the M5 traffic barely a Katherine Brunt slog sweep away. I'd arrived a few minutes earlier, reassured that I was in the right place by the fleet of Kia cars provided by the sponsors for the England girls' use.

The early sighting of one of England's most experienced players – twenty-nine years old, 219 international games – was hardly a surprise, given that I'd just read an online article where her teammates identified her as the player most likely to be first for everything. 'A few of them might be in the gym,' she said, casting her eye across the clusters of empty grey armchairs and over to the restaurant area. 'It's quite nice. We have our own cars so we can go when we want, as long as we are at the ground by 8.45. I will go early and get a change of scene.'

Having been in this situation many times before, Jenny had slept well, although she was aware that 'a few of the younger ones might not have', especially after a five-month wait since England's last competitive game. 'We were ready six weeks ago,' she said as Becky Grundy arrived and they headed for the breakfast buffet.

Unusually, the Australian team were staying in the same hotel, which meant that by about 7.30 groups of cricketers clad in both green and grey and the red, white and blue of the home team sat around tables more usually occupied by David Brent-type salesmen. It necessitated hushed tones when Paul Shaw arrived at reception and, having presented a bag of washing to the front desk, explained that Jenny, Laura Marsh and Lauren Winfield were the three girls who had been left out of the team. Jenny had told me that they knew the eleven but not mentioned her omission. I felt daft now for having asked her how she had slept.

'I like to give them twenty-four hours, so that they all know their roles,' Paul said, explaining that they had opted for three frontline seam bowlers; Grundy ahead of Marsh as spinner; and Amy Jones at number four because 'we felt she gives us a little more in the field; if we need something at the top of the order then Lauren gives us that option'. Winfield had been averaging 205 for Yorkshire, meaning Jones's selection would cause raised eyebrows in the press box later in the morning and offer further evidence of the perceived unreliability of the county game as a barometer for international potential.

As the players began to gather, Charlotte Edwards sat and scrolled through the latest messages on her phone. 'It's amazing the number I am getting. That's Luke Wright who has just texted and [England soccer captain] Steph Houghton and I have been messaging. There are a lot of people coming out of the woodwork. I am getting messages from numbers I don't recognise, and I have had this phone for two years now.'

Putting it down on the table in front of her, Lottie offered an additional perspective on the process of announcing the team. 'It's better for the girls to tell them the night before. They can get emotional and it gives them time to get it out of their system by the morning. It's different to the men, partly because the girls are all close friends so they do feel it for each other.'

Lauren seemed to be coping well enough with her disappointment when she greeted me with a cheery 'I'm your chauffeur' and began looking around for the others who would be riding to the County Ground with us, Kate Cross and Sarah Taylor. By the time those two had arrived, Lauren had disappeared, only to return looking flustered as departure time neared. Katherine Brunt, her roommate, had overslept. 'She's still asleep. I need to get her something to eat. I told her when I got up that I was going to the gym "so set your alarm".'

Coffee and granola having been duly delivered to the awakening fast bowler, we set off on the ten-minute drive to the ground, during which Kate amused herself by trying on the considerable collection of sunglasses stashed beside the driver. 'It's like being in the car with John Lennon,' said Sarah after her friend settled on a round pair with tinted lenses. As we pulled into the car park, Sarah's phone rang.

'Crossy, have you got a spare training top?' she asked.

'Yes, I've got my long sleeves and short sleeves with me.'

'Crossy's got one you can use,' Sarah said back into the phone. 'Jenny's forgotten to pack her training top,' she explained as she ended the call. 'The bag she has had packed since the end of the New Zealand tour!'

Late risers and forgotten tops. 'Honestly, it's not always like this,' Lauren laughed.

Around the home dressing room, vacated by the likes of Marcus Trescothick and Peter Trego for the England women, was the end product of those team discussions at Loughborough to identify the defining values of their cricket. Five different posters were spaced around the walls, each with a different heading, printed out in capital letters, followed by a series of bullet points. These were their pledges, made chiefly to each other, about the manner in which they would approach the coming contests. The girls saw them as important statements of intent, a way of ensuring unity of purpose, not mere rhetoric. They held these values close, and were the only aspect of the dressing room I was ever asked to keep private.

Another series of posters offered more specific reminders of the way in which they had agreed to bat, bowl and field. Positivity jumped from every sheet. On another patch of wall were laminated A4 pages highlighting each of the Australian players. Wagon wheels displayed scoring areas; strengths and weaknesses were listed; and additional factors noted, ranging from fast bowler Holly Ferling's lack of recent cricket to notions that captain and team superstar Meg Lanning might be 'separated from the team' and that the Aussies could become the 'Lanning and Perry Show'.

'I wouldn't mind a bat,' Sarah said as she looked out from the pavilion balcony at stands that were filling nicely, 'although I quite like knowing what we have got to chase.' Lottie seemed similarly relaxed when Lanning correctly called 'heads' and Australia chose to bat. 'I am happy,' she said a few minutes later, pulling up shin pads under her navy trousers. 'We would have had a bowl; we have got the three seamers.'

One of that trio, Kate, was giving off a far greater air of nervousness than she had on our journey to the ground. 'I don't really know,' she said when I asked her if she was happy to be bowling first. She was one of those who admitted she'd struggled to get off to sleep.

Final preparations continued. Amy Jones was getting a last-minute massage from physiotherapist Sue Dale. Lottie stood by a magnetic board and moved small discs around to create an attacking field for a left-handed batsman, although she never shared her creation with anyone else. The coaches fretted that the computer screen upon which they logged their game analysis was not receiving the Sky Sports feed. Paul opened a notebook and wrote the numbers one to fifty in columns down the left of the page, ready to log the significant events of each over.

The girls gathered in front of the pavilion for a fiftieth cap presentation to Heather Knight – Beth Wild counting heads like a primary school teacher on a field trip – and then filed out for the national anthems, Sarah ruffling the hair of the young girl assigned to her for mascot duties. Nerves, she had told me, were more likely to strike later in the game. 'If I am keeping I love it. Batting, I get the occasional anxiety. I would rather be like that than sat there and not feel anything. I don't mind a bit of nerves.'

The music played; players and staff locked arms. At last, after hours of nets and shuttle runs at Loughborough and thousands of miles heading to New Zealand and back, the moment that had been circled in the girls' 2015 diaries had arrived. The Ashes were beginning.

* * * * *

Undoubtedly the official attachment of the 'Ashes' brand to the England-Australia matches had achieved the aim of building interest and awareness. The men's Ashes had existed in public consciousness for almost a century before the women's contests were similarly identified in 1998, the same year in which the MCC first admitted female members. Miniature bats signed by both teams and a copy of the old Women's Cricket Association Constitution and Rules Book were ceremonially burned in the Harris Gardens at Lord's and the ashes sealed inside a ball-shaped trophy fashioned from 300-year-old yew. The ball had since been mounted inside a more photogenic framework of golden stumps.

An eighteen-year-old Charlotte Edwards had witnessed the formalities and had seen the event inflate in importance until – aided by its unique format – it threatened to dominate the women's cricket calendar in her country in a similar manner to the men's competition. 'The Ashes is just an iconic event and it is the pinnacle for most cricketers,' she'd said.

The Australians had turned up a week before the 2015 series saying pretty much the same thing. New head coach Matthew Mott, previously in charge at Glamorgan, was not about to discount the team's hard-won status as 50- and 20-over world champions, but he did admit, 'The one thing that has eluded us is the Ashes. It was 2001 the last time the team won in England. There's a lot of payback ready and the girls are really excited about this opportunity coming up. This is the time for these girls to capitalise. They've played together for a long time, they had success and they're all at the peak of their careers.'

This being the Ashes – gender irrelevant in this case – there was a bit of trash-talking to add some spice to the anticipation. 'The group that we've got at the moment has endured a lot of hardship with the Ashes losses,' said Southern Stars all-rounder Jess Jonassen, eliciting sympathy from pretty much no one in England. 'In that last Ashes series we won more games but were behind in the points. We sort of played better cricket.' It had stuck in the Australians' craw that England picked up six points for winning the Test during the previous series. Immune to accusations of sour grapes – or perhaps just playing along with the promotional hype – they argued that it had been an unfair weighting. This time around, however, the longer game would be worth only four points, much to Mott's approval. Yet the arithmetic

Glamour shoots in the Lord's Long Room are an important part of the England women's team's public projection. Left to right: Danni Wyatt, Heather Knight, Katherine Brunt, Kate Cross, Charlotte Edwards, Becky Grundy, Lauren Winfield. *(Waitrose Weekend)*

Sarah Taylor and Charlotte Edwards, cornerstones of many England successes, do battle in a controversial early-season match in the women's county championship, the Royal London Cup, at Beckenham. *(Don Miles)*

Clare Connor outlines her vision for the future of women's cricket to the television cameras. *(Don Miles)*

Paul Shaw carried the weight of the England team's fortunes in his role as Head of Performance, but always saw himself as more than just a cricket coach. *(Don Miles)*

Charlotte Edwards takes a catch off the bowling of Katherine Brunt to give England the first wicket of the Ashes series at Taunton. *(Don Miles)*

Kate Cross, fresh from her success in the men's club game, celebrates a wicket with Sarah Taylor, Nat Sciver, Heather Knight and Charlotte Edwards. *(Don Miles)*

Ellyse Perry, one of Australia's toughest competitors, goes on the attack against Becky Grundy. *(Don Miles)*

Nat Sciver (left) and Lydia Greenway (right) steer England towards an opening-game victory with their differing batting styles. *(Don Miles)*

Australian captain Meg Lanning on the attack during her century at Bristol. *(Don Miles)*

Heather Knight in full flow at Bristol, before her run-out helped change the course of the series. *(Don Miles)*

The Girls of Summer: England's Test squad at Canterbury. Back: Becky Grundy, Lauren Winfield, Amy Jones, Anya Shrubsole, Nat Sciver, Kate Cross, Georgia Elwiss, Fran Wilson. Front: Sarah Taylor, Laura Marsh, Heather Knight, Charlotte Edwards, Katherine Brunt, Lydia Greenway. *(Getty Images)*

Anya Shrubsole's success in the Test included the vital early wicket of Ellyse Perry, caught by Sarah Taylor (right) to the delight of Lauren Winfield. *(Don Miles)*

Sarah Taylor is bowled for a duck in the second innings of the Test, completing a pair in the match. *(Don Miles)*

Georgia Elwiss marked her unexpected Test debut with a brave attempt to save the game on the final day. *(Don Miles)*

Anya Shrubsole bowled superbly throughout the Twenty20 games to be named Player of the Series and was eventually named England's Player of the Year. *(Don Miles)*

Sarah Taylor recaptured her best form in the shortest format to keep England's Ashes hopes alive with a victory at Chelmsford. *(Don Miles)*

Katherine Brunt's big-hearted bowling was a feature of the summer. Here she celebrates a wicket at Hove with Dani Hazell, called up late in the year for the T20 games. *(Don Miles)*

The moment the Ashes were won – and lost. Australia's players begin their celebrations after the dismissal of Lydia Greenway at Hove gives them the series-clinching victory. *(Don Miles)*

reality – given that England only needed a drawn series to retain the Ashes – was that a home win over four days at Canterbury would leave the Aussies needing to win five of the six limited-overs games to take home the trophy: the same scenario whether the Test was worth four or six points. Ironically, it was Australia, as the team needing to chase a series win, who stood to benefit more from a six-point Test. You do the maths, Mr Mott.

Jonassen, apparently designated to play the Glenn McGrath wind-up role, added, 'With us being world champions and beating them quite convincingly in the T20 World Cup final, I think there's going to be a few psychological scars for them that I think we can potentially open up.'

Behind the bluster, of course, there was the obvious threat of a very good team. Players such as Lanning, all-rounder Ellyse Perry – a multi-sportswoman who could have been playing for her country in football's World Cup – and nineteen-year-old Ferling, even in recovery from back surgery, were every bit as revered in their country as Edwards, Taylor and Brunt in English cricketing circles. But, Paul said, every player had some kind of flaw that could be exposed. 'One of the things we focus a lot on is identifying the weakness of the opposition – really looking to attack them – as opposed to focusing on their strengths. We will look to put their batters under pressure in their areas of weakness and put bowlers under pressure so as to generate more opportunities to score runs.'

It sounded simple enough. And, Paul hoped, it would prevent his players building up the opposition too much in their own minds, making it easier for them to concentrate on their own performance. 'There is a very fine balance between focusing wholeheartedly on the opposition, what we think they are going to do and the plans we have for them, and ensuring that we leave no stone unturned to make sure the players have the confidence to play to their strengths. It is easy to go one way or the other so we are continually trying to balance that.'

Lottie had aimed to simplify things even further when we had discussed that balance. 'Sometimes, especially with a bowler, it is just a question of doing what they do the best. It's not rocket science. Top of off stump will get most batsmen out. Your best ball is your best ball against anyone so bowl that most of the time. There might be certain fielding positions we will do differently, but we have played Australia so many times now it is about delivering and executing those best balls as often as you can, and knowing when to use any variation. Keep it very simple and execute under pressure.

'These games are going to be very, very high pressure, but as a group we tend to really rise to it. Playing in front of not many people in New Zealand, sometimes I worried a little bit. The girls have now become used to playing in front of large crowds and that really gets everything going. I love playing cricket and I don't need a crowd, but some of the girls have grown up with it now and expect to have lots of people watching.'

* * * * *

The Taunton crowd was building towards 3,500 as Brunt delivered the first ball to cropped-blonde-haired opener Elyse Villani. A perfect line and length. 'Good start,' said Carl Crowe on the England balcony, to no one in particular. Paul recorded a dot in his book. The fourth ball yielded the first four of the innings, but the fifth and sixth both struck the pad and elicited screams for lbw. The extra hour's sleep had done England's strike bowler no harm.

Anya Shrubsole, bustling in from the end where workmen continued to piece together a new pavilion and stand, took the second over. The changing room offered a square-on view of the action, but Carl, crouched over the computer screen, confirmed to colleagues that the ball was swinging. 'A bit too much on there, Anya,' he added as one swerved down the leg side for a wide. Next over, Shrubsole prompted the biggest cheer of the day so far when the spectators showed their appreciation of the local girl's diving effort on the boundary to cut off an additional two runs. While Carl continued to offer running commentary, Paul quietly took notes, offering the odd whispered comment. 'Come on, Brunty,' he muttered as she ran away from the Sir Ian Botham Stand.

On the field, Cross played up to the crowd by pretending to claim a catch after Villani's drive popped up off the ground in front of her, a happy sign that she was enjoying herself, nerves receding. There was no pretending in the seventh over, though, when Villani lazily clipped Brunt to square leg. Edwards took an easy catch and set off, arms wide open, like a Premier League footballer celebrating a goal. Two overs later, Brunt struck again, leaving Australia 25 for 2. Jess Jonassen, promoted to open after Nicole Bolton had been hit on the head in the nets the previous day, had never looked comfortable in the role and swung wildly across a straight one after scoring only five off sixteen previous deliveries.

But now it felt like the series was really beginning. Meg Lanning and Ellyse Perry, the two most dangerous Australian batsmen, were at the wicket together – although not for long. Taking the ball for the twelfth over, Cross got her fourth delivery to nip in off the seam, missing the inside edge of Lanning as she played half forward and prompting the raised index finger of umpire Steve O'Shaughnessy.

At 35 for 3, Edwards opted to keep the pressure on by giving Brunt one over more than her usual opening spell of six. When Grundy finally replaced her she saw two lbw appeals turned down against the new batter, Alex Blackwell. Then she came close to grabbing a tough return catch off Perry before immediately spilling a relatively easy chance to her left against the same player. It was symptomatic of a growing uncertainty that was creeping into England's play as Australia, enjoying the speed of the outfield, rebuilt to pass 100 in the twenty-ninth over. It even spread to Taylor, who uncharacteristically failed to grasp a leg-side stumping chance against Blackwell off the bowling of Nat Sciver. The same bowler then dropped short twice and each time was pulled to the square leg boundary as Blackwell, an experienced campaigner and multiple World Cup winner, reached a half-century.

Shrubsole came back for the thirty-fifth over and was instantly steered past short third man by Perry. The Player of the Series in the previous Ashes, long fair hair partly obscuring the italicised number eight on her jersey, greeted the return of Brunt with another first-ball four, this one an on-drive that took her to a sixth consecutive fifty in ODIs. Australia brought up their 150 in the thirty-seventh over.

Just when England needed something to halt a partnership that had grown to 121 and was threatening to define the game, their fielding rediscovered its buoyancy. Scooping up the ball at mid-off, Knight aimed a bouncing missile at the stumps at the bowlers' end and Blackwell was gone for 58.

But with twelve runs coming off Grundy's ninth over and Cross being greeted back into the attack by a pair of Jess Cameron boundaries, Australia were still making decent progress until another run-out. This time it was Lydia Greenway who capitalised upon hesitation to remove Cameron with a throw that Taylor gathered neatly before breaking the stumps behind her.

At 205 for 5 with five overs remaining, England's balcony was quiet in thought. A strong finish by the bowlers could leave Australia with a below-par score; a final flourish could carry England's target into record-breaking territory. In the end, the innings finished somewhere in the middle. Perry gave up her wicket somewhat tamely when she lofted Knight to Sciver in the deep for 78. 'Anything under 250 at Taunton is good,' Paul observed.

Edwards hit the one stump she could see to run out Erin Osborne, although new batsman Sarah Coyte left Brunt holding her head in her hands by cutting her first ball for four. Brunt executed quick revenge, throwing in hard and flat from the boundary to make Coyte Australia's fourth run-out victim. Those, like me, old enough to remember such things had their minds cast back to a similar turn of events in the men's World Cup final of 1975.

Brunt began her final over – the forty-ninth – with a full toss that was swung for a leg-side four by Alyssa Healy, being watched by her fiancé, Australian fast bowler Mitchell Starc. 'No, Brunty,' groaned Paul, although she responded by trapping Kristen Beams in front with her final ball, giving her a return of 3 for 48.

Even ten from the final over, which began with Taylor missing another stumping opportunity off Grundy, could only take Australia to 238 for 9. It was a total that provoked a quiet sense of a job well done in the England changing room, although when I congratulated Brunt on her bowling she responded with, 'Not at the end. It was rubbish.'

Lottie sat buttering the two brown rolls that Lauren had brought her and asked whether Lanning's dismissal for lbw had looked out on TV. Having seen her slow bowlers combine to give up only four and a half runs an over, she wondered aloud, 'It will be interesting to see if they go with pace up front.' With almost twenty-five minutes until she was due in the middle, the skipper was padded up and raring to go.

'It's definitely gettable,' said Anya. 'It is rock hard out there. Their forward defensives were going for four. That's below par.'

Edwards was as quick to get off the mark as she had been to get padded up, pulling Perry's first ball to the boundary. Her suspicions were then proved right when Lanning employed the spin of Jonassen to open at the other end, her first over a maiden during which she induced a dangerous-looking leading edge from the England skipper. Then, having been frustrated by Lanning's posting of two short covers, Edwards began the seventh over by dragging Perry's delivery on to her own stumps. It didn't quite amount to the silence that used to descend over Indian grounds when Sachin Tendulkar was dismissed cheaply, but you could sense the deflation within a crowd that either feared for the damage her removal had done to England's chances or were disappointed at the disappearance of the one player with whom they were really familiar.

Knight followed her back in the twelfth over. Having driven past bowler Coyte for her first four, she got too much bottom hand into her shot as she went after the multi-tattooed medium pacer and dragged it to Lanning at mid-on. Jones, a quiet presence off the field and a less than imposing one on it, drove Coyte all along the ground for four, but in spinner Erin Osborne's first over she fell to a juggling catch at mid-wicket by Jonassen.

Taylor, meanwhile, had been progressing in her usual confident, often arrogant, manner. She had whacked a full toss back past Perry, clipped a couple over the infield to the mid-wicket boundary, deposited the first ball from diminutive leg-spinner Beams – another full toss – to the long-on rope and even attempted an ambitious ramp shot. But, after reaching 30 at a run a ball, she feathered Osborne to the keeper. England were 80 for 4 in the twentieth over and few in the press box were holding out much hope. But then Sciver stood tall and punched her first ball off the back foot to the cover boundary. 'She bowled it right in my favourite area,' she said later.

For the spectator, a Lydia Greenway innings is an exercise in waiting for the reverse sweep. She didn't keep anyone wondering for too long, hitting Osborne for four with her favourite shot. Sciver, meanwhile, seemed intent on setting about Ferling, nearly offering a catch when she toe-ended an attempted pull, but immediately thereafter executing the shot perfectly to send the ball sizzling to the square leg boundary.

Much had been expected of Ferling, who arrived on the scene as one of the international game's quickest bowlers as a seventeen-year-old, but was now feeling her way back from a stress fracture in her back. The long blonde hair tied in a trademark white ribbon bow remained, but much of her speed seemed to have remained in the treatment room. With her height accentuating her jerky approach, offering the impression of an antique Victorian toy, she bowled most balls at around 70 miles per hour, a couple slower than Brunt and several down on her pre-injury pace. She would end up wicketless in seven overs, costing 42 runs.

Having left the pessimism of the press box, I arrived back at the England dressing room just as the fifth-wicket partnership was reaching 50, with England now on 132 for 4 – another 107 needed in nineteen overs. Taking the spare seat on the balcony alongside the dismissed Edwards and Knight and number eleven Grundy, I asked whether they'd reached the stage yet where no one was moving for fear of jinxing the burgeoning partnership. They had, although Lottie admitted to having shoved along one seat.

Cries of 'Well done, ladies' greeted every scoring shot. Lottie was the cheerleader in chief, jumping up to the balcony railing and shouting even greater encouragement when Greenway put away another Beam full toss. Ten runs came from the over. 'We're in the game, ladies,' she declared.

Sciver survived a run-out appeal after she had failed to ground her bat when completing a run, the same mistake that had cost Ben Stokes in a Test a few days earlier, and then missed a swipe at a Perry bouncer. She redeemed herself by smashing the next ball to the ropes. Osborne went for two fours in her next over, another Greenway reverse and a leg-side flick by Sciver, who moved to within two of a half-century.

She played her next ball straight and sensibly. 'I like that a lot, Sciv,' Lottie chirped.

'Come on, Nat,' whispered Becky, someone whose natural expression often appeared to be one of concern.

When Sciver pushed down the ground to reach 50 those on the balcony raced forward to ensure their congratulations had more chance of being heard. The partnership was moving England into a winning position and the required rate dropped below five after Sciver bisected third man and fine leg with an edged hook off Perry and then lifted the same bowler back over her head. On the first ball of the thirty-eighth over Greenway drove through wide mid-on to bring up the 100 partnership, the second half of which had taken only six overs.

'They've not got a deep square leg,' a delighted Edwards remarked when Beam came back to bowl to Greenway. One ball later, the Australian captain remembered Greenway's penchant for scoring behind the wicket and plugged the gap.

Becky had earlier urged Sciver to try a ramp shot, but when her colleague began the fortieth over by trying exactly that, without any success, Lottie was quick to point out, 'We don't need to show everyone all your shots, do we, Grunners?' Greenway's reverse sweep in the same over was more benevolently received by the skipper. 'I don't mind that for Lydia. That's how she rolls.'

Only forty-five needed from ten overs now, quickly reduced when the erratic Beams served up a full toss to Greenway, who pulled that and the next delivery for boundaries to reach her first ODI half-century since January 2014. Two balls later Beams failed yet again to hit the pitch, but this time Greenway struck her straight into mid-wicket's hands. Edwards and her colleagues dashed downstairs to the boundary dug-out to welcome her home.

New batter Georgia Elwiss cut Jonassen square for four. 'All you've got to do is wait for the right ball to hit,' Lottie told those around her, and then watched as Elwiss advanced towards the bowler and plonked her over extra cover. 'Shot, G!'

Sciver, who had judged length so well and struck the ball straight and clean, had reached 66, one more than her highest score for England when, like Greenway, she gave up her wicket rather easily, chipping Osborne to mid-off. A few unconvincing calls between Elwiss and new batsman Brunt betrayed some nerves, but they were calmed when Elwiss split the field for four and Brunt put away a long hop.

With nine needed as the forty-sixth over began, an exchange of singles was followed by Elwiss picking up four more when she edged Osborne past the keeper. Then she sat back and forced the ball square for another boundary to reach an unbeaten 25, pumping her fist as she saw the winning runs disappearing to the distance. After ten consecutive ODI wins, Australia had been beaten by the third-highest run chase in England's history. Two points to the home team.

Sciver accepted the Player of the Match award and Greenway received her share of praise – no one having been worried by her usual slow start, they said. Edwards, meanwhile, warned that Australia would come back hard. By the time the dressing room was full once again, sandwiches and cakes had appeared on the central table, alongside the now-open box in which everyone's mobile phones, including mine, had been locked away by the anti-corruption officials while play was in progress. There were also various items sitting by a notice that read, 'Stuff to sign.'

Paul gathered his players in front of him. 'This will be brief, ladies,' he said. He was not one given to wild shows of emotion but his pride was obvious. 'That is a top game to win like that after the position we were in. The partnership in the middle was absolutely outstanding; the way we want to play – playing percentages, playing down the ground. And the way GG came in to win it at the end was top drawer. We knocked off 240, but we can still improve. We can bowl better, field better, bat better. We'll review it tomorrow. Recover well.'

A fantastic day for England had ended rather like it had begun. Shaw had been forced to wait for a minute before beginning his talk while Katherine Brunt was located. 'There is always one,' said Lottie in mock exasperation. 'And it is always Brunty.'

12

Poles Apart

'I remember our coach telling us he wanted us to score 200 in an ODI. A few of us were like, "My God, how are we going to do that?"' – Lydia Greenway

NAT Sciver had always wanted to represent her country. In a sense, she had been doing it all her life. The daughter of a Foreign Office diplomat, she had been born in Tokyo, lived in various European countries and thrown herself into sport wherever she had been. It was how, at an age when many of her England teammates were battling the boys on the cricket field, she'd found herself as a twelve-year-old surrounded by those twice her age in a Polish women's football league.

'My mum [Julia] was working in the British embassies in different countries so it was not a cricketing background, although my dad did play so we always had a bat out in the garden,' she explained. 'I started out playing tennis, alongside football, when we were living in Holland. In Poland, I wanted to join a women's football team because the boys were growing a bit more and getting stronger and I was still a tiny little thing. It was a bit scary. They were all older than me, in their twenties, and not many spoke English. One or two could get by having an English conversation and I could almost get by having a very basic Polish conversation about football. My teammates were really welcoming, though, and tried really hard to communicate. If I got any stick from the other team, well, I didn't really know because they did it in Polish.'

Nat's background saw her playing several other sports, including tennis and hockey, before finally sticking with cricket after returning to England as a fourteen-year-old. Originally enjoying the fact that the sport offered the opportunity to hit as far and hard as possible – in contrast to the geometric restrictions of tennis – she is a cricketing product of her diverse sporting background. Reaching twenty-three years old during the course of the Ashes series, she was no longer that 'tiny little thing', tall and powerful looking at the crease, loosely tied long brown hair bursting from the back of her helmet. The boundary looks a few yards closer when she is in full flow and, aided by practising some baseball-style striking techniques, she is generally acknowledged as one of the biggest hitters in the women's game. 'When I was young you were taught that it was forward defensive and a strong top hand, which was not really my game. Coming more from racquet sports my bottom hand does come through a little bit more than it should. It's definitely made me a different player – but I don't know yet whether it's made me a better player!'

While twelve-year-old Nat was taking tentative steps in a different sport in a very different country, Lydia Greenway, her match-winning partner in the opening Ashes contest, was already twelve months into an international career that had reached its thirteenth year by the 2015 season. Selected for an Ashes series in Australia aged only seventeen, her pathway had been the more traditional one of following her father Martin into club cricket in Kent, although the style of her batsmanship was anything but orthodox.

For a start, batting is the only left-handed activity in the whole of her right-handed life, the result of garden geography at her childhood home. 'My brother is the same,' she revealed. 'My dad tells us it's because when we were playing in the back garden he wanted us to play off-side shots. We had to hit it into the fence because there were bushes on the other side. So he made us bat left-handed from a very young age and eventually it just became natural.'

The reverse sweep, her signature stroke, became a part of her game via a rather more conventional course of events. 'I was at the academy at Kent and working with Paul Farbrace, my one-on-one coach, in the nets at Beckenham. We just had a bit of a muck-around with it and that was it. It seemed like a natural shot. I developed it in practice and began trying to do it in games until it became a really comfortable shot. It helps that my right hand is my naturally stronger hand. On the reverse sweep that is the dominant hand and it provides the power.'

At Taunton, during their partnership of 122, the bottom-handed big-hitting of Sciver and the angular sweeps and nudges of Greenway had proved too much for the Australian bowlers to handle. 'I think being different types of batters helps, plus having a left- and right-hander out there so that they have to change every ball,' said Nat. 'Me and Lyds have batted together quite a few times now and have definitely got used to each other and what works best for both of us. I felt confident with her at the other end. I just went out there and really enjoyed it. I was saying to Lydia, even when we were rebuilding, "Let's just enjoy it," and I think I was. I was trying to play mind games with the bowlers. Having that first ball go for four had been nice, not having to think about getting off the mark. Bowling attacks nowadays always try to bowl full and straight at me and at Taunton my drives were coming off, which set me up for the game.'

Lydia added, 'I really enjoy batting with Nat. Because she is such a powerful hitter of the ball, I think often it can relieve a bit of pressure from a team point of view and it means I can go about my business and try to work the gaps in the field.'

Personal pressure had been relieved on Lydia by scoring her match-winning half-century. Those who blog and comment on the women's game had been quick to point out the absence of such a score for a year and a half, suggesting that her outstanding fielding was not enough to ensure her prolonged presence in the team. 'I was pleased to get that score and I am aware that there are people who write about us, but I have never read one of them,' she insisted. 'I don't read good or bad press because that can lead you to thinking about negative or positive things too much and lure you into areas that are not helpful. Everyone has their opinion and the more the profile of the women's game is raised the more it is going to happen, so I don't really read it.

'I don't like to think about things too much. I try to keep my emotions in check whether I'm doing badly or well. Cricket can bring you back very quickly. If I have a bad run of form I look back at performances where I have done well and I work with a one-on-one coach so that I am comfortable in knowing I have put in the hard work. That helps you persevere and have more confidence.'

Comment and criticism of the women's game was hard to find anywhere in print or on the new-fangled internet when Lydia played her first England game in 2003, a time that now belongs to a different era, both technologically and in terms of women's cricket. 'I remember, moving on from my debut, our coach Richard Bates telling us he wanted us to score 200 in an ODI. A few of us were like, "My God, how are we going to do that?" Now we are trying to get 280 regularly. The physical side of it has changed too. Years ago our county championship used to be five 50-over games in a row, but with the way the intensity of the game has risen that is too physically demanding now.'

Professionalism, of course, seemed even further off than ODI scores approaching 300 when the young Lydia was finding ways to fund her part-time cricket. 'I used to do some coaching for the local borough in Godalming, going into schools and things like that, and then I had a job as a waitress and a few other bits and bobs. I ended up going to Loughborough to do a foundation degree and then Chance to Shine came in and so obviously that was a big boost, giving us some more income. But we weren't expecting full professionalism. I remember Clare Connor coming in to speak to us and we thought it would be about us maybe getting a bit more financial support, but we weren't aware it was going to provide a salary so that we didn't have to have another job. We are all really grateful for it.'

Money or not, Lydia had been committed to cricket 'as soon as I realised there was an England women's team in my early teens'. She continued, 'There have been a few challenges. I got dropped by England around 2008 and that gave me a bit of a rocket to make me want to continue to improve, not rest on what I had done. I went back and scored runs for my club and county and it gave me more of a hunger and desire. I realised how much I missed playing for England.'

Since her reinstatement she had been a constant feature of the team. Batting highlights included an unbeaten 125, her only ODI century, against South Africa in 2011 and 80 not out off 64 balls in the Ashes-clinching Twenty20 victory at Southampton in 2013. It had been her diving stops at backward point and circus catches on the boundary, though, that had attracted more attention, and more hits on YouTube. Few cricketers of either sex have ever been known for their fielding ahead of other skills, but Lydia – like Jonty Rhodes – had achieved it.

'Playing a lot of sports when I was younger, tennis, netball, basketball, hockey, has helped in developing coordination. With my brother and sister we used to play a lot and dad used to hit tennis balls at us in the garden most evenings and we had competitions. My brother was a footballer and he always made me go in goal so that helped. I enjoy practising my outfielding – the big catches and stops on the boundary – and in-the-ring diving techniques. I did some work with [former England fielding coach] Trevor Penney and he taught us a lot of techniques so I have tried to carry that on. But I have dropped catches and I am sure that people have got frustrated at me. Fielding is a big part of the game now. The teams are at a level where everyone is fielding better and that is down to the volume of training we have done. You have quite a lot of control over your fielding, whereas as a batter you are responding to the bowler coming at you.'

Being one of the less boisterous personalities on the team had not prevented Lydia becoming known as one of the team's practical jokers. Her role had now, of course, evolved to include that of veteran presence – although she felt that the importance of such a role had diminished over the years thanks to the England team structure. 'Because of the Academy, there is not such a big gap when the younger girls come into the team. When I first came in it was huge, a big jump from county cricket. Now the younger players have that confidence that they need to perform on the international stage. I try to give them support but they are well trained in that transition and probably don't really need it as much. Then you have people like Katherine and Jen who have been around a long time and help even more to ease the new players into the team. It is a good environment.'

Still, Nat admitted to some nerves when she first made the step up in 2013. 'Moving around all the time when I was young has helped me adapt to situations, although I was really nervous and shy when I got into the team. There were a few friendship groups then, but more recently the group has become more as one and not divided like that, which is really good.'

Having developed her football enough to be considered for a youth programme at Chelsea, it was not until her midteens that Nat, settled in England, had finally given cricket a serious try. Garden games with her father, Richard, and younger brother, Paul, developed into enrolment at a village cricket club in Surrey, Stoke d'Abernon. 'I was fourteen and still playing football and joined a local girls' team for two years. But I had school on Saturday and my only day off was Sunday. I kind of decided to stop playing football and try something else, by which time there was a local club with a women and girls' section, which not many had. I really enjoyed it and got on well with the girls.'

Nat also played some boys' cricket and was sent for a Surrey trial, which elevated her into the county age group system and on the pathway to the England set-up. Picked for England just in time to play a role in the 2013 Ashes victory, it was her 49 in the Perth Test the following winter that established her in the team.

It could have been different, however, had she not had the realisation after one year of university that she needed to devote more of her energy to the sport. Late nights gave way to early morning work-outs. 'I chose Loughborough because the cricket programme was so good and I knew that would help me. But in the first year at university you want to go out and have fun and I made the most of it. I had just got into the England Academy and my university coaches, Saliann Briggs and Katherine Brunt, said I had the potential to go further and made me realise I needed to be a lot more serious about it. Seeing Katherine do it on a daily basis spurred me on to be more professional and committed.'

That commitment included taking various exams towards her sports science degree while travelling the world with the England team, and managing not to let it distract her from her on-field performance. 'I had quite a good run when I first got into the England team. I have become a bit more established and a bit more comfortable, but I think there is more pressure now than two years ago considering the strength in depth that we have at the minute. No one's position is ever completely safe. I would like to put in more performances. In the first year or so teams don't really know you very well, they are just bowling to their default plan, but as time goes on you need to work on your weaknesses. I think there are things I can work on although in the middle of a series I don't want to get too technical. I want to relax and play my game.'

Nat's game had become an integral part of the England team. Her runs had propelled them to victory at Taunton and she would continue to be entrusted to bowl her seamers in the closing overs of Australia's innings in the ODI section of the series. 'I would say I am a batting all-rounder, although I do enjoy bowling and I think I am more suited to the shorter format. I can use my variations and I enjoy being involved in the last couple of overs of the innings.' She remained the most recent of three England women to take an international hat-trick, achieving the feat in a Twenty20 against New Zealand during a tri-lateral series in Barbados in 2013. 'I think that helped cement my place as a death bowler,' she said. 'It was towards the end of the innings and what we talk about is bowling at the stumps and being a threat. That's what I did and it worked out really well.'

Assuming that they maintained their form, there appeared likely to be plenty of Greenway-Sciver partnerships to come in future years. Nat was still only getting started and Lydia knew that turning thirty was no longer a time to consider getting on with 'real life' as it had often been in the past, in the pre-professional age. 'I would like to play for as long as I can if I am performing and contributing to England wins,' she said. 'If professionalism had not come in there does come a time when you have to think about another career, financial stability, having a family and things like that. Professionalism means we can build towards our future on our own terms.'

13

Turning Point

'I always talk about key moments that switch momentum. A brilliant bit of fielding, [and] they just grabbed hold of it' – Charlotte Edwards

MOMENTUM. It is an oft-quoted concept in sport, both on and off the field. The England and Wales Cricket Board had hoped that the women's Ashes series would create its own momentum, with media coverage, attendance and public interest mounting as the narrative of the series developed. In that regard they could not have been happier with the events of Taunton.

Not only had England won, but the game itself had been a good advert for the women's game, with the print, online and broadcast response to it phenomenal. A quarter of a million people had been watching when Georgia Elwiss hit the winning runs, not a bad number at all for a workday afternoon on Sky, and far and away the most watched sports programme at that time. Not only had BBC Radio been broadcasting every ball on its Sports Extra station, but on the drive home I had listened to a one-hour special on the series on the main Radio 5 Live channel.

The next day's newspapers had been a joy to behold for those within the ECB offices. Katherine Brunt's wicket celebration took up most of the front page of the *Daily Telegraph* sports section; Elwiss's victory fist-pump occupied *The Guardian*'s sports front; Charlotte Edwards beamed out from the back page of the *The Times* after taking the first catch of the series; most of the newspapers carried extensive page-lead match reports. More of the same was what they wanted two days later in Bristol, both on the field and in the press.

Even though attendance at the County Ground would not quite reach the levels of Taunton, it was encouraging to see the large number of young girls in the crowd – although it was a group of middle-aged men with elaborately prepared albums who greeted England's players as they made their way down a precariously slippery staircase at the front of the pavilion to warm up. The enhanced profile of the team clearly hadn't eliminated all potential for misidentification. When PR manager Beth Wild strolled out in her team uniform, she had to advise the autograph seekers, 'I'm not a player; I'm the media manager. I do have 400 Twitter followers, though!'

The pitch appeared to be another good one, although the outfield grass looked longer and slower than Taunton, and the sky emerging from above the Bristol College-owned flats that overlook one end of the ground more foreboding. It was a day for winning the toss and sticking the opposition in, which was exactly what Charlotte Edwards did. England had named the same eleven that won two days earlier, while Australia had brought back opener Nicole Bolton and included seamer Megan Schutt in place of the erratic leg spin of Kristen Beams.

As the clock moved towards the 10.30 start time I was sitting with David Capel, the only member of the England women's set-up who had played the men's game at the highest level. His fifteen Test matches included a highest score of 98 in Karachi and involvement in the infamous flare-up between skipper Mike Gatting and umpire Shakoor Rana on the tour of Pakistan. 'It was always good playing here, although in my day Gloucestershire had Courtney Walsh and Syd Lawrence so they used to keep it quite green.'

As a coach he had spent six years in charge of Northamptonshire, the county for whom he played, departing in 2012 and joining the England women's team the following year. There were times, he admitted, when he missed the day-to-day of county cricket, although the preparation time he now enjoyed with the girls was a luxury he would have loved at Northants.

'Yesterday was a medium intensity day,' said Capel, whose weathered tan bears testament to a working life spent following the sun. 'We took it easy on the bowlers, but the batters had a good knock. We let down on the fielding a bit. The work has to be meaningful; picking up and throwing well. There is an analogy with golf. If you are practising your putting and missing, then all you are doing is practising missing.'

Bolton, back from her blow on the head, took guard against Brunt. As the bowler ran away from us, Capel offered, 'Should be a bouncer first ball. I would.' It was pitched up. 'Looks like Brunty forgot the plan. Or maybe she is not loose enough.' The fourth ball was the short one. 'There it is. Well done.'

I asked Capel what he felt was a par score. 'I usually give it ten overs before I make a judgement. That's the good thing about chasing. They might think they need another twenty or thirty runs and go a bit too hard. That's another reason why I think we put them in – uncertainty.'

Bizarrely, the game was halted after two overs when someone pointed out that the fielding circle was set too far out, to the men's distance. 'Shame, they are nice chaps here,' said Capel of the embarrassed grounds crew, although he was also concerned that his own fielders appeared not to have noticed. Two maidens left Australia at 4 for 0 after four overs. 'There's a chance coming. She's getting edgy. I would rather have two slips than a slip and a gully.'

It was the first boundary rather than the first wicket that arrived, Elyse Villani hooking Brunt for four. By the time seven overs had gone and Australia had reached 19, Capel was admitting, 'We could just do with a break to get the ball rolling.' At 38 for 0 off ten overs, Capel was ready with his score projection. 'I think it will end up similar to the other day and if we can keep them to twenty below that we'll be happy.'

Villani was punishing anything short, but Kate Cross's first ball struck her on the pad as she walked across her stumps. Not out. Becky Grundy came on for the twelfth over. 'Her main strength is when she gets her flight and line right and gets that dip,' was Capel's assessment of the slow left-armer. 'Then she can beat the bat on the inside. She straightens the odd one and in one-day cricket that is all you need. She may not turn it much here, but on a pitch that is more than a day old she can get a bit of turn.'

After fifteen wicketless overs I was on my way to the press box when I passed the garishly-shirted BBC commentator Dan Norcross. 'Could do with a wicket – or maybe three,' he observed. And Grundy duly obliged, getting Villani to nick one to Sarah Taylor off the bottom edge.

With Meg Lanning at the crease, the scoring rate picked up, Australia's second 50 runs coming off 61 balls. Bolton, though, had never hinted at fluency and, when she swung across the line after 37 off 62 balls, Anya Shrubsole was rewarded for her earlier accuracy. Brunt was soon back into the attack as England's two frontline bowlers took on Lanning and Ellyse Perry, and questions were asked in the press box as the twenty-eighth over passed without the introduction of a fifth bowler.

While Perry was unusually subdued, failing to find the boundary until her twenty-first delivery, Lanning was irrepressible, using her feet against the spinners and steering the ball into the gaps. She pierced Grundy's off-side cordon to reach 48 and edged Heather Knight for a seventh boundary to pass her half-century. A fine sweep off the same bowler reached the same piece of boundary rope.

The bowling powerplay after thirty-five overs saw the re-introduction of the opening bowlers, Lanning lofting Shrubsole over mid-wicket for four. England's frustration was captured by Brunt standing with both hands on hips after being ruled to have bowled a wide outside off stump. A score in excess of 250 looked more than likely when a Lanning edge off Brunt smacked against Taylor's glove. After forty overs Australia had scored 193 for 2 and Shrubsole and Brunt would not bowl again.

Now in the 80s, Lanning drove at Cross, who dropped a tough chance and then dropped to her knees. She would subsequently have an x-ray on her hand, revealing no damage. The pain of the missed opportunity was more than enough. Both batsmen clipped Cross for four behind square leg, up in the circle, and Lanning greeted Nat Sciver for the forty-sixth over by lofting her over mid-off for two runs and cutting past Greenway at backward point to reach her sixth ODI century. At only twenty-three years old, but already almost two years into her role as Australian captain, she had a look of invincibility, a force that people would still be marvelling at a decade from now.

Perry fell two runs short of a seventh consecutive ODI fifty when losing her stumps as she charged at Knight on the seventy-first ball she faced, having hit only two boundaries in her 48. Then, at last, Lanning went for a classy 104, stumped on the leg side off Sciver. Knight picked up a second wicket in the penultimate over, Alex Blackwell seeming to trap the ball under her bat as she played on. The final over produced ten runs and a second Taylor-Sciver stumping. The end result was a score of 259 for 6. England would need to achieve their highest-ever run chase to win the game.

While yellow-shirted children embarked upon games of Kwik Cricket on the outfield, Paul Shaw reflected that it was 'a few more than we would have liked' but noted, 'It still looks a good pitch and there are plenty of twos out there. We didn't bowl or field as well as we did the other day. We bowled too many bad balls. But we'll save that for another day; we want them to stay positive now.' Knight's bowling at the death – 2 for 44 off nine overs – had pleased him, though. 'She has worked pretty hard at it,' he said of the vice-captain's conversion to spin bowling. As an afterthought he added, 'It was strange the way Perry batted.'

The top-order batsmen began padding up. Heather took some throw-downs from Capel; Lottie sat on the balcony chatting with Anya; Sarah was there too, looking less than her usual bubbly self. Eventually all gathered together again in the dressing room. Carl Crowe stood in front of a sizeable St George's flag, a word in each quadrant representing different elements of those closely-held team values. He began by asking the girls for their thoughts on the conditions.

'Any seam movement? Any spin?' he prompted. Someone offered a joke that even Heather had got one to turn, and there was a general view that it was similar to Taunton.

'What do we need to do?' Carl challenged.

'It's a big outfield; there are lots of twos and threes,' was Heather's response.

'It's a chance to put them under pressure with our running,' the coach continued. 'They ran poorly.'

'Get in and establish partnerships,' Capel chipped in.

Carl concluded, 'This could be a great day when these four words come to life. Go out and win the game.'

It wasn't exactly Al Pacino in *Any Given Sunday,* but the mood seemed to have lifted and become more confident. Taylor was now relaxed enough to stop for a photo with a fan as she headed to a seat in the dug-out.

England's start inspired more optimism, 45 without loss after the first ten overs. Perry, upright in her run-up with a long wind-up at the end of it, looked unthreatening. Schutt's bad balls were put away calmly by Edwards, who reached 33 by hitting fours on either side of the wicket to begin the final over of the opening powerplay. Knight had survived a sixth-over scare when she edged to the keeper and began making her way off the field. Umpire Martin Saggers called for a replay but signalled his belief that the ball had carried. The press box announcer had already given details of the wicket when television pictures revealed that the ball had hit the ground before settling in Healy's gloves. Spinner Erin Osborne was on for the eleventh over, Knight pulling an ugly long hop to the rope.

Watching Edwards at the crease, you do sometimes wonder how she manages to get from one end to another with such a stuttering running style, speed of thought making up for lack of explosiveness in her legs. It put me in mind of another great England captain, Bobby Moore, who always said that the first yard was in your head. By the end of the nineteenth over, England had reached 88 and Edwards had completed her half-century by squeezing a single to third man. She had hit six fours along the way.

The first ball of the twenty-first over changed the course of the game, maybe even the summer. Knight drove to leg, Lanning dived to stop the ball at mid-wicket and threw from her knees as the batsman tried to get back after realising that there was no run. Knight was out for 38. 'I always talk about key moments that switch momentum,' Edwards said later, 'and

I think that was one of them. A brilliant bit of fielding and a key partnership for us. They just grabbed hold of it then.'

For a while, things went along merrily enough. Taylor began with some breezy leg-side swipes and, at the mid-innings drinks break, England were 122 for 1. But then, with the third ball after the restart, Schutt got Edwards to swing over a slower ball; bowled for 58. Lottie was quickly back on the balcony, encouraging and advising. No sitting in the dressing room with a towel over her head, despite her obvious disappointment.

In the next over Amy Jones was bowled by Jonassen for a seven-ball duck. She looked straight ahead as she climbed the steps and walked along the players' balcony, past teammates who knew better than to say anything. She, too, was soon sat outside. Always the quietest girl in the squad – 'two years ago you could barely have got her to say hello', Ian Durrant told me – she watched the game in silent thought. She didn't know it, but her Ashes series was over.

Taylor clubbed a Coyte full toss to the square leg boundary and attempted a ramp shot against Schutt. 'No,' exclaimed Anya. 'I hate it when she does that.' Two overs later she squirted a single with the same shot. 'When can we ban her from playing that?' Anya asked.

England's keeper cleared the mid-off fielder for another boundary, but was then caught in two minds by Jonassen, stepping back after initially venturing forward and ending up trapped in front for 43. England heads turned towards the dressing-room television to check the Sky replays, Anya groaning when she saw how close a decision it had been.

Lydia Greenway clipped square for four and turned Perry through mid-wicket for three, just as Katherine Brunt, padded up, ventured out towards the dug-out. 'Got your bat?' asked Anya.

'Yes, and the right top and the right trousers,' Katherine answered, turning back towards her colleague.

'She went out to bat once with her training gear on,' Anya explained.

There were few moments of levity remaining in the day. Nat Sciver's big shots were finding fielders, the pressure, frustration and required run rate building with every dot ball. Greenway was lbw for 20 when Coyte's full delivery hit her on the toes and Georgia Elwiss was bowled by Schutt. Sciver swung across a straight one from Coyte. Schutt pinned Shrubsole without scoring and yorked Cross to pick up her fourth wicket. England had slumped from 156 for 3 to 189 for 9.

Grundy, having signalled to Knight upstairs to ask whether the ball was swinging, was the last in and last out, bowled hacking at Osborne. Brunt, who had scored 21 with cuts, pulls and reverse shots, was left unbeaten as England folded for 196 in the forty-third over, beaten by 63 runs.

14

The Ugly Truth

'If someone bowls a pie I will say so. If I
think someone is not fit and needs to lose
a bit of weight I will say. It is how the girls
want it' – BBC Radio's Charles Dagnall

SKY commentator Nick Knight probably summed up
events of the third Ashes match when he tripped over
the name of the Australian captain and called her 'Leg
Manning'. England's players, having failed to run her out
early in her innings at Worcester and then dropped her,
came no closer to getting to grips with the opposition's most
dangerous batsman. They paid the price with an 89-run
defeat. Not only did it leave them 4-2 behind on points in the
Ashes, but it meant they had lost ground in the ICC Women's
Championship and had to watch the Aussies lifting the Royal
London One-Day Series trophy.

'We just didn't play to our brand or anything,' Lottie said
a few days later, 'apart from the first twenty overs of our

bowling, when I thought we did extremely well. Then we just weren't at the races. The manner of the defeat was more disappointing than the result itself.'

It had been a particularly tough day for the England captain, dismissed in the first over without scoring and the subject of much criticism for her captaincy. Lanning was lauded by the watching media for her thoughtful field positions and flexibility – 'always moving, always staying fresh', according to the BBC's Ebony Rainford-Brent. Edwards, it was felt by many, was safe and formulaic. 'I think Lanning has looked a cut above Charlotte in her captaincy,' added Lottie's former teammate. It sounded a lot like the Michael Clarke and Alastair Cook conversation of recent years.

'I don't get too caught up in all of that,' Lottie shrugged. 'Everyone has got an opinion. I have got a job and I do it to the best of my ability. I have done it a number of times and you have a feel for things. My gut has not let me down on too many occasions. I wouldn't change anything.'

Having seen heavy rain wash out play on Sunday – during which the England girls made many new fans by tirelessly signing autographs and posing for photos with just about everyone in the New Road ground – Lottie had few doubts about sticking Australia in when Lanning called wrong at the toss twenty-four hours later. 'With all the rain around, if there is going to be any assistance it will be this morning,' she said. England had made three changes to the team beaten four days earlier, Lauren Winfield, Jenny Gunn and Laura Marsh in for Jones, Cross and Grundy, moves that looked like increasing the depth of batting. Lottie explained, 'With Gunn on this wicket, we feel she is going to be a good option. It is horses for courses. Marsh has been bowling well; we've got competition for places within the squad. Lauren was very unlucky to miss out in the first two games so we are giving her a chance.' Australia, meanwhile, brought in the experienced Rene Farrell for the young and erratic Ferling and, surprisingly, reinstated leg-spinner Kristen Beams for the steadier off spin of Erin Osborne.

Brunt opened with a maiden, swinging the ball away and then cutting one back in off the seam to catch Villani's inside edge, although her speed was a couple of miles per hour down on the previous games. Shrubsole's square-chested deliveries hinted at a touch of movement away from the left-handed Bolton, who was duly circumspect in her approach. Add a sluggish outfield to England's accuracy and it resulted in 10 runs off the first four overs.

Villani climbed into Brunt's first short ball of the day. 'If she is going to bowl that length she needs her square leg just behind square,' ventured Paul Allott on Sky's commentary. 'About there,' he added as the next ball suffered the same fate. 'I think the answer is not to bowl short.'

Brunt didn't need anyone to tell her that, especially with the track clearly on the slow side. Australia reached the eleventh over, bowled by Gunn, with just 24 on the board and the twelfth was entrusted to Georgia Elwiss, who had not seen the ball in the first two games. Her first ball was full, pitched around middle stump, and Villani politely clipped it into the hands of Gunn five yards in from the mid-wicket boundary. Take that, those who felt Lottie's tactics were not 'funky' enough.

Bolton drove Gunn wide of extra cover, but it was a rare boundary in an innings that owed more to hard work than brilliance. The latter was more likely to be provided by Lanning, even though she was a touch lucky that the ball fell safe when she edged an attempted pull to an Elwiss delivery that kept low. She was even luckier two overs later. Bolton played Elwiss towards mid-wicket and called for a run, only to change her mind and send her captain back. Lanning was yards from safety, but a combination of a tentative and inaccurate throw by Sciver and a clumsy grab by Elwiss saw the ball squirting away to give her another life.

Marsh was on as early as the eighteenth over, much to the satisfaction of commentators on both television and radio. 'I think rotating the bowlers early is always a good ploy,' said Allott. Marsh's bowling was flighty with a bit of dip, but Lanning was patient, assessing each delivery, adapting to the fact that the ball was not coming on to the bat. She shuffled down the pitch to drive over Marsh's head and found the boundary again next ball when she clouted away a full toss. The Kent spinner's two overs had cost 14 runs.

Bolton, who had seemed content to let the bowlers dictate to her, began to look a little more desperate to increase her strike rate, just clearing mid-on with an ugly hack at Sciver. She tried the same thing next ball and was bowled for 40 off 89 balls. After twenty-seven overs the Aussies seemed to be in check at 88 for 2.

Alyssa Healy was promoted to add some urgency and, even though she lasted only 18 balls before offering a return catch to Heather Knight, her 17 runs included a few big shots and did just enough to change the personality of the innings. So did the events of the thirty-fifth over, when Lanning aimed a square drive at Brunt and Lydia Greenway could not keep her hands around the ball as she came down from a leaping attempt at backward point. Lanning had survived again and she responded by chopping Shrubsole away for a single to reach 50 and then pulling her in front of square for four.

Having been employed in the batting powerplay, Brunt and Shrubsole had used up their overs before the start of the fortieth. Cue more head shaking in commentary boxes. 'I have gone with purely trying to get our best bowlers bowling at their best batters,' Lottie would explain. 'I have always followed that train of thought really. Some bowlers are used to bowling in the powerplay – for the less experienced girls it is difficult. You look at the situation of the game. Unfortunately they have had two of their best batters in at that point. You have got to bowl your best bowlers with three fielders out and then you have got to back your other, less experienced bowlers to bowl with four out at the end. I don't think it is rocket science in that respect. Those are the decisions you live and die by.'

Collectively, Brunt and Shrubsole conceded only 62 in their twenty overs, but neither had taken a wicket and Australia went into the final ten at 162 for 3. Brunt's fumble allowed Perry a boundary, an edge by the same batsman brought up a 50 partnership off 55 balls, and Lanning attacked Knight with a swept four and another boundary between the off-side fielders. Marsh's return brought a slog sweep for four by Perry and a Lanning pull through mid-wicket. When Australia reached 200, their latest 50 runs had come off only 31 balls.

Lanning missed a century this time, Sciver taking a low catch in the deep off Gunn after she had scored 85 off 89 balls. Perry continued on, cover driving to the boundary to reach yet another half-century. A flurry of late wickets – including Perry bowled by Gunn for 67 – could not disguise that fact that England had repeated their errors of the previous Australian innings; sloppy, inconsistent fielding and too many short balls allowing the visitors to 241 for 7.

'We bowled well up front, but it came away from us at certain points,' said Sarah. 'But if we play our game and start well, and someone bats through from the top three or four, we can win it.' Indeed they could have done. But by the middle of the second over both Edwards and Taylor were gone.

Perry, sporting an optimistic Adam Ant-inspired stripe of sun block, made her fourth ball cut away off the seam just enough to catch the edge of the England captain's bat on the way to Healy's gloves. 0 for 1. Taylor could have been run out first ball after changing her mind about attempting a second run on a misfield, but she survived only one further delivery, bowled via her pad two overs later after ill-advisedly attempting to work Perry to leg.

England had spoken in their team meeting about the importance of playing straight early on, but Taylor had – as is her wont – chosen to do her own thing. She is one of those players who looks magnificent when such an approach pays off, but lays herself open to criticism when it doesn't. On BBC Radio, Dan Norcross was not about to give her an easy ride. 'It is the sense of unfulfilled promise that drives you berserk,' he said. 'What Taylor does is just not taking England into winning positions. She still scores a lot of runs, but you want her to understand what is expected of her. She is one of the best players in the world, but she could be better.'

Having monitored the TV and radio broadcasts through the day, I had been struck by the frankness of many of the comments. On the positive side, it appeared indicative of the growing relevance and legitimacy of women's cricket. The players would rather be slagged off than patronised, which even in the twenty-first century could still be the default approach of much coverage of women's sport.

BBC commentator Charles Dagnall, who has covered as much women's cricket as anyone in recent years, explained, 'I approach it the same as any other game. It is a game of cricket. If someone bowls a pie I will say so. If I think someone is not fit and needs to lose a bit of weight I will say. It is how the girls want it. They are accountable, they are professional. This is what they want.'

Confirmation of that came from Anya. 'No one will have greater expectations of me than I have of myself,' she said. 'We all know we are in the spotlight a bit more as professionals and we are going to be criticised a bit more. We expect that and we want that. We want women's cricket generally to be taken seriously so we have to be prepared to take criticism and say it was not very good when it was not. No one will be harder on us than we are on ourselves.'

Kate Cross had been aware of the changing mood in the year since professional contracts were awarded. 'I have definitely seen a difference in the media,' she said. 'If we don't do well you can see that the media is noticing what we do and don't do. It is still so new for us all. You could really feel the pressure in New Zealand when we were 2-1 down. When we weren't professional, well, it is hard to criticise a team that is doing it purely for the love of the game. I think Charles Dagnall is a really good example of it. If you don't do well he is not afraid to say anything. He always had that kind of mentality regardless of whether we were professional or not. I think it is good for the game. Daggers will say it how it is.'

Back out in the middle, it was movement in the air rather than criticism on the airwaves that was posing England problems. After some confident early strokes Winfield was struggling to keep the scoreboard moving, playing and missing and then inside-edging against Perry. It was Knight, forceful off the back foot but also fortunate to survive a confident lbw shout by Farrell, upon whom the home team's chances rested. Especially when Winfield's discomfort manifested itself in an injudicious call for a single after turning Jonassen to square leg, where Bolton dived and then threw down the stumps as the batter tried to regain her ground. She had taken twenty-six balls to score her seven runs and now England were 30 for 3.

A total of 50 was not reached until the nineteenth over as Knight and Greenway attempted to repair the early damage, but Greenway burst into life with two whipped fours – one aerial and one along the ground – off Coyte. She made it three in a row with a more orthodox straight hit.

A brief rain delay in the twenty-third over proved to be a precursor to another wicket. Barely had the game restarted when Knight stepped across the crease and, as she looked to turn Jonassen to leg, was beaten by some late dip and lost her off stump for 38. With half the innings remaining and the score on only 72, Brunt, England's biggest hitter, was sent out to the middle.

While she and Greenway mounted a partnership of 51 there was still hope. Having cracked a back-foot four through off, Brunt picked up a slog sweep and plopped Jonassen on to the boundary foam for six. Greenway responded in typical style, an unstoppable reverse sweep. Lanning brought back Farrell, who had conceded only 13 runs in seven overs, and Brunt was twice thwarted by fielders in the deep. The powerplay was taken after thirty-two overs and the partnership perished in the third over of it when Greenway sliced Coyte to backward point.

England managed only 29 further runs, Brunt run out for an ODI career-best 31 and everyone else falling in single figures. Sciver, Elwiss and Shrubsole gave Beams a trio of victims, while Marsh's miserable day was completed when Coyte had her caught without scoring. The home side were all out for 152 in the forty-fourth over, an 89-run margin of defeat. 'The hard truth is they have plateaued in white ball cricket for several years while others have caught up,' noted *The Guardian* cricket correspondent Mike Selvey.

'It's disappointing because we are normally a good chasing team,' said Lydia. 'We just couldn't quite get the partnerships. I think that was the key. Hopefully the change of format will freshen things up a bit and we can turn things around.' With the Test match coming up they would not, she continued, over-analyse every aspect of back-to-back ODI defeats. 'Sometimes you can get too caught up in things like that and with the change of format some of the stuff is not really relevant. You have got to keep moving forward and not dwell on it too much.'

Anya, selected to face the media after the game, voiced similar sentiments. 'What's important now is that we go away, regroup, have a few days off and come back hard,' she said, words that are always easier to deliver than to convert into meaningful actions. 'The series isn't over by any stretch of the imagination. If we go and play well in the Test match, if we get a victory there we're right back in it.'

* * * * *

A few days had passed when I discussed the state of the series with Lottie, by which time England's men had stormed back from being humiliated at Lord's to overwhelm the Australians at Edgbaston. It had acted as a soothing balm. 'I've been sat here watching the Test and thinking it shows you that in a week in sport a lot can happen really,' Lottie said cheerily. 'I think it's probably good timing for us, this break.

'At Bristol we massively missed out on an opportunity to go two games up and then Worcester was really disappointing. But I have been able to switch off and relax, and taken a lot of heart from what has happened here. We are not at panic stations; there is still a lot of cricket to play. I think sometimes with this group they need a good kick up the arse, so hopefully it will have that kind of impact on them.

'You wouldn't be doing the job justice if you didn't sit and reflect and I did that on the Monday night. I was fortunate that I was doing a *Masterchef* type thing with Waitrose the next day and it took my mind off it and helped me put things into perspective. OK, we just lost a game of cricket, but we need to keep calm. You can have all the plans in the world and have everything in place, but if you don't go out there and apply them it means nothing. That is what we didn't do. We didn't look positive with the bat at Worcester. I know we had lost wickets, but in overs five to twenty we didn't really go anywhere. We have got to be positive.'

Lottie echoed Lydia's view that a full post-mortem would wait until England approached their next ODI rather than distract them from preparation for the four-day contest. 'You have got to acknowledge what went on, but it has gone now and you have got to move forward. There are some fundamentals we have got to carry through in terms of hitting straight and bowling straight and taking our chances and we will pull things we think will help us. It is about us delivering what we are meant to. We haven't. I know we will bounce back. I have seen the girls and I know that sometimes it takes something like this to kick them into gear.'

Lottie was enjoying a few days of rest before the team reconvened for more preparation and a three-day game against Warwickshire's youth team. The Australians, meanwhile, were embarking on two- and three-day games against the England Women's Academy.

'Those gaps between formats,' Paul Shaw had ventured, 'I think the team that pays most attention to those gaps and works appropriately away from the matches in those periods is going to give their team the best chance of being successful in the Ashes. For Katherine Brunt, for example, what kind of rest and recovery will she have after the ODI series to make sure she is ready for the Test match? In the past, we have given them quite a lot of rest, but we are quite eager to get going again, make sure we balance the rest and recovery with appropriate preparation. How we manage players through that off time is going to be really crucial.'

In the case of Brunt, she would bowl only four overs in the first innings of the drawn game against Warwickshire because of a septic toe and did not appear at all in the second innings. The most notable individual performances were first-innings fifties for Knight and Edwards, who were both out in the forties in the second knock. Taylor needed to bat three times in order to achieve time in the middle, allowed to score 49 from number seven in the second innings after being out for 2 and 0 in her regular number three position. Becky Grundy achieved eye-catching figures of 3 for 4 in five overs as England just failed to take the final wicket they needed for victory.

A couple of days later, it was Amy Jones who excelled with an innings of 155 for the Academy against the Southern Stars in the three-day game at Beckenham. It was too late, however. Her place in the England squad for the Test match had already been given to the non-contracted Fran Wilson, who followed up her consistent form on the Academy tour earlier in the year with a half-century against the Aussies in the two-day warm-up. It was the only change to the squad that had contested the 50-over games, Jones's ineffectiveness in that series outweighing the three-figure score she had made in the intra-squad four-day game earlier in the summer.

'Coming out ahead after the ODIs is obviously our intention,' Shaw had said before those games, 'but we also have to ensure that if we are not ahead then we hold on to perspective and we are clear about what we have to do to get back in the Tests and T20s.'

Now was the time to put that objective – and Lottie's optimism – into practice.

15

Get Ready For It

'Some days I wish I still played [football].
Like when you get out for a duck and don't
bowl very well and have to sit around for
five hours' – Jenny Gunn

THE choice of Canterbury as the location for the singular Test in the Women's Ashes could hardly have been more appropriate. The Spitfire Ground, still better known locally as the St Lawrence Ground, might have been selected to take advantage of Charlotte Edwards and her Kent colleagues in the England squad, but it had been literally just down the road in a barn in Tonford that, so the tale goes, an early nineteenth-century woman pretty much invented cricket as we recognise it by hastening the change from under-arm to over-arm bowling. Wearing a fulsome skirt as she practised with her brother John, a Kent cricketer, Christina Willes found it less cumbersome to adopt the latter style and – much in the manner of William Webb

Ellis picking up the football at Rugby School – legend was made.

Edwards is the type of player who, like Webb Ellis, may well end up having some kind of trophy named after her, such has been her contribution to women's cricket. For now, though, she had more immediate concerns; sleep for one. England had checked into a hotel barely a cricket field's distance from the cathedral and she was not expecting her nights to be undisturbed. 'I find Test cricket quite hard,' she admitted. 'I have many sleepless nights playing Test cricket. We are not used to playing four-day cricket domestically. There are situations you have not been in and you are not quite sure how it is going to pan out; you don't have that experience to fall back on. But that is why I really love it. I think we love it because we play so little of it. We get to play in white and there is a special feel to it, although I am not saying I would want to play it week in and week out. I love the format of the Ashes. I think it should be played across all the international series we play now. There is a place for Test cricket within women's cricket and it would be great for other teams to get the chance to experience it.'

Swathes of blue had been elbowing the morning cloud aside like a determined shopper on the first day of Harrods' sale as the England team staged their final training session before the Kia-sponsored Test portion of the Ashes began the following day. The players had arrived at the ground after a morning meeting in which Paul Shaw had told them who would be in the team, 'because we wanted them to be able to practise their roles out there today.' The eleven names he had read out, in planned batting order, were: Knight, Winfield, Taylor, Edwards, Greenway, Sciver, Marsh, Brunt, Gunn, Shrubsole and Cross.

Laura Marsh had been chosen as spinner ahead of Becky Grundy, partly for the form Paul felt she had been showing with the ball, but also as a lower middle-order batter. 'We will miss the left-arm spinner and I would have liked to have got Becky in,' he shrugged. It meant that the expected return of Kate Cross for Georgia Elwiss was the only change from the team that played the third one-dayer. Elwiss had been the first-choice extra seamer-cum-batsman in the 50-over matches but now Gunn, the tall, dark and angular veteran of Nottingham, was the one being entrusted with that role. 'She has never let us down in Test matches,' said Paul of someone who had played eleven games in the format and been her team's top scorer with an unbeaten 62 the last time they had worn white.

If all cricketers owe something to their environment and upbringing then Gunn's long England career, which at age twenty-nine had been going for eleven years and earned her an MBE, could be put down partly to the great football manager – and cricket lover – Brian Clough. Her dad Bryn had spent a decade playing as a defender under him at Nottingham Forest, winning a European Cup winner's medal in 1980, a few weeks after Kate's dad had lifted the FA Cup.

'My family never pushed me towards anything and we played every sport possible growing up,' said Jenny, who had been in the academy system at Notts County before concentrating on cricket. 'Dad played cricket as well so that helped and I just found I was good at it so I pursued that a bit more. I think my dad's background helps with the competitiveness. We didn't realise we were being tested from a young age. But even just talking about his experiences, like playing at the Nou Camp, it is just crazy. I could listen to my dad's stories all day because it was a different era of football, especially under Brian Clough, who was such a tough manager. Like when Steven Gerrard lost his last game at Anfield and they still paraded around, Dad said that if Clough had lost that game no way would he have allowed a parade. Why should you celebrate when you have lost? He has some stories which make me glad our coaches are not like that. But they were successful so it worked.'

And somewhere along the way some of it rubbed off on Jenny, making her determined enough, and good enough, to have played cricket for England or – as her former Notts County teammates did a few weeks before the Ashes – in the FA Cup final at Wembley.

'There is nothing better than playing cricket for England so I can't really complain, but I love football and I always will. It is in my blood. Some days I wish I still played, like when you get out for a duck and don't bowl very well and have to sit around all day for five hours. Football, you play the game and go home. I would like to see how fit I would be if I played football now. I am certainly stronger now than I ever have been. And a few of the girls I grew up with are playing in the Super League now and one of them has gone on to play for England. I would like to know if I could have made it. One day when I have retired from cricket I will probably go back.'

Cricket began taking a grip on Jenny's sporting ambitions when representatives of Nottinghamshire visited her school in West Bridgford for a coaching session. From there she found herself in a youth competition at Trent Bridge and on the pathway into the county team, even though her family made sure she had finished her homework each night before she was allowed to go and play any sport.

She was still at South Notts College, studying sports science, when, at age seventeen, she was selected to tour South Africa with the England team. A four-wicket haul against India later that year helped establish her international credentials and the following summer she was playing an important role in an historic Ashes victory, including a marathon twenty-seven over spell that produced figures of 2 for 35.

A member of the victorious World Cup squad in Australia in 2009 she returned with mixed memories of the tournament, having missed the final after injuring her calf during pre-match warm-ups. Prior to the event, she had her bent-arm bowling action officially investigated for its legality, having been banned from Australian domestic cricket while playing for Western Australia and reported after the opening World Cup game against Sri Lanka.

'The first time it happened was in my first game for England,' she sighed, her voice revealing her resignation to years of constant scrutiny. 'I had gone through the nerves and excitement of being called up at age seventeen and then I had to go to the umpires' room with Clare Connor, the captain, thinking, "What the hell have I done wrong?" The umpires said they didn't think my action was legal. I went from the amazing emotion of making my debut for my country to thinking, "Am I ever going to play again?" I was tested by the ECB centre and I was fine; it was proved that my elbow doesn't bend that much so I was cleared to carry on bowling. Then I got called again.'

With heavy sarcasm, she continued. 'Shockingly, it was Australia who said it was not quite right. I was playing state cricket out there. It was just before the World Cup and they said, "You need to go and be tested." They said I had been clocked at 100 kph, but back then I didn't even bowl at 60 mph. I felt I was being forced to bowl a different action than I was used to. It was weird that it was right before the World Cup. It felt like they were trying to stir things.'

Jenny passed the ICC's video analysis, but was forced to endure the same examination after an ODI in New Zealand three years later. Clare Connor said at the time, 'Jenny Gunn's bowling action was independently analysed and confirmed as legal by the ICC in 2009 so it is unfortunate for her that its legality has been called into question once again.' This time the ICC observed a 'high degree of hyperextension' in her bowling arm, but accepted that it was something she could not control and again ruled that it was within the

'ICC tolerance threshold'. 'I physically can't change,' Jenny explained. 'I hyper-extend my elbow and my arm doesn't come down straight; my right hand comes out to the side. My arm goes beyond straight and comes back, which is why it looks from certain angles like I throw it. Then my wrist splits at the end, which also makes people think I throw. I can see where people are coming from, but if you see my action in super slow motion you will see it. It frustrates me that people want to say I throw it rather than looking at my action in slow motion.'

Jenny quickly discovered that the best way to cope with the jibes from opposition was to embrace them. 'They just do it to try and cause a stir so now my own teammates call me "Chucky". Sarah Taylor has always said "let's get in there first" and called me that. It makes me laugh. If they are calling me that, then it says to the other team, "Who cares?" It has been dealt with.'

The experiences, good and bad, and the longevity of Jenny's international career – 201 wickets and close to 2,500 runs in 220 matches – made her a valuable sounding board for the younger members of the squad, even though she had seen the role of vice-captain passed on to Heather Knight in 2014. 'I'm old, thanks,' Jenny had said one day when I'd asked how she was. 'I don't really feel old, but I get told about it,' she clarified. 'They keep me on my toes and it is all good fun. I don't think it has made any difference not being vice-captain. I was approachable then and I am approachable now. A lot of the girls talk to me. I don't think that side of me has changed over the years. We're playing the kind of cricket now where I think everyone knows their role, but I am always happy if people want to talk to me. If they need me I will always be there.'

In any case, as Lydia Greenway had stated, Jenny also felt that the new players were coming into the squad with more confidence and less need for mollycoddling than in the past.

'They have more pathways now. They start directing them right through the age groups. That benefits them. I made a massive jump up to international cricket, but now they get all the help they need, which was not quite there when I was growing up. There is a lot more support for the youngsters.'

So far, it had been a funny old year for Jenny, reduced to a bit part player on the New Zealand tour, where her skipper seemed to have lost all faith in her bowling. 'It was an odd tour, but one that you probably learn from. I need to get a bit smarter on certain tracks, setting different fields. It's knowing what to do if that happens again. The key is to keep learning from it.'

It had led to her being left on the sidelines for the first two one-day games of the Ashes series. 'I think you are always wondering what management are thinking and you never know to be honest. Will players be picked for different formats? Is it going to be three different teams? There are so many questions. You have just got to relax and keep enjoying your cricket. You play your best cricket when you are not worrying and, with the men playing so well recently, cricket is back on track and it is an exciting sport to be involved in.'

It was sheer enjoyment and love of the sport, more than the welcome new-found professional status, that kept Jenny striving to achieve more, despite the niggles that age and seam bowling were guaranteed to bring with them. 'My dad has always said that as soon as you stop enjoying it you have to stop. I got injured with my back and that helped me realise I wanted to carry on.

'We are not blessed by the best conditions in England and my body just said it didn't want to do it any more. I had issues in my lower back and had a few injections in it two seasons ago. I have had to make myself a bit stronger, in my core and my back, and it has been all right. Without that I might have got bored with it. I still felt I had more to give. I had that competitive side that I don't think playing county cricket would have satisfied. I have a competitive edge.'

Paul and his fellow coaches and selectors wanted that edge on the field in the heat of a four-day Ashes contest and Jenny felt she was better equipped than ever to meet their expectations. 'I am a bit smarter with my bowling,' she suggested. 'I used to just try to put it in the right spot, but now I try to figure out batters and be a bit more positive. I have a lot more self-confidence.'

Lottie admitted that Jenny had 'struggled with the ball in New Zealand and didn't really stake a claim' although she acknowledged that 'they were flat tracks over there'. But she warned, 'When she gets on a wicket where it nips around she will come into her own.'

* * * * *

It was two days since the men had retained the Ashes on the third day of the Trent Bridge Test and the excitement of their female counterparts in the midst of their own battle was obvious. 'We all love the four-day games but you are knackered by the end of it,' said Jenny. 'We just don't play enough of them, especially against Australia. Hopefully we will get more games and also play more practice games so our bodies get used to them. That is the biggest danger; getting injuries with bowling so many overs.'

'It's a shame we don't play more Test cricket,' said Paul. 'It is great for their overall development as cricketers.'

'It tests your skills in a lot of different ways,' said Lydia, 'and obviously we prepare for that as best we can. We have had a couple of three-day games, which has helped us, and it comes down to holding your skills for a long period of time and winning as many sessions as you can. That is what we have been working on. You try not to look too far ahead and just focus on what you can control in that moment in time.

That is really relevant with Test matches, hour by hour and session by session. If you are doing the right things in a short period of time hopefully that will look after things over a longer period.

'Because we don't get to play Test cricket much it makes it more of a big event. I remember my debut was in an Ashes series played over three Test matches and we don't do that now. The attention is more on the shorter formats because it seems to be where we get more publicity and media interest.'

Anya Shrubsole, similarly, acknowledged the realities of the modern cricketing era. 'We would like to play more Tests,' she said, 'but we understand that the marketing of ODIs and T20s is what has sold the women's game at the minute.'

While the girls went through their various cricketing drills in preparation for this most special of occasions, strength and conditioning coach Ian Durrant scurried from group to group. 'I have been trying to find a little gym so I can keep them working,' he said, concerned that the girls' days off prior to reporting to Canterbury needed redressing. 'Women lose muscle profile after four days' inactivity, which is quicker than men.'

A former basketball player for Crystal Palace, Kingston and Edinburgh in the British League – 'I went to the US a few times trying to get into a college, but I was about a foot too short' – Ian said that he loved the cricket environment and added, 'If they all click then this team can do anything. I really believe in them.'

Beyond his immediate concerns around this match, Durrant was thinking ahead to when several of the girls would slip beyond his sphere of influence when they travelled to play in overseas domestic cricket. 'The challenge in the winter will be communicating with the Australian teams. There will be times when they are carrying injuries, but they are being paid by the teams out there so they will expect them to play. We'll be working with the Australian strength and conditioning coaches, but I hope the girls know the value of certain things that we do and would keep them up even if the Australian coaches don't want them to.'

Kate Cross, one of those who would be heading Down Under, chatted with Georgia Elwiss as the final few shots were struck on a practice strip placed as close to the Test pitch as possible, specifically to help the players get accustomed to the slopes and undulations of the ground. 'It feels so different, putting on the whites. I love it. It's a different atmosphere,' said Kate, before adding, as she usually did, 'How's the book going?'

'It will be all the better for you guys winning here,' I told her.

'Actually I have got a really good feeling about this week. I think we come back better than they do after a loss.'

Georgia added, 'I played against them in the two-day Academy game and I didn't think they were anything much. I think their bowling is ordinary. If we can get Lanning and Perry out early...'

I asked Kate about England's intentions for those two. 'We have got plans for them, but we didn't execute them in two of the ODIs. Lanning is a real lbw candidate early on. Until she has scored a few she looks a very average player. That's the great thing about Tests; you don't have to chase things. You can just stop them scoring and be boring, really.'

Lottie had given me what amounted to a similar view about both the batting and bowling of the Aussies when we had spoken after the one-day matches. 'We put them under pressure in the first game and they didn't react very well. After that we have not taken probably six chances that Meg Lanning has given us. If you don't take those chances they are going to make you pay for them and she did. She has been the difference, with her strike rate and the way she goes about things. They are heavily reliant on her and we sense that. If we can make a few inroads like we did in the first game then a few cracks appear. When we have put them under pressure they have been vulnerable and I think that is something to hold on to.

'There are no demons in their bowling attack. There was all this talk about them bowling bouncers, but they bowl full and straight and we have got to hit back straight. Once you get in you can get more expansive on your shots. I thought they would stick with their spinners a little more, but it looks like they are going to go with seam at us.'

The re-introduction of Holly Ferling after her omission at Worcester was, Lottie felt, an intriguing possibility although not one that was filling her with dread. The fast bowler had followed up her wicketless ODI performances by spraying it about a bit in the subsequent warm-up games, including five wides in an over at one point.

'I have been really surprised,' Lottie admitted. 'When I faced her two years ago she was a really raw young bowler and she had that point of difference; her pace, height and bounce. When I faced her at Bristol she seemed to be lacking in confidence. She has remodelled her action and is not bowling at the pace I thought she would. They might just edge towards her for the Test purely because she is a little different to the rest of their bowling and we won't underestimate her at all. She is probably going to take a little bit of time to get into the series. In general they have probably been a little bit more disciplined than us and we haven't had much luck with the ball. Anya and Katherine have bowled well and if we get a little bit of luck going our way we can make inroads into their batting.'

The Australians' pair of 50-over victories and their 4-2 points lead in the Ashes made them Test favourites in some people's eyes. Others stuck to the conventional wisdom that England were traditionally the stronger team in the longer game, despite that loss at home to India a year earlier. 'It is hard to really have any evidence other than we won the last Test match against them,' Lottie suggested. 'I think our bowling attack is probably suited towards Test cricket, and potentially our batting, but we are going to have to play well. I am really confident, even though we have not performed well so far in the series. I think you will see us bounce back.'

Of her own form, despite a duck in the third ODI, she said, 'I feel in really good nick. First game I was a little bit unfortunate to drag one on and I felt bad about missing out on a big one. I was bitterly disappointed at Bristol after getting myself set and playing well. At Worcester I was gutted to get out in that manner really. But I don't get too down. I have played enough cricket to know there is always a big score around the corner. There is a lot of cricket still to be played and lots of runs to be scored. I am pretty confident.'

As the captain made her way out of the nets, Beth Wild – having managed to remove a local BBC television reporter from standing on a good length on the match pitch – asked, 'What have you got left to do, Chedwards? I've Henry [Moeran] from *Test Match Special* waiting.'

'Nothing,' Lottie replied, before quickly correcting herself with, 'Oh no. I've got my short leg work.' BBC Radio would have to wait while David Capel thrust his pad down the track – much as he had done against Abdul Qadir in Lahore nearly three decades earlier – and Lottie and Lauren Winfield cheered each other loudly whenever they took a catch.

Nat Sciver was one of the few batters to come out of the one-day series with a big innings behind her and, even after two defeats, was excited about the challenge of the coming week. 'The time off has given me a chance to reflect and I feel comfortable in my role,' she said. 'Preparation has been more about the mental side of the game, dealing with the pressure rather than working on technical things. The three ODIs showed the increase in popularity and recognition. There were loads of people at the games, more than ever before, so the pressure increases a bit. Having not done as well as we would want, now we will see what effect that has on us.'

The fact that the Test was taking place in the middle of the series for the first time, instead of as the opener, appeared to have been welcomed by all. 'I think the move is a good one,' said Heather Knight. 'It will be the team that transitions better and holds their nerve for the big moments that will come out on top.'

Once the training session had ended, and before Lottie was ushered to the pre-match press conference, the players once again gathered around Carl Crowe and the dressing-room music was silenced. This time the coach was intent on finding out what they had learned from batting and bowling at opposite ends of the ground to the previous day. Lauren suggested that the gradient meant batsmen would need to be strong in holding their positions. 'That slope can pull you away a little bit,' Carl agreed. When it came to the bowlers, Katherine warned, 'When you are bowling up the hill you have got to stay strong and upright and drive as hard as you can towards Sarah and the batsman. You can be pulled away.'

And then Lottie stood up from her position at the back of the room. Paul had wanted her voice to be the last one they heard before match-day. 'You have seen how passionate I am about these next four days,' she began as every eye locked on to her. 'What an opportunity we have. This is the pinnacle of what we do, ladies. Remember that feeling at Perth? That was one of the best feelings I have had and I want it again. We are better than this lot. I know we will fight; that is a given. But we have got to show discipline as well. We have got to totally believe in one another. Fucking enjoy it. It's the first women's Test ever shown on Sky so let's show them we are enjoying it. This could be the best fucking four days of your life. You have seen what the men have done at Trent Bridge. We can have some of that. We can nail it.'

To round things off a video appeared on the TV screen. Over Take That's 'Get Ready For It' was a montage of shots of the girls from the one-day series. In the room they cheered at the wickets and big shots, laughed at the close-up reactions of their teammates, and finished with a collective cry of intent and determination.

'Come on, ladies,' yelled Lottie as the din subsided. 'We have got this.'

16

Canterbury Tales: The Wife of Bath

'Outwardly I am a little more laid back. I like to save my energy and use it when I bowl' – Anya Shrubsole

THE sky was as grey as the slate roof of Canterbury Cathedral, the cobbled city centre streets made shiny by the early morning drizzle. Inside and out the atmospherics were oppressive and heavy. You could feel the weight of the Ashes Test match bearing down as the England team came and went from breakfast.

Having spent a quiet evening, eating in small groups or with family and friends in the many High Street restaurants, a lot of the girls came down complaining of bedrooms 'like a sauna' after a steamy night prior to the freshening rain. This felt different to the morning of the first one-dayer of the series. More intense, not much lightness to be found;

just an obvious sense that here we were at the crossroads of the summer.

'Morning, David,' said Heather Knight. 'You look nervous.' I hadn't realised it was getting to me as well.

Discussion of the unexpected turn of weather helped distract a few minds from the upcoming events; days that could define the career of some of these players. Strength coach Ian Durrant bounded down the stairs with a big smile and a fist pump. Further relief arrived in the shape of Charlotte Edwards carrying her England blazer over her shoulder. 'I am wearing it for the toss,' she declared. 'It's an extra half-point if Meg Lanning doesn't wear hers.'

And then Katherine Brunt, a guaranteed mood-lifter, turned up with, 'You're in my car. I hope you like singing. Do you know any Jess Glynne?'

'Put your seat belt on,' Kate Cross warned as I headed to the car park with Katherine, Fran Wilson and Nat Sciver, who ended up driving. 'I can't believe we only have time for one song,' Katherine complained as we set off on the short drive; the tune of choice being the aforementioned singer's 'Hold My Hand'. 'Nat is the best singer in the team. She used to be in a choir. If she doesn't sing loud it is because you are here. Write that she has the voice of an angel.' When I mentioned how much I kept hearing about the skipper's karaoke exploits, Katherine shot back, 'Lottie is terrible!'

Maybe it was Katherine's singing and passenger seat dancing. Perhaps it was getting out of the low lighting of the hotel lobby. Or it could have been the obvious pleasure the team took from coming out for warm-ups in their sparkling white sleeveless sweaters. Whatever it was, things appeared brighter.

Not for Jenny Gunn, though. She had felt the warning signs of a stiff neck as soon as she awoke. By the time she was up and about she was having a real problem in turning her head to the left and was now walking around with her left shoulder raised a long way above the right in an attempt to find some comfort. Twenty minutes before the toss she was ruled out. It was the 2009 World Cup final all over again. Edwards handed a first navy blue Test cap to Georgia Elwiss.

Jenny couldn't have looked any more downcast. 'I didn't think I was coming here to watch for four days,' she said as she stood in the dressing room. 'I've not had this before; it's usually the other side I have trouble with.'

Paul Shaw had delayed ruling her out until as late as possible in the hope that the passing of time and some treatment would loosen things up. 'It went the other way,' he explained, with Lottie adding that 'we couldn't take the risk'. Australia, meanwhile, were grouped in a circle on the boundary while baggy green caps were presented to Test debutants Kristen Beams, Nicole Bolton and Jess Jonassen. Lottie watched the ceremonies and quickly huddled with her coaches, their expectations of their opponents' line-up apparently confirmed. At the toss, Lottie's hunch that fast bowler Holly Ferling's potential would be trusted in the four-day game was also proved correct.

Lanning, minus blazer, called correctly and decided that Australia would bat. A few eyes were raised to the sky – not a sign of blue – and a few English batters smiled as their bowlers quickly switched from fielding drills to practising their run-ups. 'That's not a bad toss to lose,' said Lauren Winfield as she headed upstairs to put on the padding she would need for short leg duties. 'I think before the rain we would have batted, but now, if we can get them three down early...' Lottie duly confirmed that she would have elected to field.

'You need to be down there for the anthems at 10.54, ladies,' called Beth Wild, playing teacher as usual. 'Not 10.53, not 10.55.'

As the girls obeyed instructions, Nat dithered over whether to wear a sweater or not and wondered if there was time for a final trip to the loo. Katherine was the last to leave the dressing room, emitting a warrior-like shriek, long and high, before she did so. 'I feel like I am going to explode with all this energy.' That force seemed to have permeated the rest of the team as they threw themselves lustily into 'God Save the Queen', laughing together when they realised they had raced through it so quickly that the music was still playing long after they had finished singing.

Brunt opened from the Pavilion End – not her preferred option – with three slips and a gully, and set about a superb, luckless, hour of bowling. By the end of it, BBC's Charles Dagnall was telling me, 'That is the best spell I have ever seen her bowl. She looks fitter than ever and if there had been a little more pace in the pitch she would have had a couple of wickets.'

Approaching the crease with her left shoulder slightly to the fore, all the better to get herself into the best position to swing the ball, Brunt was moving it away from right-handed Elyse Villani from ball one. Anya Shrubsole, auburn hair bouncing in its pony tail, was also making it bend; too much as it passed harmlessly behind left-hander Bolton. She quickly changed to bowling round the wicket. Bolton edged the first run of the innings off the final ball of the second over and only just jammed her bat down on the first delivery she took from Brunt. The third hooped in and brought about a loud appeal for lbw, although she had just managed to get some bat into play. 'Tell you what,' said Carl Crowe from behind his computer screen. 'Something is happening.' By way of emphasis, Brunt found the edge again with the final ball of her over. As she arrived at fine leg and looked up at the team balcony, Paul gave her a double thumbs-up, also signalling to her confirmation that Bolton's bat had saved her from the lbw appeal.

Brunt's third over was a masterpiece. Twice she swung the ball in to strike Bolton's pads. The first would have missed leg but the second, television suggested, would have clipped the stump. Both appeals were denied. After Bolton clipped a three to register her first runs it was Villani's turn to hold her breath as Brunt reversed the direction of her swing to thud into the right-hander's pads. Not until the seventh over did Brunt eventually bowl a loose delivery, allowing Villani to pull to the leg-side boundary.

A radio was located so that the England staff could hear the BBC commentary without an internet delay and the microphones were quickly picking up yet another Brunt appeal, a little extra bounce saving Villani this time. Two balls later the batsman left what she assumed was the outswinger and was nearly bowled by one that went the other way. Australia had made 19 from nine overs, but you could not help sense that England were in danger of missing the chance to get the dangerous Lanning in early while the new ball was playing tricks.

Further shape away from Villani by Brunt, but then another slap for four; this one through mid-on, the opener's third boundary. Bolton clipped a full Brunt delivery to the rope, but was immediately trapped by a straighter one. Another appeal turned down. 'I am not sure what was wrong with that,' the England balcony heard BBC's Alison Mitchell comment. By drinks, Australia were 47 for 0 off fifteen overs and appeared to have ridden out the opening storm, with Brunt replaced by debutant Elwiss and the pitch too slow to offer much encouragement once the ball stopped swinging.

Villani, as strong as always on anything short, enjoyed a couple of Elwiss long hops and Shrubsole returned in place of Cross to bowl the twentieth over, again from Brunt's favoured Nackington Road End. Taylor, helmetless, stood up to the wicket. The fifth ball of her second over, ninety minutes into the day, was full with a hint of swing and Villani pushed forward to offer Knight a catch at first slip. 66 for 1 and suddenly England were running into position between overs, the decibel level on the field rising.

Third over of Shrubsole's spell; fifth ball again. Same delivery, same shot offered by Lanning and the same result; the ball in the hands of Knight via the outside edge. The big batsman had gone for 3. Now came the dangerous Perry, surviving an lbw shout first ball and helping her team to 84 for 2 from twenty-eight overs as lunch was called.

During the break David Capel discussed field placings with Lottie and suggested that Laura Marsh, given one over before lunch from the Nackington Road End, from where the slope assisted her off spin, might be tried at the Pavilion End. Anya looked at the analyst's computer screen; Crowe, Capel and Shaw ended the interval comparing notes in their respective jotters and the latter declared the morning had been 'reasonable' as the players returned to the field.

It got better than that in the first over after lunch. Bolton aimed to drive through mid-wicket as Shrubsole fired one in at her pads and ended up without a leg stump, her 36-run vigil over. It took Australia twenty balls before scoring their first run after lunch. They had added only three when Perry pushed forward to Shrubsole and inside-edged against her pad. Taylor was already leaping in celebration as the ball settled in her gloves. Shrubsole had taken four wickets for only 21 runs, including the big two of Lanning and Perry.

'It was especially pleasing to get their two main players the way we had planned,' said Paul. 'We wanted to bowl full to Lanning early on and we always felt Perry was a candidate for bat-pad or lbw. It is fantastic when you have talked about something and you see the girls execute.'

'There is no better feeling,' Anya said later of that moment when a plan comes together. 'We spend a lot of time analysing these players, going over footage and coming up with strategies, and you would be surprised how many times it doesn't pan out how you hoped. So when it does and it happens, it is really special.'

* * * * *

A four-wicket haul equalled Anya's best return in Test cricket. There were some who felt that a bowler with her international experience and skill should be taking more wickets for England, but, she had to remind herself, she was still only twenty-three, younger than teammate Georgia Elwiss, who was playing in her first Test. 'I am definitely a believer that no one ever has nothing to improve upon. I am no different. I forget how young I am to be honest. I made my England debut at sixteen so I have already been in the squad for seven years. Sometimes I have to stop myself and remember how old I am so hopefully I have got many years ahead of me. The last two years have, without a doubt, been the most successful of my England career. Injuries early on meant I didn't play the number of games I could have done, but I have got over that and in the past couple of years feel I have given what I expect of myself.'

Born in Bath, the daughter of a minor counties cricketer, Ian, Anya made her debut for Somerset's senior women's team aged twelve, barely four years after a local coach visited her school and offered her the chance to turn the interest she already had in the sport into something more tangible.

'I was always a bowler,' she explained. 'When I got to about twelve or thirteen I just had a growth spurt and got a lot bigger than I had been. I was always big and tall for my age. I was playing for Somerset boys at under-12s and it all kind of started from there. It was a little bit daunting playing for Somerset women that young, but to be honest I have played for them so long it all just seems so normal now. I remember the county championship used to be a five-day thing at Cambridge. I missed the first two days because

I was playing for the boys' team and then played the next three days. The first day we played Berkshire and I got Claire Taylor out [for nought] and got another.'

She bagged two more wickets the following day and was on the fast track to the England team. The only thing that delayed her progress was her health. 'I had a lot of back injuries when I was younger, but it is almost inevitable. It was a stress reaction. I managed never to have a stress fracture, always managed to stop just before. It is almost a rite of passage for a fast bowler.'

By 2008, at the age of sixteen, Anya was making her England debut in an ODI against South Africa at Shenley and earning a place in the winter World Cup squad in Australia, where she took two wickets in her only game, a group match against Pakistan. 'I was massively shocked when I got selected for England. I thought I was a good couple of years away. It was a brilliant experience to be there and to say I was part of a World Cup-winning squad is a huge part of my career. One of the great things about this group is that you couldn't be made to feel more welcome when you come into the squad. And because we play a lot of cricket against each other, you know who everyone is so it didn't feel like a massive transition for me.'

Off the field Anya is one of the more studious, discreet members of the England squad. While others are killing time between action with pranks and party tricks, she is often to be found, as at Canterbury, with her nose in a *Puzzler* magazine. While Katherine is screaming at the world to get herself fired up, Anya will sit in quiet contemplation.

Like her opening partner, Anya believes the constant battle against injury has given her the ability to maintain a certain equilibrium when it comes to events on the field. 'You have to accept that as a fast bowler injuries are going to come around every now and again. Even the fittest fast bowlers in the world get injuries. You have to look at it as an opportunity to come back stronger. It is hard going through injuries, but I don't tend to be too bothered by stuff on the pitch so much because I know there is worse off it and I have potentially already gone through it. There are tough situations where sometimes I come out on top and sometimes the opposition come out on top. There will always be another game and another opportunity to put it right. It has helped me deal with the pressures a bit more.'

If that doesn't sound like the cut-throat attitude one expects from a fast bowler it was reflective of the opposite personality neighbourhoods inhabited by Shrubsole and Brunt. 'Outwardly, Katherine and I are quite different,' Anya acknowledged. 'I think it was the Worcester game in this series, we were about to go out and Katherine was up and about making a lot of noise and I was bordering on lying down, really relaxed. Lauren turned round and said, "We could not have two more differing opening bowlers." But I think when we get the ball in our hands we are the same. We are both aggressive and we want to take wickets even if outwardly I am a little bit more laid back. I guess it is what you need to get yourself going. She needs that; I don't. I like to save my energy and use it when I bowl.'

When I asked Lauren about the bowlers she confirmed, 'They have been very good for such a long time and you sometimes forget how good they are. I mean, Anya is a quiet character; she is not loud and in your face. She goes about her business in her own little way and she is so understated. You sometimes forget that she does it time after time and you almost don't notice sometimes.'

Anya prides herself on being something of a student of sport – 'the girls joke that if you need to know anything sport ask me; I seem to know a lot about things I shouldn't really know about' – and of fast bowling in particular. 'I watch a lot of cricket now, although I don't remember watching a lot when I was younger because I was down at Bath Cricket

Club. I massively admire the West Indian quicks. I know they were before my time, but I still watch videos of them bowling because a lot of them were just brilliant. I particularly like watching Michael Holding, just the way he eased in and bowled at the speed of light. But all of them were brilliant. Especially since I have been playing for England, I watch a lot of cricket because there is always something to learn by working out what is going on and applying it to your game. I definitely look out for things I can add to my own game. Everyone is different and no two people bowl the same, even if they do vaguely the same thing, but you try to pick up bits and pieces where you can.'

The kind of knowledge that came only from personal experience was how to ensure that she remained healthy enough to keep playing for England. 'Keeping on top of things, making sure you are fit and strong and doing the things you are asked, making sure you do your recovery right,' were what she cited as the keys. 'Knowing your body and working closely with the physio and strength and conditioning coach is vital. You might go to a session and say, "I don't feel right today," and not do so much. Some sessions you feel really good and do a bit more. It's about knowing the right times to put the foot down and the right times to hold up.'

As the 2015 season unfolded, Anya was one of the few players in the England set-up to be playing Division 2 county cricket. Those emotional Bath ties had kept her tethered to Somerset, even as she had seen former teammates, such as Fran Wilson, head to more elevated homes.

'I remember a coach called Tom Baker visiting our school. He was coaching at Bath and was a brilliant coach with kids, very enthusiastic, and he really instilled into me that I was good enough. He gave me confidence at a young age to take cricket seriously and I went on to spend a long time at the Somerset academy. I owe a lot to Somerset; I have done a lot of my training down there. I want to be able to help the girls who play there and have put a lot of time and effort into Somerset so that they have the best chance of going up. It could be this year, which will make my decision easier next year about whether I stay or go. I also get the opportunity to captain down there and I probably wouldn't have that at another county. It does benefit me to stay there and hopefully it benefits the girls to have me there to lead the way.'

Anya had led the way for England on this day and with four wickets down it was now all encouragement and movement in the field. 'I don't think I bowled very well with the new ball, but I was happy with the way I came back,' she said. 'That is the beauty of Test cricket. You have a spell that didn't go so well and you have time to evaluate and work out how to get better, and you get another go. It is brilliant to bowl spells when you feel everything is coming out right and you get the reward. Picking up Lanning and Perry cheaply after they gave us the run around in the one-dayers was brilliant.'

Shrubsole was now bowling with three slips. The second of them, Sciver, added to the vivid red steak on the back of her trousers by vigorously polishing the ball before it was returned to the bowler, who saw Jonassen slide it away off the outside edge.

Interest in events in Canterbury had seen '#WomensAshes' trending on the UK version of Twitter for most of the day. And while 2,000 were in the stadium, the Sky Sports audience was growing towards a peak of close to 150,000 viewers late in the day. Midway through the thirty-ninth over they saw Brunt get her reward, Blackwell trapped lbw on the front foot for 7, leaving Australia in trouble at 99 for 5. The fans in the Colin Cowdrey and Frank Woolley Stands gave the bowler a merited ovation as she made her way to long leg at the end of her over.

This all felt like the reverse of what had seemed likely earlier, when most had assumed that batting would become easier as the day went on. Order was about to be restored, though. Fifty minutes into the session, Jonassen drove Shrubsole for the first boundary of the afternoon and England were going to have to wait until after tea to strike again.

Taylor whipped off the bails with another effortless take, her keeping far more assured than it had been in the one-day games. It did not elude the attention of one of England's finest glovemen, Jack Russell, who had set up behind square leg with a sale of books of his paintings. At the end of the day he tweeted, 'Enjoyed watching Sarah Taylor today live for the first time. Top wicket-keeping. #classact' – which the chuffed player announced she would have framed.

Jonassen, the dark-haired left-hander, was also beginning to impress in her first Test innings. Still at the crease and quick to burst forward into the drive, she twice sent a tiring Brunt to the ropes, while wicketkeeper Alyssa Healy found the boundary off Shrubsole. England needed a tight spell from Cross to keep up the pressure, but her first ball was a loopy half-volley, a gift for the Jonassen drive. Marsh also returned, the flatness of her default delivery showing her background as a seamer, but proving impossible for the Australians to dominate. It took them twenty-eight balls to score a run off her. Before long it was spin at both ends, but Knight's first ball was heaved for four from outside off by Healy. There was a sense now of killing time before the strike bowlers, Brunt and Shrubsole, were ready to return. Was this where England, as Paul feared, were missing the left-arm turn of Becky Grundy?

Suddenly, a chance. Marsh found a little more flight, Healy drove square and a diving Cross spilled the catch at cover point. There were already cries of joy in the air before teammates realised the ball was on the floor. The fifty partnership was reached in just over an hour and Healy celebrated by hoisting Knight over extra cover, the Australian fans in front of the café beyond the boundary cheering heartily as the ball sped towards them. Two balls later Healy swatted away a full toss with similar results. Tea arrived at 162 for 5 and the 78-run session had flown by, despite the relative lack of incident in the second hour.

Sciver bowled the first over of the evening, seeing the second and third balls dispatched for fours by Jonassen. Marsh seemed no more likely to make an impact when her second ball was square driven to the boundary, but then she got one to hurry through on Healy, who played across it and was given out leg before for 39. The 77-run partnership was ended, the score 176 for 6.

Jonassen reached her fifty by cutting Cross to the rope and then working her ninety-third ball to leg for a single. The Lancashire bowler had been guilty for much of the innings of bowling too full with a lack of devilment, but she fired one in to bring Sarah Coyte forward and Taylor, standing up to the stumps, claimed a catch. Umpire Alex Wharf concurred and the joy of her teammates indicated their empathy with the tough day Cross had been having until then.

The score passed 200 shortly after Megan Schutt slashed Cross through the slips and Jonassen punished the bowler for over-pitching. But then Marsh struck again, a similar dismissal to her first as Schutt was rapped on the pads. Australia had slipped to 206 for 8 and England had thoughts of winning the day and having to bat before the close.

Australia had other ideas. Jonassen, even when tied down by the spin of Marsh and Knight, had no thought of doing anything rash and risking her wicket. The uppish drive back over Marsh and a waft at the final ball of the eightieth over were rare moments of impulsiveness. Marsh made way after her nineteen overs, which cost only 37 runs, for the new-ball pairing of Brunt and Shrubsole, but neither was able to break the partnership of Jonassen and Beams, who edged short of slip to the fifth delivery of Brunt's return. Brunt was left kicking the ground after she gave up the first boundary of her spell to Jonassen in her third over and, with the floodlights now on, the same batter edged Shrubsole past Knight at slip.

Ten overs with the new ball and still no breakthrough, although Marsh, diving to her left at wide mid-off and reaching the ball with both hands, might have caught Beams off Brunt. A pushed single by Jonassen brought up the 250 and when Beams nudged Brunt to complete a half-century stand the partnership had developed the feel of a match-changer. Brunt took out her frustration by bowling a couple of bouncers at Jonassen, who missed the first with an attempted hook and steered the second for a run. Asked about the confrontation later, Jonassen replied, 'I find [Brunt] a bit funny. If I show her I can hold my ground she can't roll over the top of me.'

Capel commented, 'I couldn't understand why Brunty bowled two bouncers at the end against someone in the 80s. If you're going to do that, then do it against the number ten. She's a number ten for a reason.'

For a while there had been a flurry of shots that hinted at a possible early Australian declaration before stumps, but such thoughts had been abandoned as Jonassen settled for knocking singles down the ground and making her way steadily towards three figures. A two-minute delay while the Australian physiotherapist and twelfth man both stood in the middle chatting to the batsmen ensured that play ended with ninety-seven overs of the day's scheduled 100 having been bowled, Australia on 268 for 8 and Jonassen unbeaten on 95. The inescapable feeling was that the final hour and a half, and a partnership of 62, had sent the Ashes a good deal further back towards the southern hemisphere.

'Frustrating,' said Capel as he watched the girls leave the field, adding his own applause to the generous acknowledgement of Jonassen. 'There were a lot of good things today and you look at that score and think they could have got that many for five with Lanning and Perry getting runs, so it is frustrating that they got there with the others getting them. I thought we were a little naïve at times, bowling our frontline bowlers in those long spells. It is a shame we couldn't get that wicket because I don't think the number eleven can bat at all.'

The final words of the day went to Shrubsole, selected after her twenty-three overs with the ball to be the team spokesman at the close-of-play press conference. She, too, used the word 'frustrating' to summarise events. 'I am a little bit tired,' she confessed. 'I am not going to lie. But that is what we do the training for. You have to back the preparation you have done and all the running. You know you are going to be at your limit. I love to play Test cricket, as hard as days like these are.'

17

Test of Patience

'The girls might not always appreciate it, but in years to come it would be nice for them to look back at this time and feel it helped develop them as people' – Paul Shaw

A MOTLEY collection of coloured towels draped over the two benches placed just inside the boundary of the Spitfire Ground told the tale of the second morning of the Test match. As rain soaked into the makeshift seat covers, England's players remained in the dressing room instead of taking their places for the team photo. Spectators huddled under umbrellas and in the various shops and refreshment centres.

It would take more than a bit of bad weather to stop Charlotte Edwards putting on her pads, though, and she was the first to head off to the Kent academy's indoor nets behind the pavilion, stopping to chat to the family members of the Australian players on the way back. The rain had already been falling for longer than forecast; but then again the same forecast had, a week earlier, been predicting several days of twenty-five degree sunshine.

Paul Shaw chatted with groundsmen and pawed with his foot at the grass by the boundary marker like an impatient colt. 'We leave it up to the players whether they want to go to the indoor nets or not,' he explained. 'Sometimes it is not always helpful to have a knock on a fast, hard surface that has no bearing on what they will have out there. But some just like the feel of the ball on their bats.'

We talked about the first day. 'I think we ended about even. It's a shame we didn't get the last two wickets – it just got away from us a little at the end. I thought Katherine and Anya both bowled exceptionally well.'

In the dressing room, Sarah Taylor was passing the time by taking on challengers at FIFA on the games console, while Laura Marsh had resorted to hiding in the lockers. 'If it goes on for a long time people will start jumping out of bags and scaring people,' Katherine Brunt explained. 'Lydia is one for that. She is the joker. We were at a hotel once and Heather was walking backwards into her room with a cup of tea and Lydia jumped out at her. The tea went everywhere and we got it all on video. We were trying to scare Fran [Wilson] in the hotel yesterday but she barely flinched. I am sharing with her and as she is the new girl it my job to break her. I think she is a bit gullible. If I told her I had webbed feet or said the reason I bowl fast is that I have a metal shoulder she would believe me.'

While her teammates were killing time, Katherine had addressed a more serious problem – the colour of her sports bra. On day one she had attracted comment, and the disapproval of her family at the close of play, by wearing a bright pink one that had been clearly visible through her white shirt and shown up more as a shade of tangerine. Beth Wild said she had taken various messages throughout the day about it. 'These shirts are so see-through,' Katherine said with faux embarrassment. 'I have put a black one on today,' and she pulled out the strap by way of proof.

'It was too warm to wear my jumper, which was a shame because those are very precious, our version of the baggy blue caps the men get. We don't get them, but we should. The caps we wear are designed so that we can get our hair through, which we need, but we should get a baggy blue to keep, like the men.'

Eventually the rain relented and the call came to start play at 12.30. 'Hopefully we are not out there for long,' said Anya after changing into her whites. 'I don't know how much more my legs can take.'

'The wicket's not doing much,' added Heather Knight. 'The outfield is slow, though, and it will be like that all week with this rain around. Big day, this.'

Jess Jonassen added to her overnight total by edging a couple of runs off Shrubsole, while Brunt bowled too short and wide at Kristen Beams, allowing her to play comfortably off the back foot. Jonassen moved to within one of a debut Test century, only to miss a drive against Brunt, who crouched and roared like a Maori warrior in mid-haka as her opponent was given out leg before. The applause that accompanied the Aussie girl back to the pavilion was more sympathetic than celebratory.

Holly Ferling walked out, played and missed at one ball, and returned to the pavilion as her captain signalled a declaration. England would have to face one over before lunch. A declaration when the wicket fell would have meant two overs, so goodness knows why the number eleven was sent in to bat for a single delivery. 'They weren't prepared for her getting out,' suggested David Capel. 'They hadn't thought about it.'

'I was just thinking the only way we were going to get her out was lbw,' said Lottie on her return to the dressing room. 'Gutsy decision. One of those where if it had not been on TV it might have been given not out. Credibility is at stake when the cameras are here.'

Credibility was an issue for Lauren Winfield, opening in an Ashes Test match for the first time and determined to prove that she deserved the honour. 'I think there are certain formats I have proved myself in more than others,' she'd said. 'Having made my Test debut last summer and been given the opportunity to open the batting through Arran Brindle's retirement, that is still something that massively excites me. Thinking about, dreaming about that first hundred; it's something that I am pushing towards. I want to show I can be adaptable and score runs in all formats.

'The main thing for me is to keep it really simple, not over-complicate, not premeditate anything, simply watch the ball. Naturally I am an aggressive player and if it is there your instinct takes over and you play it with conviction anyway. So it is mainly about not trying to force anything, backing my natural instincts, being relaxed at the crease and not thinking too much about the scoreboard or the situation.'

It was her senior partner, Knight, who faced the first ball of the England reply, playing and missing as Ellyse Perry moved one up the hill. There was a feeling of relief among her colleagues when she drove cleanly to the cover boundary and amusement at her over-elaboration between balls. 'I love people's ways of wasting a bit of time,' laughed Lottie. 'Anya does her hair; takes it out just to put it up again.'

'I used to favour the gardening or the shoelace,' Capel chipped in. 'There was always a shoelace to do up.'

Despite Knight's efforts it appeared there might be time to start a second over, but the umpires had no such intention and headed to the dining room. 'They love a bit of early lunch,' said Lottie. Little did she expect to be joining them in the middle in the second over after the break.

Perry bowled it, the second ball popping off a length. Winfield tried to get her bat out of the way, but could only edge it to the keeper. In came Sarah Taylor, and out she went first ball, lbw playing around a straight one. England were 7 for 2. Edwards was struck on the pad as she took on the hat-trick ball, but even the pumped-up Aussies could muster only a token appeal.

Perry's first three overs after lunch were scoreless and it took Edwards seventeen balls to squeeze a delivery from Megan Schutt into the off side for her first two runs. As I watched her battle I remembered what she had told me about the early stages of her innings, especially those played when she did not have a stack of runs behind her. 'Inevitably you are going to go through dips in form,' she'd said. 'It is just how quickly you come out the other end. Mentally you have to be really positive and not beat yourself up. If you are thinking positively, your movements become much more positive. You have just got to park it and not feel sorry for yourself. The minute your mind becomes cluttered and not thinking positively is when you come unstuck a bit.'

Edwards finally unfurled a cover drive down the slope for her first boundary and clipped another ball from Schutt off her toes and up the hill for another four. Then she drove a Perry no-ball through mid-on. 'If I am hitting the ball straight down the ground I know I am in a good place. Even just leaving well sometimes is a good sign. Equally, you have got to be focused if you go out there and hit the first couple of balls for four. You have still got to be very disciplined. I think that is where I have improved. Every game I try to make the most of it.'

Knight looked composed at the other end, prompting memories of her Ashes Test century two years earlier. It made it more of a surprise, therefore, when she drove loosely at the gentle medium pace of Sarah Coyte and was caught by Lanning at first slip. Coyte was immediately pulled out of the attack for Perry. Australia were going for the kill and their leading bowler almost inflicted another wound when she appealed loudly for lbw against new bat Lydia Greenway. The ball had pitched outside leg, replays showed. Greenway got off the mark by sliding an over-pitched ball through the leg side for two. Edwards punched Perry down the ground for four and jumped on a short one a couple of overs later for another boundary, taking England to 51 for 3 in the twentieth over.

I was finding this a compelling and gripping passage of play, one that was again bringing home to me how much I cared. As I had walked back to my hotel the previous evening I had even found that my teeth were aching, so much had I been grinding them while waiting anxiously for a wicket. Looking around the press box, from where I had been watching since lunch, I found it hard to find real kinship with those around me. Everyone seemed too neutral, too professional. They would file their reports and fill their websites, whatever the result, and move on to the next story. And they would be in the same seats next year to do it all again. For them this was a matter of business; for me it had become an issue of the heart. And it was now or never; no next year for me. I went back to the England balcony.

Edwards, on 30, had seen her scoring slowed again by Lanning's thoughtful posting of two short mid-wickets, forcing her to change the line through which she was looking to push her shots. Maybe it was playing on her mind when Schutt got one to nibble back in towards the stumps and clip the leg bail, the umpire superfluously signalling out, presumably in the belief that it had been the bat with which contact had been made.

It took another twenty balls before England added to their 61 runs. Already it felt like they were playing for survival. Nat Sciver, still and upright as the bowler approached, was finding it tough to time the ball until she waited on one from Schutt and hit it with a flourish through extra cover – the only scoring in the seven overs after Edwards departed.

Greenway survived another appeal, struck on the pads again off a full, flighty ball from Coyte. Lanning, a bowler short with Beams off the field with a calf injury, snuck in an over before tea and England went in at 81 for 4 off thirty-eight overs. Greenway's 16 runs had taken 65 balls and she had scored only two in the fifty minutes since losing her skipper.

Next batter in, debutant Georgia Elwiss, sat alongside Edwards and Knight listening to their post-tea anecdotes and chat, smiling along but with the distant look of someone who had more important matters on her mind. A couple of times her heart skipped as Coyte appealed for lbw against Greenway. In the forty-fifth over, though, she was away down the pavilion steps as umpire Alex Wharf finally put up his finger to remove Greenway for 22. Perry was the bowler this time and the decision was a poor one, the ball clearly pitching outside leg stump according to television replays. At 93 for 5 it was impossible not to sense the English team's optimism disappearing down the stairs with the ingoing batter.

Elwiss scored her first run off her eleventh ball and Perry telegraphed a harmless bouncer at Sciver, who lofted it clumsily into the leg side for no run. Finally, Elwiss shaped up as someone who wanted to take the initiative away from the bowlers, slashing Schutt through the slips for four and executing the shot she'd really wanted to play next ball, cover driving for another boundary.

On one of the balcony benches, Sarah picked up Anya's discarded *Puzzler*. 'I have to do something,' she explained. 'I am not good at watching. I get too nervous. I have to do something to take my mind off it. I am doing a missing link puzzle.' If the cameras had picked up Sarah laughing over her attempts to find the word that connected three other words it would have been easy for viewers to get the wrong impression; that she didn't care that she had been out for nought. At Worcester, she had been filmed joking with teammates shortly after her dismissal. It didn't look good.

But it was an unfair impression. Sarah desperately wanted to score significant runs in the one format in which she had a record of consistent disappointment. Her quirky personality and nervous energy was an effective mask, maybe even a protective blanket.

It seemed to me that she was held to a higher standard to most of her teammates. As gifted as she was, expectations of her ran high. If a colleague was out, often it went unremarked upon. If Sarah failed she was wasting her talent. 'Yes, it is a bit like that,' she agreed. 'But it goes with the territory, I suppose.'

Kate Cross spoke quietly in her friend's ear, laughing and turning to me to warn, 'That conversation's not going in the book.'

Perry returned with a short ball that barely got above stump height. 'What are you leaving it for?' Katherine asked aloud. 'Bosh it.' With that she grabbed the magazine and demanded, with her usual competitiveness, 'Let me have it. I have got to get one.' And then, 'What time are we playing until. Half seven? Blimey, we're almost playing until midnight.'

Sciver dragged attention back to the field by putting away a Jonassen short ball, but failed to do anything with two more loose deliveries, hitting to the bowler and then to short leg. Elwiss inside-edged past leg stump as Jonassen continually tried to tempt her into a loose drive and Lottie noted, 'It's getting dingy out there.'

'Engine,' barked Katherine, linking the words 'driver, oil, search' and celebrating as though she had taken a wicket. She was soon off into the dressing room to pad up, though, as Sciver played over one that kept low from Schutt and was bowled for 35, scored off 125 balls. Almost immediately, Brunt was bounding out to the crease, Elwiss losing middle and off for 17 as Jonassen got the ball to spin sharply from outside leg stump.

Anya sat tapping her spikes nervously on the concrete below her feet. 'I don't fancy myself as a batter as much as Katherine does,' she noted as Brunt pulled Jonassen through mid-wicket. A couple of runs later Marsh was out without scoring when she fended at Schutt and touched the ball to the keeper.

Shrubsole almost went to another ball that kept low, as more and more were doing when bowled from the Nackington Road End. Yet she was to stay around for forty-seven balls in compiling the third-longest duck in the history of the women's game as she and her bowling buddy put on 37, almost every ball greeted by cries of encouragement from the watching Elwiss.

Lauren encouraged the waiting batsman, Kate, to 'get stuck in' against Perry, something she was unafraid to do verbally when Perry was batting. Sarah explained, 'Crossy is the worst for that. She says, "I am number eleven, what do I care?" In general we just try to create an environment where they know we are out there.'

On the field, Brunt, quick of feet, took four to long leg off Jonassen and then slogged a full toss to the long-on boundary, bouncing a foot short of the rope. The score reached 150 when Brunt flipped a Ferling bouncer just beyond the grasp of Lanning running back at mid-off. Ferling tried the same tactic at Shrubsole, but nothing could disturb her. Ball after ball she prodded forward without the hint of a run. Brunt played a late slash for three runs and stepped into Ferling to pick up two more, but when she played back to Perry the ball scuttled through and dismantled her wicket. Her 39 runs had included five fours and had been the most purposeful knock of the innings. One over later, Shrubsole was trapped in front by Schutt and the innings was over at 160, a deficit of 106 runs.

England had been dismissed below 200 for the third consecutive time in the Ashes series, but had yet to do the same to their opponents. Surely they would have to do that now if they were to have any chance of winning the game.

* * * * *

When I had left the ground at the end of the second day, which concluded with the fall of England's tenth wicket, Paul Shaw had been staring intently at the computer analysis screen. He had ended up not moving for about an hour.

'It's what you filter,' he explained early the next day when I asked whether recent events around the men's team had made such dependence on 'data' something a coach should no longer own up to. 'You might look at forty pieces of data, but then you prioritise and take away two or three. We spent a long time looking at things on the screen. We are looking for common themes and we look at individual dismissals, and we will look at their dismissals as well. Then I went back to the hotel and out to dinner with Capes and we talked about what we were going to say to the girls. Capes is great in that respect. He has been there and been under pressure in Test matches. The girls don't play much so you need to remind them they can win the game from here. Bowl them out for 120/150 and they can win it. We had a very good meeting with them. The girls were very honest about their shortcomings. At the same time we have to keep them positive.'

Paul had clearly been disappointed with his team's performance; any coach would have been. In particular, England's batting had rarely matched the 'positive brand' of cricket to which he wanted the players to aspire. 'It is a very slow pitch,' he said. 'I have to be careful what I say here, but we had wanted a faster pitch. Then when you lose three early wickets you have to go into survival mode to a certain extent. What I did feel, though, was that there were bad balls that could have been put away if the girls had not been thinking so much about survival. We had a couple of people get in, but we didn't get one or two big scores. We needed a big partnership or two. Even at the end if, say, Nat and Brunty had stayed together, they are the type of players who can put the bowlers under pressure and change the game.'

It was hard to imagine Paul ever throwing teacups around the dressing room in anger. 'I think in two and a half years there have been three times when I have said, "Come on, this is not good enough." What makes me cross is when we don't live up to our values. But I work hard at being measured. I don't think it helps to come down too hard on them. They know if they have not performed, and they need to be lifted. Their self-esteem can drop very quickly so you have to be careful.'

Shaw was also cautious about what he said to the girls on a one-on-one basis, he explained, because players liked to 'gossip'. Many a time he had heard what he had thought were private conversations being discussed among others. That was less to do with gender than it was with the insecurities of the professional athlete.

'We are developing people here,' he said, returning to a theme we had discussed often in the past. 'We have a higher purpose. Yes, we are working in the game we love, but it is about more than that. The girls might not always appreciate it at the moment, but in years to come it would be nice for them to look back at this time and feel it helped develop them as people.'

It seemed an appropriate time to ask Shaw where he saw himself in ten years' time: working in men's cricket perhaps? 'I want to continue to work with people, to bring the best out of them. When you look someone in the eye and see you have made a connection that is so rewarding.'

With twenty minutes to go before play began, Anya's nose was back in the puzzle book and she had to be stirred to join her colleagues for the delayed team picture on the field.

Sarah helped Beth Wild carry the benches off the field, which I am sure Alec Stewart never had to do.

When play began, Brunt took the new ball from the Nackington Road End, a change from the first innings, when she had bowled all her overs from the Pavilion End. Later she told the media that Anya had graciously offered it up to her, which was not exactly the truth. She had demanded it after being denied its use earlier in the game. 'That was where I wanted to bowl,' she told me. 'I am the senior strike bowler so I should get the choice, but they said they wanted me to try the Pavilion End so I didn't have any choice. Fair enough, Anya bowled really well, but I said, "Let me have a go at some point," but then Laura ended up bowling a nineteen-over spell. I think we let Jess get too settled. I know that when I bat I love it if they delay bringing back the strike bowler. She batted well, but I think we let her have too many.'

Elyse Villani played and missed at the third ball. Two balls later she played back and had her off stump flattened by a delivery that cut back down the slope and through the gap between bat and pad. Australia had lost their first wicket without a run on the board and Lanning was exposed to the new ball. She let her first ball go past off stump, risking the incline of the pitch, and Brunt's arms shot up, suggesting that it had been closer than it was.

To the second ball of Brunt's second over, Lanning nudged forward, was rapped on the pads and given out without scoring, a second wicket gone for only 2 runs. Brunt was sending them down at 75 mph. Not bad for someone who claimed that her eyes had barely closed the previous night.

'I had only about three hours' sleep because my roommate had night terrors,' she'd said laughing. 'Fran was racing around the room because she thought there was a giant genetically modified tarantula on the ceiling.' At this point

I'd looked at Katherine as though she was trying to convince me she had webbed feet. 'Honestly, at one point it looked like she was going to throw herself through the full-length mirror. I had to rugby tackle her. She woke up and was like, "What? What?"'

Perry got away with an inside edge before forcing away the first boundary of the innings. Edwards posted a second gully; Perry cover drove for three runs and Nicole Bolton dropped her bat on a yorker. And then, as thunder began circling the ground, the umpires brought the players off for bad light. Within minutes a full blown storm would begin, forcing spectators to run for shelter, flooding the bottom end of the ground, wrecking the Sky signal to the press box, taking the scoreboard and floodlights out of action and sending BBC Radio off the air in favour of taped segments as lightning forked perilously close to their elevated commentary position.

Before the rain began sheeting down, Sarah looked across the field from the balcony and called it a 'great start' to the day. 'We wanted to give them a different look and thought the slope would help Katherine bring it back in and maybe Anya moving it away. That ball to Villani really cut back.'

Lanning, of course, had been the big prize of the brief session, which had ended at 15 for 2 in the eighth over and changed the personality of the match again. 'With Lanning, you can't give her any width early on,' Sarah continued. 'But for the first ten or fifteen balls she doesn't move her feet. I don't feel so bad about my dismissal now.' The priority when play resumed would now be removing Perry, whom I heard described at various times in the England dressing room as 'a princess', as someone who batted for herself rather than her team, and in somewhat blunter anatomical terms. It was hardly an unusual stance for a team to adopt against their most dangerous opponent.

The assault on Perry looked likely to have to wait, though. It was pouring down. 'I feel sorry for my mum and dad,' said Sarah. 'They only got here today. Right, FIFA anyone?'

* * * * *

By 3.45, the ground had dried enough for a restart. Paul took up his usual position, hunched forward on his seat, elbows on knees, jaw working on a piece of gum, and Perry forced the first ball square for four. Two balls later Shrubsole was short and wide again, and this time Perry slashed and edged into the eager gloves of Taylor.

Alex Blackwell squeezed one into her pad, to a yelp of torment from Brunt, and Shrubsole had a half-appeal for a leg-side strangle against Bolton turned down. England were full of energy once more and Edwards was happy to crowd the new batter with close fielders. Bolton edged Brunt to third man and then slashed a full toss to the same neighbourhood, while Shrubsole struck Blackwell on the pad three times from around the wicket.

In the eighteenth over of the innings she did it again, but on this occasion the ball ended up in the hands of Edwards at short leg and England made loud and lusty claims for a bat-pad catch. Not out. Blackwell had scored only a single off twenty-eight balls before she jabbed a cover drive to the boundary.

Cross came on with a maiden and then saw Bolton drive loftily and Blackwell edge a lifting ball short of the slips. Shrubsole rested after a ten-over spell that cost only eleven runs. After the players had been on for little more than an hour, third umpire Martin Saggers warned his colleagues via the radio of the possibility of more rain. 'It is building up over Calais, but might miss us.'

'How far is Calais?' came Alex Wharf's deadpan reply.

Cross had been bowling with more direction and intent than in the first innings. The first ball of the twenty-seventh over brought her a wicket as Bolton, on 25, went after one that was full and wide and managed only to spoon it to Brunt in the covers. Australia were 51 for 4 and England's run rate on the second day didn't seem so bad.

Jonassen came in – 'she has used up all her runs for this match,' Taylor had said earlier – and quickly pushed a two that she wished she could have scored the previous day. Marsh was struck high and deep over mid-on by the left-hander before Shrubsole returned and, so we all thought, struck with her second ball.

Blackwell fished and edged, Knight caught the ball, the umpire put up his finger and the batsman departed. She was more than halfway to the pavilion when the third umpire called his colleagues and told them he was checking the replay. To my, admittedly not totally neutral, eye it appeared that Knight had wrapped her fingers under the ball. Besides, England believed, the umpire on-field had sent the batsman on her way without recourse to television and there was no DRS in this match. Blackwell had been given out; she should stay out. 'Not out' appeared on the stadium screen. Brunt was predictably furious and the crowd booed.

It was the last meaningful action of the day. By 5.40 – a few minutes after the umpires had warned Edwards that she was four behind the required over rate – the weather had arrived from Calais. As the girls sat around waiting for confirmation that the day was done and they could get changed and leave, the non-catch was the only topic of conversation. 'The umpires gave it out,' said Taylor. 'Blackwell should have gone on Trev's word – spirit of cricket and all that.'

I picked my way around and over kit bags to reach Knight's seat. 'It was a catch,' she insisted. 'But as soon as they go upstairs on those you know you might lose it because of the way the cameras make it look.'

'Shakes, stretches and cool down,' Ian Durrant called out as the players began taking off their boots. 'Do the right things.'

In front of the pavilion, Paul shrugged. 'It was a shame but there is nothing you can do about it. What is the forecast for tomorrow?'

'Currently saying no rain until the evening,' I reported. 'Is that good or bad news?'

'Get a couple of wickets early and they could be in two minds,' he smiled back. 'I think it is going to be an interesting day tomorrow.'

18

The Day the
Music Died

'It's been two years, I miss my home,
but there's a fire burning in my bones' –
Charlotte Edwards singing Rachel Platten

GEOFFREY Chaucer, author of *The Canterbury Tales*, claimed that women wanted six things: 'their husbands to be brave, wise, rich, generous, obedient to wife and lively in bed.' Having said it in the fourteenth century he could be excused his political incorrectness. Besides, if he had been able to hear the conversation in the hotel meeting room that bore his name early on the final morning of the Ashes Test he'd have realised that one group of women had somewhat different desires. They required their fellow England players to be bold, smart, disciplined, supportive, true to the game plan and lively in the field. It was the only way they would come out of these four days without finding themselves on the brink of a series defeat.

The girls squeezed themselves behind the desks that stretched around three-quarters of the white-walled room and gazed ahead at the projector out front. Clips from the previous day's play appeared and the viewers became animated.

'That was out,' said Lottie as she watched herself appeal at short leg. 'It got her on the way back through. That was why she looked up.'

Groans went around every time the ball was shown banging into Alex Blackwell's legs. 'She must have been hit on the pads thirty times,' Lauren Winfield complained before Ellyse Perry was seen being caught by Sarah Taylor off Anya Shrubsole.

'That was such a shit shot,' said Lottie.

'That was such a shit ball,' responded Anya, sat next to her.

Cheers greeted Katherine Brunt's catch and laughter accompanied the sight of Lydia Greenway jumping into her arms. 'Look at the bum grab, so inappropriate,' someone piped up. 'That wasn't a bum grab,' Katherine shrieked in protest. 'It was below. Where's her bum?'

The screen went dark and Carl Crowe, still smiling along with the girls, turned to face them: 'Straight into yesterday. What did we do well?'

Becky Grundy: 'Our energy was really high. We didn't take any time to get into it. We were constantly challenging the batters and we always seemed to be on top.'

Carl: 'Great. That's a good summary. Anyone else?'

Sarah: 'Our energy was ridiculous. Everyone was talking every ball. It shows what energy can do and create.'

Carl: 'The enjoyment was there and it shows that that's when we play our best. We definitely won the day. Win today and you never know what will happen.'

Kate Cross: 'We have got into Perry's head. A couple of low scores for her and Lanning, and their tour starts to fall away. It's definitely good to have that in the bank.'

Carl: 'So how should we approach today and what have we learned from two days ago?'

Lydia: 'They are hoping to bat their areas and to be picking up more singles. But the bounce seems to be getting lower so they are going to have to be a bit more watchful.'

Lottie: 'They are going to want to declare with ninety-two overs left. If we can't get them out we want to make them go to about eighty-four before they can declare.'

Carl: 'When we bat, the situation might be anything, but we play best when we are positive. Think about Nunny in the first innings. Being positive affected them. Whether we are going for the win or playing out a draw we need to be positive. Run the singles.'

Lottie: 'Against Coyte we have got to be out of the crease by a couple of feet.'

Katherine: 'And when the keeper comes up still get in a big stride. You think she is a slow bowler so you just want to twat her, but she does bowl good lines.'

Carl: 'Get your bat out front, hitting the ball. Make Healy stand up; it's not her first choice. Cross-bat shots: what thoughts?'

Lottie: 'Put them away for a bit.'

Carl: 'And be wary of the drag on when you play the cut shot.'

David Capel: 'You have to have discipline when it is a good length, but a half-volley is a half-volley and a short one is a short one whatever the situation.'

Katherine: 'Jonassen gets flustered. She gets pissed off if she gets hit for a boundary. She can get herself into a bit of a tizz about it. Use your feet and take the opportunity.'

Lottie: 'Even today, be careful with Perry's short ball.'

Capel: 'You have to earn the right to be in a position. We have got to bat hard and bat our way into that position.'

Paul Shaw, responding to some questions and confusion about the number of overs in the day: 'We will come back to you with an assurance on how many overs we are playing today as soon as we get there.'

Lottie: 'And unfortunately we can't slow it down – for my sake! We are already at minus four.'

Carl: 'First fifty overs, you are batting to your strengths. We have got ourselves back into this position through high skills. If we win the day we could be having a long, cold beer tonight.'

The final word went to Shaw: 'The performance yesterday has got us into the game and all results are possible. The fight, determination and character we showed yesterday has got to be seen today, and more. Go well. You have deserved the right to play some good cricket today.'

* * * * *

Whenever I had travelled to grounds in the players' cars, the selection of music had been of paramount importance. Today, Lottie was driving and she was feeling pleased with herself. 'I have a new one,' she said excitedly before she began to sing along to 'Fight Song' by Rachel Platten, turning up to full volume as a thump of drums signalled the chorus kicking in. 'Cos I've still got a lot of fight left in me,' was the pay-off line. It was, I concurred, a good choice for the occasion. 'These are the days you play for,' Lottie agreed.

First to arrive, first one padded up, Lottie's day was off to its typical start. So was Anya's as she lay down outside the dressing room with a book. Lauren informed me she had slept well, despite knowing that she would have a vital role to play up front with the bat. 'I don't mind,' she said. 'You know you have done all the prep. I like opening, knowing I can just get out there. I am excited. The weather looks good so that should help us if we are batting most of the day. I don't think the ball will move around too much.'

Whether or not it would end up factoring significantly into the result, the decision to rob Heather Knight of her slip catch off Blackwell continued to be a much-discussed event. 'There are too many grey areas,' said Lauren. 'It definitely feels like we have had the worst of the umpiring decisions.'

Confirmation arrived of the overs to be played: 109, including seventeen in the final hour. When the bell sounded to summon the players for the first of them there was a simple 'Come on, ladies' from Lottie. No need for big speeches now. I followed the girls down the stairs towards the field, stopping behind them when they paused near the bottom before being given the word to emerge into the bright light. 'We are going to get a sun tan,' chirped Katherine.

I was not the only one to notice an unpleasant stench hanging around, like a club player's kit bag opened for the first time in spring to find last season's gear still festering unwashed. 'Is that actually someone? It stinks,' Lauren complained. 'I hope it isn't someone,' Anya responded. And then they were out there; their Ashes lives at stake.

Blackwell pushed the first runs of the day through mid-on to take the Australians' lead to 200 and Brunt's first ball was a sloppy full toss that Jonassen clubbed to the cover boundary. When the Yorkshire opener got the chance to bowl at Blackwell, the first, second and sixth deliveries all slammed into her pads.

Shrubsole disappeared off the field briefly after her fourth over and Marsh took over. Blackwell skipped down the pitch at her, missed the ball and was hit on the legs yet again. Then Jonassen reached her second fifty of the game by giving a full toss the leg-side treatment it deserved. Shaw agreed it had been a 'strange' innings played by Blackwell on day three, but now she had a more purposeful air, moving into the forties as she looked to attack Marsh.

The partnership had reached 92 when Jonassen was out for 54, caught low by Greenway at extra cover after not quite getting to the pitch of Marsh's delivery. With ninety-two overs left in the match, the point at which Lottie was expecting a declaration, Australia led by 258. In the next over, the first after drinks, Alyssa Healy was bowled by Knight attempting a reverse sweep and Lanning called her team in at 156 for 6. England would have eighty-nine overs in which to chase, if they chose to, a women's Test-record target of 263 at 2.95 runs per over, well in excess of the rate of scoring in the match so far.

* * * * *

'Bat fifty overs, see where we get to,' Carl Crowe reminded the dressing room as Knight and Winfield went out. Perform well and they could get close to the target, at worse get a draw to bring the Ashes down to a straight winner-take-all Twenty20 series. A bad forty minutes before lunch and it could be pretty much all over.

Lydia and Nat, frequent partners in the middle, were the first to take their places on the seats outside the dressing room. Lottie was soon out there as well, seated as usual alongside the coaches. Sarah, padded up, plonked herself on a bench at the further end of the balcony. All were greatly relieved when Ellyse Perry served up an amicable half-volley first ball and Knight tucked it through the leg side for four.

Winfield faced the second over, bat aloft, squatting in her stance as Megan Schutt approached. The wind blew off the bails, just to add to the tension, before she was off the mark with a quickly run single. That took her down to face Perry, bowling faster than in the first innings, and twice she was beaten outside off.

Only seven runs were scored in the first six overs; and the first wicket fell in the eighth. Sarah Coyte bowled full and the ball tailed in to hit Knight on the pad. Umpire Neil Mallender ruled in Australia's favour and England were 11 for 1. Taylor went in to bat and Kate Cross came out to the balcony to watch her friend. Neither were in their respective places for long. Fourth ball, Taylor drove without foot movement at a ball well wide of off stump and achieved only an ugly inside edge on to her stumps, her second duck of the game.

Edwards took guard, settled into her familiar wide stance – from where she could play back or forward with only a mere shift of weight – survived a second-ball lbw appeal and eventually got off the mark streakily against Coyte. As lunch was reached she patted Winfield on the head and the batters left the field at 16 for 2 off ten overs.

Just as it had been the spell immediately after lunch that had seriously undermined England on day two, so it was on the final day. First ball, in fact. Edwards groped forward at a wide one that she had no need to go anywhere near and managed only to feather Perry to the keeper. Disbelief consumed her and she remained leaning forward on her bat for several seconds before heaving herself away from the crease. Even Greenway's clipped four off the first delivery she faced couldn't ease the feeling of impending doom. She appeared fortunate to live through an lbw shout later in the same frenetic over.

The Aussies were swarming all over the home team, to the point where Winfield was unsettled enough to almost allow herself to be run out on what should have been a comfortable single for Greenway. Perry tested the middle of the wicket twice against the newer batsman, but was hooked for four when she attempted it against Winfield. A further twenty-two balls went by without a run.

Schutt had come on for Perry and in her second over she swung the ball in at the stumps and Winfield was given out leg before for 12 as she tried to whip it square. There appeared a distinct possibility that it was missing leg, which I suggested to her when she was back as a spectator. 'I actually hit it,' she argued. 'It's frustrating. I was feeling good out there.'

Two overs later, the benefit of the doubt favoured Australia once more. Again, Sciver probably should have ignored the full, wide delivery served up by Schutt, but there seemed to be a good chance that she had caught the ground rather than the ball as it scurried through into Healy's gloves. The umpires halted her while they held a brief discussion, but quickly advised her to resume her course back to the pavilion. England were 29 for 5 in the twenty-first over.

Elwiss at least harboured notions of changing the tempo of the action, flashing unsuccessfully at her first ball, helping a full toss on its way for four on her second and sending the fourth trickling into the rope. There were even some exchanged smiles between the batters at the end of the over. Holly Ferling gave way after conceding only five runs in four overs and Elwiss twice forced Jonassen off the back foot, for two and four.

The partnership extended until tea, taken at 76 for 5. Greenway was either measured or unambitious, depending on your viewpoint, scoring 15 off 124 balls, while Elwiss – who had looked far more comfortable than her partner against the leg spin of fit-again Kristen Beams – had reached 36. After almost an hour and a half without a wicket, there was a whiff of optimism in the England camp that the remaining forty-one overs could be survived. When play resumed, people went back to the seats from which they had been watching the partnership develop.

Elwiss scored another two off the edge. 'You know what looks good on the board?' asked Katherine. 'Forty. Once you make it to that everything is easier to live with.' She was soon critiquing the Australian field, arguing, 'If I was Perry, with five wickets down and bowling to Lydia, I would have two short legs.' Immediately, the ball jumped off the pads to exactly where Katherine had suggested posting a fielder.

The next ball climbed and Greenway deflected it away with a mixture of bat and ribs. 'She will wear them all day,' Katherine continued and, looking at me, added, 'Here's some insight for you. I was bowling indoors at Edgbaston. I was raging and it reflected in my bowling. I gloved Sarah and I broke Lydia's rib. She didn't flinch and she didn't mention it to the physio for two weeks. She is hard as fucking nails. She is covered in bruises, including one I can't tell you about.' Her single brought up the fifty partnership.

Yet, a couple of overs later, Greenway chose to duck rather than wearing a Perry short ball. As her knees touched the ground, the ball got up only just enough to loop over her shoulder and drop down on the stumps. Her 137-ball vigil was done; out for 16. Marsh was out the very next ball, playing back and having her off stump flattened; another one to bag a pair. Red-faced and looking distressed, Laura was soon sat alongside Lottie once again, her eyes gazing emptily at her feet. She looked like she needed a hug.

Perry attempted a couple of bouncers at Elwiss – anything might happen with the bounce the way it was now – and Brunt, having got off the mark with a pleasant on-drive, resisted the temptation to 'twat' a Coyte wide one. She ignored a Perry bouncer, practised a hook shot and, next ball, top-edged exactly that shot for a boundary. She was soon trying it again. She thought she had missed; the fielders didn't, claiming a catch to the keeper. Alex Wharf gave her out and she stood, arms spread wide in incredulity, before muttering all the way to the pavilion.

'Are you kidding me? You're kidding me,' she announced as she barged open the dressing-room door. She was fighting against tears by the time she sat down on the balcony, ripping up a cardboard coffee cup and then dishing out the same treatment to a plastic water bottle. 'He's given that out and he hasn't heard a thing. He's given it out on their appealing. And I have probably got myself banned.'

Elwiss had reached 46 by leathering Coyte through the covers, but then she weakly chipped Perry to mid-on, an insipid end to an inspiring knock. Perry had her sixth victim and England were one wicket from defeat with 97 on the board. They stuttered into three figures when Cross played consecutive balls through mid-on for twos. 'We can do this,' she urged as she tapped gloves with Shrubsole in mid-pitch. 'Imagine if we did this; how good it would be if we could save this Test match.'

A low ball from Coyte immediately pinned Shrubsole and that was the end of Cross's fantasy. With thirty overs still in hand, Australia had wrapped up a 161-run victory, the last five wickets having fallen in fewer than seven overs for 20 runs. The details were quickly taken off the electronic scoreboard, as if too painful for prolonged viewing.

There was no avoiding the post-game formalities. Players and staff dragged themselves down to the boundary for handshakes and to stand around awkwardly as Mark Butcher conducted interviews with the captains. Putting disappointment aside, Beth Wild, switched on as always, had rushed to the field to give Edwards her 'media cap' to wear. 'Some of our shot selection wasn't good enough,' Edwards said, unable to avoid an obvious truth. 'The bowlers performed really well, but the batsmen didn't back them up.'

Just as I had followed the players out at the start of the day, I followed them back upstairs after Jonassen had been honoured as Player of the Match. There were no jokes this time, just an anxious silence, broken only by the scrape and clank of spiked boots. Heads remained dipped as the girls dropped on to dressing-room chairs. They reminded me of misbehaving children for whom that 'wait 'til your father gets home' moment had arrived. As Paul allowed them to settle I made a point of catching his eye, making sure he knew I was there and giving him the opportunity to kick me out if he felt I was intruding on private grief. He didn't.

'It's hard to know what to say at a time like this,' he began, his voice calm but unequivocal in its disappointment. If he really had only been truly angry with his players three times in the past, as he'd told me a couple of days earlier, everything about him suggested this was the fourth occasion. 'We are all hurting. But that wasn't good enough. You have got to take responsibility. We have let ourselves down.

'We're still in this. If we win the three T20s then we can still win the competition. So we'll work hard next week and in the warm-up games against the boys. But we have, all of us, got to look at ourselves. We are professional cricketers and we have got to take responsibility.'

An uncomfortable, accusing silence hung in the air. 'I've got nothing else to say right now.'

* * * * *

He had plenty of words the following morning when the girls reconvened in the room where, twenty-four hours earlier, they had stated intentions that they had so disappointingly failed to deliver upon. When, a few days later, I was telling Clare Connor about the team talks and meetings I had been present at she raised her eyebrows and remarked, 'Not the Saturday after the Test, I assume.'

'It was a meeting that needed to take place,' Paul explained. 'I was just really disappointed, to be honest, that we weren't able to play as we wanted to play. That said, when you are 29 for 5 it is difficult to play the kind of cricket you want – you have to play to the situation and rebuild. But I was disappointed with some of the decision making and some of the shot selection. And the way we managed the pressure situation as a team and as individuals was not the way we train. So from that perspective I was disappointed.'

The theme of the meeting had been set up by Paul in the dressing room immediately after the game. The next day the girls were reminded, leaving no room for doubt, that they needed to 'take responsibility for their own performances', while Paul also conceded that 'as staff we need to take responsibility for the preparation and the way we work with the players'.

'We spoke about the game, but we also spoke about our values,' he said. 'Whether we were contributing to the environment and delivering on our values as we have done for a long time. As players and staff we had to have a good look in the mirror and we shared home truths about ourselves and each other. We felt we could all improve in a number of areas.'

Paul had gone into the meeting confident that his players would respond with honest self-appraisal. Certainly, I had seen no evidence of a blame culture within the group, never heard whispers that the bowlers, for example, were blaming the batters. They seemed to be a team that would put their own hands up before they pointed fingers. 'I think that is fair and hopefully the environment we have created has encouraged that,' Paul continued.

'We are a team and we work so hard together that we would never shove the blame on anybody,' said Kate. 'It was a really difficult meeting, quite an intense chat, but I came away from it thinking that we will be a stronger team because of this. There was no time throughout the series where we were frustrated with each other.'

Paul continued, 'We are not about making excuses at all and I think that is why we have been successful for a period of time now. There are reasons why certain things happen so you have to take responsibility. It is important that that happens. It is not about personal relationships; it is not about whether I offend this player or that player. It is about performance and looking at the areas we need to improve and how we improve, and which are the areas we do really well in so that we continue doing so. We stress all the time that it is not a personal thing, it is about performance, so that takes away the emotional side of things. But we also recognise the things they have done well. They need to keep seeing that.

'I think what you have got to do is identify the key areas you have done well in and the key areas you didn't and agree that as a group. That is first and foremost, and then you agree to move forward. If you are dwelling on past performances all you are doing is diminishing any confidence that you have got. It is about building that confidence. Going forward and setting your sights on how you are going to perform in the next phase of cricket. How we are going to do that as a group and individually. By the end of the meeting we were very much focused on looking at that.'

Our conversation had been the one occasion during my time around the team that Paul had been careful, even cagey, about what he said. Even though he had stressed to the girls that 'it is not personal' there had clearly been views expressed and criticisms aired that he felt were better kept within the walls of the Chaucer Room. The impact of those words would likely be clear for all to see when the Ashes resumed in Chelmsford.

19

Fight for the Right

'I did not find that Canterbury put me off cricket for life. In the same way that Chris Tavaré did not put me off cricket for life in the 1980s' – Andy Zaltzman

I WHEELED my suitcase into Canterbury East station, took my seat on the first London-bound train that arrived and browsed gloomily through my notes from the previous few days of Test cricket. The insalubrious environment of a provincial commuter carriage managed only to make my mood more melancholy.

I thought about those I knew would be feeling considerably more miserable; like Anya Shrubsole and Katherine Brunt, the opening bowlers who had performed with such skill and heart. I felt sorry for Sarah Taylor, who had been brilliant with the gloves and bloody awful with the bat, wanting so badly to score significant Test runs and managing not a single one. I felt sorry for Georgia Elwiss, who had been thrown into a Test debut at less than an hour's notice and played England's only significant innings, and for Charlotte Edwards, whose captaincy and, yes, even her batting would now be questioned.

I felt sorry for Clare Connor, whose vision had been to have the women's Test match televised by Sky Sports and for the country to be captivated by what it saw, yet had been rewarded by too many passages of attritional cricket and, ultimately, a dismal home defeat. And I felt sorry for Paul Shaw – and Carl and Capes – whose plans and hopes had been undermined by the players' shortcomings and whose methods would now be scrutinised. All of Paul's talk of developing people and 'playing to our values' was in danger of coming across as empty jargon, shallow rhetoric. He deserved better than that.

To be honest, I realised that I felt sorry for myself as well. This unwanted turn of events would force me to confront a question I had hoped to avoid: how much to criticise, or defend, a group of players I had grown close to and felt protective towards. There was little point in trying to gloss over much of the batting. Balls had been played at that should have been ignored in a four-day game, obvious scoring opportunities had been squandered, run rates allowed to slide into flatline territory and basic flaws in technique exposed too frequently.

I was not having it, though, that the England players had not cared, or played without heart or passion. It was an easy accusation to make and I had seen such remarks aired more frequently as the week had worn on. I had seen the girls often enough in the gym or pushing themselves through sprint sessions to know how much they wanted to succeed, how hard they were prepared to work towards the goal of victory. I knew how disciplined they were. Never, Paul said, did he have to worry about them going out and getting drunk at inappropriate times or turning up late for training or meetings. I knew how proud and privileged they felt to be in their position, how aware and appreciative they were of the support that had put them there, how acutely they felt they had let people down.

The biggest failing, if you could call it that, I had noticed was a lack of swagger and arrogance about them. Sometimes it felt like a bit more devilment and a little less diffidence would serve them well. There was rarely a sense that they were going to go out and dominate and bully. They were, to put it simply, too nice at times, and maybe that was a reflection of their coach. Often they could appear too tentative, too happy to wait for things to develop rather than shaping their own destiny.

Perhaps you could argue that it was a form of laziness, or lack of guts and application, to fail to achieve the concentration needed to bat out eighty-nine overs for a draw. But in the main it was their execution, rather than their determination, where fault could be found. It wasn't desire that was missing; it was discipline of thought in the heat of battle. I knew that was what upset Paul the most, given all the time he and his staff spent trying to get his players into the habit of thinking for themselves. When the Aussies had wrecked that satnav Paul spoke of, with a key partnership or a crucial wicket, the girls had looked lost.

My sympathy for them grew when, over the next few days, their right to play Test cricket was questioned. There was no escaping the truth that in spite of some intriguing periods – and even if you had a strong vested interest in the match – it had not been a great spectacle. Scoring rates had been abysmal.

The highest-profile critics were ex-England captain Mike Atherton and the former England seamer Mike Selvey, cricket correspondent of *The Guardian*. Atherton said the Test had been 'tedious' and had 'set back the cause of women's cricket'. Speaking on the Sky Sports show *Cricket*

Writers on TV two days after the conclusion at Canterbury, Selvey said that 'what I saw the other day was excruciating' and argued, 'I don't see why there is a desperate desire to play the long game. The women's one-day game is vibrant. People who just saw that as an exhibition of how women play cricket will be sorely disappointed. It was a poor advertisement.'

Cue indignation from the staunchest supporters of women's cricket, although even they would have struggled to contradict Selvey's further comments: 'I saw some really poor technique. I saw poor mentality, the way they played the game. I think England have got problems in all forms of cricket. I think other nations have caught them up... they are full-time professionals now so the level has to go up on the basis of that.'

Wisden editor Lawrence Booth, on the same broadcast, suggested, 'The mood around the men's team has been exciting and the women had the chance to grab on to their coat tails a bit and show that it has spread to the women's game too. To score at one and a half or two an over felt like old-fashioned cricket. I felt like they had missed a trick and gone backwards. It is a shame; there is a lot of resource being poured into it and there are a lot of talented players there.'

Show host Paul Allott even floated the possibility, whether genuinely or deliberately provocatively, of lighter balls and shorter wickets in the women's game, although if the issue was that bowlers were on top too much then it was difficult to see how shortening the wicket would do anything but give them an additional advantage. Even Selvey gave him short shrift on that one.

More reasoned was the concern expressed to me before the match had even started by the BBC's Charles Dagnall. 'I hope the ball goes through a bit,' he'd said. 'I would rather have an exciting game over in two and a half days than a boring four-day game. This is a showcase.' Yet midway through the match, he'd sighed, 'The wicket is killing it. People must have been switching off.'

Shaw had also suggested to me his dissatisfaction with the pace of the surface and Dagnall, a former county seamer who had become one of the biggest champions of the female game within the British media, continued, 'The best game of cricket I have ever seen, men or women, was the Perth Test [in 2013] and that was because you never knew from one ball to the next which way the Test was going to go and because it was a fast wicket. The biggest thing the women's game needs is good, fast pitches. If you get a really slow one then – and I am not saying anything out of school here – they don't have the same power as the men. The wrist play and technique that they have can be neutralised by a slow pitch.'

Meanwhile, Cricinfo columnist Andy Zaltzman endeared himself to the women's cricket community when he stated that much of what he watched was 'engaging, at times engrossing'. And, echoing Dagnall, he said of the Perth Test, 'If it had been a men's match, played out on television instead of an internet stream, it would have been revered as a classic.'

Noting that much of England's batting was 'counterproductively tentative', he cited various examples in recent years when the same could have been said of their male counterparts. 'Picking on the dull phases of a single match as evidence of a general malaise is a risky approach,' he wrote.

Part of the problem appeared to be that the teams were engaged in a format of cricket they rarely played; England their first Test for twelve months and Australia their first for a year and a half. That offered no excuse for the home team performing so much worse than their opponents, but did offer some mitigation for the uncertainty of much of the play. As Zaltzman noted, 'There was an understandable degree of learning on the hoof.'

More Test cricket, not less, would appear to be the way to achieve higher performance. Paul even suggested it would benefit all forms of the game. 'Our players and the women's game around the world could learn so much from playing Test cricket. Players can develop their mental skills, physical skills and cricketing skills to a far greater extent than they can in the 20- and 50-over game. They understand and accept and enjoy being part of other formats – that is really important because that is far more commercial and marketable and there is really, really good cricket in those formats – but I still think in Test matches players develop more. It would enable them to be multi-dimensional cricketers, not just doing it in limited-overs games.'

Clare had admitted before the series the battle she faced to get more countries to buy into the notion that the longer form should feature more often in the calendar. 'I would never want to be part of an administration that strikes a line through Test cricket,' she stressed. Canterbury had done nothing to make it easier for her to break the long game out of the vicious circle of 'fewer games, lesser skills' in which it was trapped. Some would argue that her desire to keep Tests going 'for the players – it's sacred for them' was an ex-athlete speaking rather than a hard-headed administrator. Yet Zaltzman concluded by urging the ECB and other boards to 'embrace the Test format as the ultimate test of cricketing skills, regardless of its run rates, audience or perceived lack of modernity'. Alongside the barbs about women's Test cricket in general, the debate about the England team's performance was a more valid one; the criticism unavoidable. 'We have preparation with three- and four-day games, but that is nothing compared to being in an Ashes Test match under that type of pressure,' said Paul. 'How do you cope with that and then how do you excel? I can understand that, but with the players we have got I would expect them to perform a little better than they did.'

Lottie admitted, 'The top order didn't perform. There is no point in people beating up the lower order after we are 27 for 5. What are they supposed to do? We feel like we should have been able to bat out the final day, but, look, it's a format we play once a year so there is no point spending too long on it. We need to focus on the games we have left to play.'

'We make no excuses for our performance,' said Kate Cross. 'We know we let ourselves down with the bat in both innings and it is something we will take individual responsibility for.' She said that the players were unsurprised by, and actually took heart from, the level of scrutiny and criticism. 'It is incredible to see so many people talking about women's cricket and having an opinion. It shows how far the game has come.'

Of course, victory on live television and radio would likely have prompted even more discussion and coverage so one had to view Kate's comments through the lens of someone working hard in unfortunate circumstances to promote her sport. Likewise when Katherine Brunt said, 'We understand that with the increased profile comes a higher level of expectation and we accept and embrace this. It is a sign of how our sport has progressed.'

No one had taken defeat at Canterbury harder than Katherine, someone who had tattooed the highs of her career on her torso, but who was now contending with one of the low points. 'The feeling at the end of the match will live with me for a long time,' she confessed. 'We are a tight unit, a family away from our families, and underperforming over four days was hard to accept.'

Clare had admitted on Twitter, 'Criticism is part of professional sport; we've fallen desperately short this week despite wonderful support from so many. So we will take that criticism and we will all improve.'

Test Match Special had started its dissection even before the game had finished, spending the final tea break analysing the shortcomings. Fingers were pointed by the likes of Ebony

Rainford-Brent and Middlesex captain and journalist Izzy Westbury at the structure of the English women's game, suggesting that the current county system was not producing international quality players. This, of course, was not exactly news to the ECB. It was why Connor had spent so long developing the contents of her blue file; the outline of the Women's Super League. It was why, when I saw her in the England team hotel on the first day of the Test, she had been buzzing at having been approached by twenty-eight parties interested in being operators of one of the six proposed teams. That breadth of choice offered the ECB the opportunity to appoint entities that best embodied its own vision of the commercial and developmental opportunities created by the new competition.

The volume of cricket played by the contracted England players was also questioned; the notion being that they spent too much time training at Loughborough rather than engaging in meaningful competition. That, too, might be addressed by the introduction of a new level of domestic cricket, along with the more balanced calendar of international contests that Clare was striving for.

All were important discussion points, but as far as the England girls were concerned, such issues could wait for another day and sit in another person's in-box. They still had three matches to prepare for.

* * * * *

It was an easy equation: three wins to save the Ashes. A trio of victories in the NatWest-sponsored Twenty20 series at Chelmsford, Hove and Cardiff would level the summer contest at eight points apiece and allow England, the holders, to retain the trophy. It was a somewhat harder task to achieve than to explain. Australia were merely winners of the last two World Twenty20 events and, having spent the week after the

Test beating Ireland three times, had taken their winning streak in the format to sixteen matches.

'We are effectively in a World Cup quarter-final situation,' Kate said. Except if you beat the champions in that first game you might expect the task ahead to get easier in the semi-finals. In this scenario there would be no respite, no easier opponent.

When the ECB announced the fourteen players who would comprise the England squad for the series, Cross was one of those who had not made the journey from the longest to shortest formats. She had said at the start of the year that she didn't think the team management fancied her as a Twenty20 bowler and – even after she and Lauren Winfield had been named as overseas players by the Brisbane Heat in the Women's Big Bash League – she joined Fran Wilson as the players to miss out post-Canterbury.

'I found that really difficult because I almost felt like I was leaving the girls in their hour of need,' Kate explained later. 'I know it sounds ridiculous because it is a game of cricket at the end of the day, but I wanted to be there all the way throughout it because we had done the journey as a team, but I had to step away from it and was no longer in the bubble any more.'

Included in the England squad for the first time in the series were batting all-rounder Danni Wyatt, prolific in the county Twenty20s for Nottinghamshire, and Yorkshire off-spinner Dani Hazell, the world's top-ranked T20 bowler. Some felt Hazell had been unlucky to be excluded from the Test squad, especially after the way she cleaned up Meg Lanning in one of the Aussies' warm-up matches. 'It has been frustrating watching the series, but it is good to be in now,' she said.

Wyatt had offered a final nudge to the selectors by scoring 62 against Surrey on the final day of the county T20s on the weekend after the Test and was herself in the process of securing a BBL contract, with the Melbourne Renegades. Kent's Tammy Beaumont had done even better, reaching three figures against the same opposition on the same day, but was destined to complete 2015 as she had begun it, as an outsider. Hazell, meanwhile, had spent the day after the Test equalling her season's best figures in men's cricket when she took 4 for 17 off twelve overs for Durham City in a Durham Senior League game against Horden.

'Together they offer us a lot of international T20 experience, with well over 100 caps in this format between them,' Paul had said of the new players as part of the official team announcement. 'We know that we face a huge challenge to get back into this contest, but there is a lot of pride and fight within this squad.'

Wyatt was something of an enigma. Prolific at the top level of county cricket since moving from her native Staffordshire to Nottinghamshire in 2013, she had worn England shirts of various hues eighty-nine times yet had never scored a half-century, averaging 13.16 in her fifty-six T20 internationals. A member of the Ashes squad in Australia in 2013/14, her innings scores had been 6, 0 and 6, since when she had batted only twice for her country. She had played all three T20s on the New Zealand tour without getting to the crease. She did offer an additional off-spinning option, though, having taken forty-six wickets in the shortest format.

It was only eighteen months earlier that she'd harboured real doubts about the continuation of her career. Out of form in Australia and troubled by back pain, she was omitted from the World Twenty20 squad in Bangladesh. 'It was a nightmare,' she said. 'I felt like I was sixty years old and believed I would never bowl again. At one point I thought about giving it all up. Missing out on selection was just what I needed. I had no choice but to change my bowling style and now I have adapted to that I feel like it's all turned around.'

Reconstruction had involved eliminating much of the backward lean and twist that had placed strain on the spine. 'I've started getting forward more. It's more loose and natural and it seems to have done the trick. I pushed on after that, had a really good county season [540 runs in fourteen innings] and did all I could to get back in with a chance of playing for England.'

Another of the England squad encouraged by an older brother to start bowling, Danni had originally thought 'no way' until the coach at her local club Whitmore in Staffordshire stuck her into the boys' team. Yet football could also have stolen her away, having played in Stoke City's academy teams. 'I was actually better at football and everyone thought I could play for England,' she admitted, opting to focus on cricket because she felt it was a more sociable game. 'With football we just used to train and go home.'

It was football, or at least the fact she had dated a couple of footballers, that earned her the nickname 'Waggy' among the squad. Yet it was when she posted 'Kohli, marry me!' on Twitter in April 2014 – an expression of her admiration of Indian superstar Virat Kohli's batting in the World T20 – that she earned global notoriety.

Dani Hazell, meanwhile, was already spoken for, unique among the England contracted players in being the only married one, having wed a Durham City teammate, Jake McCann, in 2013. An opening bat and wicketkeeper for Durham City, he was an Aussie, which made for interesting domestic dynamics during a double Ashes year. 'I hope he wants us to win,' she laughed. 'It's not like the men's series. Then it is different.'

Dani described herself as coming from 'a competitive background', adding, 'I wanted to bowl as fast as I could, hit as far as I could and eventually turned into a spinner.' Her first games were within the family, with echoes of the memorable *Fast Show* 'competitive dad' sketches. 'My dad

[Geoff] never let me bowl him out when I was a kid. I had to earn the right to bowl him out. He was good enough to keep me out when I was twelve or thirteen, but not anymore.' Quickly, garden games and watching her dad play at his local club, Bearpark, was not enough. 'I got bored of doing that so I had a go myself. I played in the girls' and boys' teams and it just propelled from there. Men's cricket helped me progress and be a bit tougher. People try and whack you as far as they can.'

Having made her debut for her native county of Durham a few days short of her fourteenth birthday, Dani had made the move to Yorkshire in 2008 and been introduced to the England Academy in the same year. Since her international debut on the West Indies tour late in the following year she had played thirty-nine ODIs, three Test matches and sixty T20s, a format in which her 65 wickets at an average of 18 and an economy rate of a little over five an over had earned the ranking of number one bowler in the world.

Both newcomers looked likely to play a role in the three Ashes matches, even after Wyatt failed to get a bat in two warm-up matches against the Northamptonshire youth team, one a victory after they had totalled 157 and the other a tied game after England scored 167.

When I caught up with Paul again he expressed satisfaction with how those games had gone and how the girls had responded to the events of Canterbury. There had been time, too, to think harder and deeper about that disappointing week. 'I went home for a couple of days and reflected on the performance. Any coach, along with his coaching team, you are always searching for those excellent performances and those passages of play where you fight your way through it. You reflect on the game and there are a few sleepless nights, as there always are, and you look at yourself first and foremost. I thought about what we could have done, what preparation we could have changed. The preparation for the T20s has been batting, bowling and fielding, of course, and really focusing our mindset. We picked a squad that has given us options in all disciplines of the game to play positive cricket and then we have put that into action in some tough sessions and the boys' games. There has been lots and lots of good stuff.'

The girls would need a lot more of the good stuff if the Ashes contest was to continue.

20

The Short Way Back

'Historically we have a knack of playing our best cricket when our backs are against the wall, and we have no choice now but to deliver' – Katherine Brunt

THEY referred to it constantly as 'Fortress Chelmsford', indicative of the fact that England's women had won all five of their matches at Essex's home at the County Ground over the previous five years. The fans there took pride in the title, took seriously the role they could play as the home team's 'twelfth man'. They couldn't wait to get started either, queues beginning to build thirty minutes before the gates opened and two and a half hours prior to the scheduled start time. Not even the late afternoon rain, which was continuing a good hour beyond its forecast time of cessation, could deter them.

The England team, meanwhile, were yet to arrive. At least they were within walking distance when their coach driver informed them that the reason he couldn't complete the sharp turn he was attempting was that his vehicle had broken down. The girls zipped up their jackets, grabbed their kit bags and made their way as briskly as possible down the street and into the shelter of the pavilion.

'I don't like having to walk,' declared Dani Hazell, looking so happy to be back in the squad that one suspected she'd have happily walked down from Durham to wear the England shirt.

'How is it looking?' asked Anya Shrubsole, leaning forward over the wooden barrier on the players' balcony with its 'No bottles, cups or glasses' warning. A patch of clear blue sky, approaching from the south and visible above the Hayes Close End, lifted the spirits of the English girls, for whom a wash-out would have meant relinquishing the Ashes. It was still cold enough, though, for Danni Wyatt to climb up the steps flanking the pavilion carrying two steaming cups of tea that she had just made. 'No sugar,' she told Dani, who declared that that was 'perfect'. The usual gaggle of middle-aged autograph hunters stood below the balcony, laden with all kinds of signature-ready paraphernalia. Spotting a particularly garish sweater that looked like it had once been a Christmas present, Sarah Taylor pointed and declared, 'I love a retro jumper.'

Once Paul Shaw had finished pacing around the outfield and checking it for moisture, he declared his confidence that his team was ready for the challenge ahead. 'Absolutely they are in the right frame of mind,' he said. 'Honestly, I thought they were in the right frame of mind before the Test match, but then it was about how the game went. We didn't deal with certain situations as well as I and the staff would have liked.'

Danni Wyatt had a situation of her own to deal with. 'I have got a spot and it needs to go. Put that in the book,' she told me.

'Either do it or we'll get the ones on your neck,' warned Sarah.

'Yeah, we need to get that,' said Lottie.

'I have done it five times today,' Danni added. 'I need to do the root. But I've just seen it in the mirror and it is not that bad.'

I wondered how many similar conversations had featured during the men's Ashes series.

Skin issues aside, Danni was clearly thrilled to be back. She had already been told that she would be playing, as would Dani Hazell, with Georgia Elwiss, Becky Grundy and Laura Marsh the ones who would be forced to ferry drinks around. 'I am here finally,' Danni said, 'and I love Twenty20. I went to the first ODI and then I watched most of the others on TV. But I am not great at watching.'

Word came through that the players would be able to begin warming up at ten minutes past six and that the start had been put back fifteen minutes to 7.15. Third umpire Martin Saggers appeared, looking for someone to select the match ball England would use. 'I will pick it,' offered Sarah.

'In T20 you want the oldest, shittiest one you can find so that it breaks up,' Anya told her.

Anya and I began chatting about American football and it turned out that she was a New York Jets fan. 'My family has a history of supporting teams that aren't very good,' she explained. 'We are all Portsmouth fans.'

England's analyst, Chris Sykes, reported that he was happy with the wooden construction, like a large bread bin, that had been built to house his two computer screens outside on the balcony. As usual he would be logging every occurrence in the match, noting the line, length and outcome of each delivery. 'Every ball is an individual event,' he said, checking as he spoke that Sky's feed was working so that he could match up video with the data. The combination of keyboards, wooden housing and elevated stool gave him the appearance of Rick Wakeman about to embark on a concert performance.

'The girls are feeling good,' Lottie confirmed, as the floodlights began taking over from daylight as the chief source of illumination. 'We like being at Chelmsford. It will be rocking and it feels familiar. Although Australia have played better than us, we don't feel like they are a team we can't beat. I have played against some Australian teams in the past and you just knew you had no chance of beating them. This team is not like that. You look at things like Heather's run-out at Bristol – that changed the whole series.'

In the days between Test and T20, Lottie had been, as her position and her personality dictated, talking up England's hopes of resurrection. 'We believe we can win these three games,' she said in the pre-match press conference, although even she could not avoid the obvious truth that 'we've got to play a lot better'. She added, 'If there's one form of cricket where we can turn things around it's T20 cricket. We have to put in a strong performance here and who knows what happens after that? We've got to connect back to the first game of the tour, where we played brilliantly. It's about character now; it's about seeing how much we want to keep hold of these Ashes and from what I have seen from the girls they are desperate to do that.'

Katherine Brunt had insisted, 'I don't think the story of this summer is finished yet.' She'd explained that 'we have all been very open and up front about how we are feeling' and insisted that the Test match had been laid to rest. 'We are now completely focused on what is coming up. Whatever happens during the next three matches, I know that every single player in this squad will be fighting to put their hand up and be a match-winner. There is a really big feeling of belief in ourselves and in each other. Everybody wants to do well, and we owe each other and the public a lot.'

Lottie duly won the toss and invited Australia to bat. Lauren Winfield wasn't happy, however, when Sky's sound technician attempted to fit her with the microphone and earpiece she would need to be able to speak to the commentary box while on the field. The contraption included an unwieldy elastic and Velcro waist band, which housed the power pack. Lauren pulled a face to indicate her discomfort, just as Lottie was passing on her way back to the dressing room. 'Are you going to be all right up in the ring with all that?' she asked her player. 'I don't know,' Lauren replied, and was soon shedding the equipment.

Beth Wild was summoned to explain to the broadcasters that they would not be able to have a player wearing a microphone. 'I think Sky are OK with it,' she explained. 'The problem is that the girls are not used to it. It is more cumbersome on them than it is on the men.'

Having changed into her tight-fitting 'solar red' England T20 shirt, Dani Hazell stood looking at her reflection in the full-length dressing-room window. 'Not very forgiving these tops, are they? They leave nothing to the imagination.'

Brunt, grateful for the coloured jersey to save her any further sports bra embarrassments, took the first over from the Hayes Close End. 'They turn out here, don't they?' said David Capel. 'Good atmosphere.' Capel and most of the team staff were stood out on the chairless balcony. Paul was alone with his notebook, perched on a makeshift seat in the entrance to the dressing room.

Having watched Brunt keep her first few balls pitched well up to Villani and Perry, Capel looked across at the information overload on the electronic scoreboard and commented, 'It's an improvement on the old one, but it's a bit bunched up.' We eventually found the area of the board showing the overs and agreed it could do with some additional spacing.

There was not much wrong with the cricket we were watching. Where Brunt angled the ball in, so Shrubsole shaped it away. The crowd appeared as energised as the home players, willing England towards peak performance and applauding every stop and pick-up in the field. They were cheering when Wyatt made a stretching, diving stop at short third man on the edge of the fielding circle. And they were on their feet when Villani tried to steer the fifth ball of Shrubsole's second over into the leg side and a leading edge offered up an easy caught and bowled, leaving Australia 5 for 1.

The girls were bouncing around in the field and Brunt was forcing Perry to play everything to Lydia Greenway at backward point. Jenny Gunn threw down the stumps from mid-on, although Perry was easily home, and Meg Lanning finally scored her first run with an ungainly uppish shot behind square leg. After four overs, only 11 runs had been scored. 'Really good so far,' said Capel. 'It only takes one or two changes to make the whole unit stronger. Wyatt in there makes a difference.'

It was almost the end of the fifth over when Lanning inside-edged Brunt for the first boundary of the innings. Shrubsole bowled the sixth over, Edwards again wanting her two frontline bowlers to take the burden of the powerplay against the Aussies' two best batters. 'With Jenny in the team you can afford to do that,' said Capel. 'A lot of the time, if you win the first six overs you can win the game. We often mix it up and have Dani Hazell bowling in the powerplay, but it's often down to the conditions.'

Lanning took two fours in the over, flicking a slog sweep to deep square leg and edging a drive to third man, taking the score to 26 for 1. When Gunn came on for the seventh over Lanning, accelerating ominously, went down on one knee and deposited her first ball over long leg for six.

Hazell came on to bowl the eighth over, making the Australian captain play and miss to her first ball and tying her up with the second. Capel went to look at the computer and television monitor. 'Is she spinning it?' I asked.

'A little bit. Not much.'

Heather Knight's first over relieved some of the pressure on the visitors by going for thirteen runs, including a full toss that Lanning banged to the mid-wicket rope, before Hazell was left hopping around from the impact of a Lanning drive that cracked into her left ankle. But it was the Aussie captain, on 28, who was in pain one ball later when she lifted Hazell's low full toss out toward the leg-side boundary, where Greenway held on to a catch at the second attempt as she dived forward.

Perry could have gone next over when she didn't quite get to the pitch of Knight's delivery, but Gunn couldn't get under the swirling ball as it arced up into the sky. Perry then found the gap between two fielders in the deep on the leg side and Australia reached 67 for 2 with eight overs remaining. Perry was soon out, though, to Nat Sciver's first delivery, driving over a full one and departing for 30. Sciver picked up another with the final ball of her second over, Jess Jonassen hoiking it into the leg side and Gunn this time able to take the catch.

Alex Blackwell had earlier been denied a boundary by typical Greenway brilliance, but she managed to get one through mid-wicket to move her team into the 90s. Grace Harris, a squat and powerful addition to the Australian team for the T20s, was run out as a result of her own doziness after Shrubsole fielded a drive at mid-off and the visitors had only just made it into three figures when the final three overs began.

Gunn was brought on – tonight Edwards would be praised by the media for her bowling changes – and was instantly lifted by Blackwell to Shrubsole. Another wicket fell in the nineteenth over, Brunt, the bowler, making a sliding stop as Alyssa Healey tried to drive her and throwing down the stumps from her backside. Two balls later: another run-out – a horrible, panic-stricken mix-up leaving Taylor the simple task of gathering Greenway's throw and removing the bails with a theatrical pause and flourish. There were no more wickets, but ones and twos off the final few deliveries left Australia with a very mediocre-looking 122 for 8.

Paul offered only a quiet nod when I asked him if he was happy with that outcome, although Carl was a little more effusive. 'We've given ourselves the best chance, haven't we,' he said as he departed to watch the England innings with the girls in the dug-out. 'That was brilliant.'

England's plan for these short games had been to promote Brunt to number five behind a top order of Edwards, Winfield, Taylor and Sciver. 'We have got a solid top eight,' said Paul. When I asked about the process of changing the order on the fly, he explained, 'I will make the call in communication with the bench. I will get their feel for the situation from down there.'

Up a short flight of stairs leading up from the back of the Chelmsford pavilion balcony was a small room with a treatment table and a few work spaces. As I sought some warmth up there I found Beth working on her latest social media updates and Clare Connor, coughing and spluttering her way through the evening instead of speaking to the Sky Sports viewers in the analyst's role she had been filling throughout the series. 'I doubt I'll do it in the future,' she said when I asked her about mixing the detachment of the commentator with her position as head of the English women's game. 'It has been very difficult. A real conflict. I have to speak honestly and criticise players if necessary, but it is getting more difficult. I think it is because there is more of it. When Sky only showed a couple of games then it was important; a chance to promote what we are doing.'

Having the night off sick from such duties meant she was liberated to cheer and groan her way through the England innings and give voice – what was left of it – to her partisanship. All of us in the room held our breath, though, as Edwards chipped the first ball of the innings only a few inches short of Sarah Coyte at backward point. As the official attendance figure of 3,450 reached Clare mid-way through the third over, England were about to lose their first wicket.

With only five runs scored by her team, Winfield looked to force things against Perry, but became the latest player to offer a simple catch after not getting close enough to the shot. Villani was the recipient. After Taylor's pair in the Test, nerves were running high at seeing her march out to face Perry again – and were hardly eased by the single she squeezed out to get off the mark. But at least England's two premier batters were together and when Edwards executed her favoured square drive late in the fourth over it brought the first boundary of the innings. 'This was never going to be easy,' said Beth with a nervous sigh. 'It was always going to be a scrap.'

Taylor, however, appeared determined to prove Beth wrong, dropping to one knee to flip Perry over her shoulder and down to the fine leg boundary; then walking purposefully towards Coyte and driving her through mid-off. Never still at the crease, always looking to make something happen, she swept Jonassen for three. Edwards, meanwhile, had flicked a Perry full toss for four and neatly cut Jonassen for another couple and England reached 43 for 1 from seven overs, 37 having come from the most recent four. It had the feel of the home team's night when Villani, stretching above her head at mid-off, missed the chance to dismiss Edwards in the next over.

Taylor continued on, plonking Jonassen's full toss back over her head, while Edwards pushed herself to come back for a second after another late cut. A cracking on-drive by the skipper raced to the rope; Taylor laid back and belted Coyte away. 80 for 1 from thirteen overs.

Two runs later, Edwards was gone. Again she tried to run the ball down to third man, this time as she advanced towards the bowler, Erin Osborne. Healy took off the bails and to the naked eye it looked fatal, although replays suggested she might just have slid her bat into the crease in the nick of time. The screen showed 'Out' and England needed 41 from 38 deliveries with their captain departed. When the equation became 32 from 30 balls, Clare insisted, 'We want that from 24 balls. We don't want it going into the final over.'

Sciver slammed Osborne to the mid-wicket boundary and Taylor reached 50 off 42 balls when she pulled the same bowler behind square. 'Mentally I wasn't quite there in the Test and it showed,' she would admit. 'The more positively I play, the better. I needed to get into better positions.' The raising of her bat had a feeling of self-vindication and, when she directed it towards the bench, an acknowledgement of the support she had received from her teammates.

One of them, best friend Kate Cross, could only cheer at her television screen as she sat at home in Lancashire. 'I felt like a proud parent when she came back and got that fifty,' she would explain. 'I felt awful not being there, but the thing that people should see from that is the character that she showed. I have felt really sorry for Sarah this summer because obviously she is one of the best and most well-known players in the world and that brings an expectation to do well. But that is not how it works. You can't perform every single time you step out on that pitch. Sarah has been struggling with the things going on and being said off the pitch, and not doing well on the pitch has made it a big battle for her as well. You know, because you are there, that we talk a lot about character in the dressing room and people who will stand up. Sarah is one of those people who will do anything for the team. It was unfair that she got singled out a lot for criticism.'

For now, though, Taylor was vindicated. Perhaps she was still dizzy with it all when she ran down the wicket next ball and was stumped by a distance.

The seventeenth over began with England needing 17 runs, four of which Brunt chalked off with a square cut off Perry's first ball. A drive was intercepted on the rope for two, another cut shot flew square to the boundary and a clipped full toss brought two more. Sciver took care of the rest in the next over, clubbing a full toss from Schutt past long-on and slashing the third ball for four more, taking her side to a victorious 125 for 3 with two and a half overs left of a perfectly-paced run chase.

Fists pumped, players and staff embraced. The crowd's excited applause and cheering was returned by the girls. 'They played it nicely,' said Capel. 'A steady performance. We are in the semi-final now.'

'A great performance under extreme pressure,' was how Lottie described it to Sky while her players stood around in the evening chill waiting for Sarah to be honoured as Player of the Match. 'But it is only one game. We are pleased with how we played tonight, but we know Australia will come back hard at us.' She had been unconcerned, she said, at the slow start to the innings, saying that 'I have been in those situations many times and you know you can catch up'.

While Sarah was left behind on the field for further interviews, the girls returned, all back slaps and excited chatter, to the dressing room. They sat contentedly on their benches, below various printed items highlighting the individual achievements of the Essex team throughout the season, while they waited for their teammate to return. 'The good news is we won,' Carl chipped in. 'The bad news is we have to walk back to the hotel.' Amid the feigned groans, Sarah turned up, a mixture of apology and delight, and Paul was ready to speak to his team.

'OK, girls, listen up. That is one of the best performances I have seen in a long time.' He paused and looked around the room, aiming for as much eye contact as possible. He was pleased with every one of them and wanted them all to know it. 'With the ball, in the field and with the bat, all were outstanding. What has made me really proud is that you made everyone in this ground tonight proud. You showed heart, character, bottle, as well as class. Do the right things now and rest up. We have still got two games to win, but do you know what is the most important thing? We are still in this fucker! Honestly, fabulous performance.'

21

Sinking by the Sea

'Hope in reality is the worst of all evils because it prolongs the torments of man' – Friedrich Nietzsche

JOHN Cleese's character in the movie *Clockwise*, Brian Stimpson, had another take on Nietzsche's theory. 'It's not the despair,' he said. 'I can take the despair. It's the hope I can't stand.' The despair of Canterbury had been turned into hope by the events of Chelmsford. And now I could recall few sporting occasions where my guts had been as knotted as when Charlotte Edwards again won the toss and once more put Australia in to bat under the setting sun at Hove. What could have been a carefree, meaningless match now had the potential to take the Ashes to a decider in Cardiff three days later. As an author chronicling the summer, it would be everything I could have asked for; as a supporter of the England team it offered the tantalising prospect of dreams fulfilled in the most dramatic of circumstances.

When Australia were restricted to 107, hope was moving towards reality.

But fate can be a right bastard, taking that hope and whacking you around the head with it.

A dry pitch with bare patches had prompted England to include Becky Grundy in place of Jenny Gunn. The sight of the Warwickshire spinner warming up a couple of hours before the start offered a clue about the selection to the early arrivals, of whom there were a lot. A sold-out crowd of 5,740 would be inside the County Ground, long lines of mascot- and flag-bearing fans having again preceded the players' arrival. Australia, meanwhile, left many scratching their heads by bringing in a seamer, Rene Farrell, for a slow bowler, Erin Osborne.

Katherine Brunt achieved immediate outswing and was soon hollering an appeal for lbw as she got one to nip back in at Ellyse Perry. Anya Shrubsole provided her usual contrast, bending the ball in the opposite direction, and, even though Elyse Villani indicated her intent by coming down the track, only seven runs materialised in the first couple of overs. Perry straight drove Brunt for the first four and survived another shout from the field when Shrubsole swung the ball too much to elicit a decision. There were whoops of delight all round, though, when Perry tried to work the final ball of Shrubsole's over into the leg side and chipped an easy catch to Dani Hazell at mid-on.

Meg Lanning made an eventful entry: missing an attempted cut off Brunt to her first ball; producing a brilliant two-handed boundary stop by Lydia Greenway when she connected with a similar shot on her third; and cover driving the next ball to the boundary. A score of 19 for 1 off six was improved by Lanning taking six runs, including another cover driven four, from Grundy's first over. Australia were still only one wicket down by the mid-point of the innings, but an inability to get the ball away from the boundary fielders, some good length bowling by Hazell and a failure to cash in on a couple of full tosses by Grundy meant they had scored only 42.

Lanning's solution was to sweep, but when Grundy, getting a hint of turn, beat her shot, umpire Nick Cook had no hesitation in giving her out leg before. New batter Alex Blackwell got away with the same shot at the end of the over. It was Villani's turn to attempt it off the first ball of the next over, but Hazell's yorker-length delivery got through to the pads. She, too, was given out and Australia were 45 for 3.

Another wicket fell in the next over. Blackwell drove back at Grundy; the bowler flinched, but clung on to the catch. 'It was all instinct,' she explained. 'I'm glad it stuck.' The manner in which Grace Harris swung at her first ball – she should have been caught by Shrubsole at mid-wicket – demonstrated the panic being felt by the visiting team. A few days ago, the Ashes had been there for the taking. Now they could see them scattering into the Brighton sky.

Jess Jonassen, whose batting at Canterbury had done so much to set up their winning position, tried to rescue things by using her feet to drive Hazell down the Hove slope for four. Harris had her own method, heaving the same bowler over deep mid-wicket for six. She ought to have been out when Nat Sciver came on to bowl the fifteenth over, but Lauren Winfield spilled a skier at mid-off.

A partnership of 26 was threatening to make a significant difference to the game, but Shrubsole broke it when Harris walked across her stumps in an attempt to whack the ball to leg and was an easy lbw victim. Anya's four overs had brought her figures of 2 for 9.

Jonassen slashed a four off the edge, but was run out next over when Sciver dived to stop the ball at mid-off and her throw was gathered neatly by the bowler, Brunt, who then threw down the wicket. With the penultimate ball of her spell Brunt took the seventh wicket when Healy, swinging across the line, was beaten by pace. No further wickets fell and a valuable 15 runs were added off the final over, Cameron playing a series of inventive shots off Sciver. But 107 for 7 was a better result than England would have dared imagine. Hope was running rampant.

Katherine and Anya slapped hands in mutual acknowledgement of jobs well done. 'That is brilliant for us,' said Becky. 'Starting from the first six overs; it was brilliant up top.'

England were 108 runs from taking the series to the decider. The target was quickly down to 101 as Edwards took seven from Perry's first over with various steers through the vacant slip area. Jonassen's left-arm spin was employed for the second over and her accurate leg-stump line, allied to Lanning's field placings on that side of the wicket, kept things tight for four balls. The fifth was a long hop. A gift for the England captain. Yet all Edwards could do was bottom-edge her pull shot, via her pad, into her stumps. It was a setback, for sure, but here came Taylor, in form and confident, with an easy target to chase down. She was on the move from ball one, skipping outside off stump to work away a single.

Winfield had been waiting all summer to make a meaningful contribution with the bat, yet her poor run continued when she tried too hard to drive Perry over the top and offered Jonassen an easy chance at mid-off. In came Sciver, to be bowled first ball as she played around a full delivery. At 10 for 3, that winning total, and my vision of a nail-biting final chapter, was turning into Michael J. Fox's dissolving family photo in *Back to the Future*.

It was something of a surprise to see Brunt still entrusted with the number five spot at a time when consolidation and rebuilding was needed. She allowed Perry's hat-trick ball to pass perilously close to her off stump. Mind you, a few overs of Brunt would be a big step towards victory and she clearly had that in mind, coming down the track to Perry and scooping Jonassen away for three. After a couple of wicketless overs and with the score on 24 for 3, things appeared to be calming down.

But when Farrell, the surprise selection, came on to bowl the sixth over, Taylor connected with a full toss low on the bat and gave Villani an easy catch at mid-on. Heather Knight would be a steadying influence, surely. She edged her first ball for four past Healy, standing up to the wicket, but three deliveries later was deceived by a back-of-the-hand slow yorker and played down the wrong line. Bowled. England were 28 for 5. Going for the kill, Lanning allowed Perry to bowl her fourth and final over. The batters survived.

On the bench, Edwards blew out her cheeks, Taylor bit her nails and Danni Wyatt, next in, tried to hide the tension by standing and singing along to the stadium music. In the middle, Australia continued to bowl fuller and straighter than their sloppy performance at Chelmsford, although Greenway finally brought the crowd to life with a swept four. Brunt, though, managed only to find the boundary riders when Megan Schutt dropped short and by the end of the eleventh over the score had tiptoed along to 46.

Harris, who valued her Aussie cap too much to remove it when bowling, did get punished by Brunt for a half-tracker, the batter's pull shot dropping just in front of Schutt at square leg and disappearing under her body for four runs. But when Brunt tried to run Schutt's first ball of the next over to third man she, like her captain, was bowled off the bottom edge. It had been too close to the stumps for the shot that she tried and she was gone for 20.

Yet suddenly it seemed like a different game. Wyatt turned a full toss behind square for two, conjured up a third leg bye with her urgent running between the wickets and slammed another full bunger to the cow corner boundary for four. Despite the early wicket, ten runs had been added in the over and Wyatt, all energy and intent, had the look of a match-winner.

Fate had other ideas. Greenway leant into a drive to take Farrell straight for four and two balls later connected crisply with another shot down the track. Farrell, bowling round the wicket, extended her left arm, made the merest contact with the ball and saw it take the stumps at the bowler's end with Wyatt out of her ground. England were 71 for 7 off fourteen overs, needing 36 to win. 'I felt for Danni because obviously she had come in and was playing well, going along quite quickly and all of a sudden to get out like that was gut wrenching for her and for us,' said Paul Shaw later. 'We were right in the game. That is tough, but these things happen.'

As the number of balls remaining came down below the number of runs required, the decision to keep Brunt at number five seemed even odder. Where she had been forced to play the role of consolidator, more suited to Greenway, so Greenway now found herself having to swing for the fences, something for which Brunt was better equipped. Shrubsole fell to a mid-wicket catch in the sixteenth over and Hazell went in the next, trying a ramp shot that she lobbed up in front of the wicket. It was 78 for 9 and many of the crowd were heading for the exit, along with England's Ashes hopes.

With every dot ball and squeezed single the situation became more hopeless. Taylor held her hands in front of her face, like a child who could only bear to watch a scary movie through the cracks in her fingers. Brunt concealed her head inside her sweater and, when she emerged, revealed the tears that were now beginning to form. She saw through them to witness Farrell, bowling the first ball of the last over, struck cleanly by Greenway to long-on, where Jonassen slid under the ball to take the catch that finally broke English hearts and what little resistance there had been in this innings. All out for 87. So much for it being Australian cricket's unlucky number. Brunt buried her head in Wyatt's left shoulder as she tried to hide her grief.

The Australian reserve players stormed the field to join the bouncing bodies that formed their team's victory huddle. England strolled out behind them, offering each other consoling hugs. Lottie knew she had a captain's job to do, smiling professionally through her disappointment and leading the congratulations to the opposition. Katherine was still crying, as now was Danni Wyatt. Heather repeatedly puffed her cheeks, as though she intended to somehow blow away the misery. Sciver's faraway stare suggested she would rather be anywhere else than right here, right now. There was no escaping, though. There were post-game formalities to attend to and the England girls stood around shivering with hands in pockets, the cold now suddenly hitting them along with the chill of defeat.

Katherine was further frustrated by the cold shoulder she felt she received from Perry. 'I went to congratulate her. Fast bowler to fast bowler. You would expect some mutual respect. I might as well have punched her in the face. They have all been lovely except her.'

Finally they were allowed to slouch back to the dressing room. They sat and picked at boot laces, or stared unseeingly at the walls opposite them. Paul knew this was no time for the 'hair-dryer'. Instead he acknowledged their disappointment, said how well they had done for much of the game and praised their effort. 'It is tough for us at the moment,' he told them. 'But we stick together as a group and we look to see if we can finish the series on a high in Cardiff. Even though the Ashes have gone there is still a T20 series to be won. We need to finish on a positive note. This is the first step towards the World Cup.'

Later I asked Paul if he had allowed himself thoughts of victory at the mid-point of the match. 'No,' he smiled. 'In performance sport things can change very quickly – and they did. It didn't go our way. At halfway the bowlers and fielders had done an exceptional job. It's gutting that we weren't able to get over the line after we had set it up brilliantly. The shot selection and some of the decision making at times wasn't great, the players know that.'

Watching at home at the other end of the country, Kate Cross had struggled to believe the images on her television screen. 'I never at any point thought we were going to lose that series, which probably sounds really daft,' she said. 'I always saw this incredible comeback. We were going to do it. On reflection, the turning point was the last ODI at Worcester. Losing that meant we went into the Test match under more pressure. If we could have won the third one-dayer we could have gone into the Test leading and with our confidence up.'

Lottie called the events 'bitterly disappointing' and admitted that Australia had 'completely outplayed us in this series'. She added, 'Today we fought hard and I thought we did brilliantly with the ball, but our batting just hasn't been consistent enough. We made early inroads and we started well in the first over, but there were some poor shot selections and a bit of bad luck with the run-out. I thought with Danni and Lydia there we were going to make a late charge.'

That charge had been halted in the time it took for a deflected drive to cannon against the stumps, the ache of hope giving way to the vacuum of loss. In a way it had been a blessed relief, a release from purgatory. Yet I missed that death grip of helpless desire for victory.

'You didn't get your fairytale ending,' said Laura Marsh. No, none of us had.

22

The End of Days

'I know every series from now on will get bigger and better, but this one was the first of the biggest ones. The vastness of the series will never be forgotten. For the team it wasn't a great series, but it will still go down in history' – Kate Cross

THE final morning of the Ashes series began as the first one had, with Jenny Gunn the earliest arrival at breakfast. Located a short walk from Cardiff's Millennium Stadium, the walls of the Marriott Hotel's restaurant area featured various quotations from famous Welsh sporting figures, although I wasn't sure how much the England girls would have agreed with the words of football legend John Toshack that 'winning all the time is not necessarily good for the team'. Outside it had been raining on a city centre that had been packed the night before by those making the most of the Bank Holiday weekend, although the forecast was for it to clear up well before the start time of 10.30.

The girls came and went, the urgency and sense of anticipation of previous days notably absent, before gathering to get on the team bus. On the way back down to reception four of them had been in the lift when Australian captain Meg Lanning stepped in. Lydia Greenway delighted in recounting, 'She looked down and said, "This is going to be awkward." Nat said, "I don't feel awkward." Shall we say that to her when she gets to the crease?'

'Or when we get her out,' Katherine Brunt suggested.

On the coach for the ten-minute ride to the Swalec Stadium, several of the players sat on their own, their Bang and Olufsen-sponsored headphones detaching them from the chatter of a couple of groups of four who gathered round tables. There was talk of the end-of-series night out after they had watched the men's T20 international that followed their own match.

'So where are we going to go?' asked Katherine, before shrugging, 'I bet a lot of people might think it is inappropriate.'

Someone mentioned a well-known bar chain, to which Heather Knight quickly responded, 'No, don't go there.'

Laura Marsh added, 'I saw a story where one of their places in London was found to have rats in the freezer.' It was dismissed as a potential destination.

When the coach approached the stadium car park at 8.30 the floodlights were on. Where had the summer gone? 'The weather has been a bit shit for us. I couldn't live anywhere else, though,' said Beth Wild, who would be ending the year by marrying her partner Eliza in the Long Room at Lord's.

'I could live in Australia,' said Dani Hazell, married to an Aussie. 'I could get my green card.'

The presence of the England and Australia men's teams in the stadium's dressing rooms meant the women were relegated to what amounted to little more than a couple of store cupboards in the indoor cricket centre, bare walls and no windows. Anya Shrubsole was one of the first out of there and on to the playing area, reporting back that it was 'not too bad'.

While a few of the girls had some early throw-downs in the indoor nets, Paul Shaw remarked, 'Today is a good test of character and a good test of our unity – important values. Another one of our values is pride and for them to come out and play with some pride, that can only be a good thing. It can galvanise us as we move forward towards that T20 World Cup.'

He explained the team changes he'd made for the final match of the summer. 'Danni Wyatt gets her chance at the top of the order and Lauren Winfield misses out,' he said. 'And Georgia Elwiss will come into the lower middle order.' It meant that, having begun the year left at home while the team went to New Zealand, Elwiss had played in all three formats of the Ashes series. 'She has had a good summer and she is one for the future. It is important that people see there is a pathway and an opportunity to break in.'

Lauren's exclusion meant there would be no final opportunity to claim some form of personal achievement from a summer that – despite her high hopes, a mountain of county runs and an eventual 50-over county championship triumph with Yorkshire – had delivered overwhelming frustration. 'This is the first time I have been involved in a series that didn't go the way I wanted and it hurts more than I thought it would,' she admitted. 'You can't hide from what has happened and sometimes you learn more from defeats than success. We have got to be better. By our standards we have been quite average at times and not been at our best for twelve months.

'It has been the most disappointing series I have been involved in from a personal point of view. In the other series I have played in I have managed to score some runs. I ran myself out in my first opportunity in the ODIs, which puts you under pressure. I think it makes you play a little bit beyond what you need to do. It is a good learning for me. There will be plenty of series where you are not going to get off to a flyer, but you don't try to go outside of your game. I need to stick to my game and forget about things that are not natural.'

Out in the middle, to the amusement of even her opposite number, Edwards won the toss yet again. England would bat second, as they had done in every match of the series. 'The wicket has been under the covers,' she said, which was indisputable, adding, 'it is something that has worked well for us,' which wasn't. Sure, England had mostly performed brilliantly when given the responsibility of bowling first but the batters could hardly be said to have been accomplished chasers throughout the summer. Even so, it was a decision that no one could argue with. Sarah Taylor had some last-minute practice with Shaw, who finished by laughing and putting his arm around her in encouragement, and the final match was ready to begin.

The crowd, the vast majority of whom had bought their tickets with the men's game in mind, had mostly not bothered with the England women's early start. After the sell-outs at Chelmsford and Hove it made you question the wisdom and necessity of coupling the two games. Even if the women's series had been alive the chances are that most ticket-holders would still have been late arrivals and the decider would have begun to a backdrop of empty seats and apparent disinterest, an injustice to both sets of players.

After seven runs were scored off Brunt's first over, Shrubsole swung a wide past the leg stump of Lanning, promoted to opener. When she produced another in-swinger the visiting captain somehow managed to play inside it and lost her off stump. The delight of the bowler made it clear how alive England's desire for victory remained, despite the loss of the Ashes. Elyse Villani tied herself up by trying to cut one that was too close to the stumps and then attempted to negate Shrubsole's swing by coming down the track. She succeeded only in swiping the ball up into the air and Lydia Greenway settled under it at point. Australia were 9 for 2 after two overs and once again appeared to have little idea how best to approach building a twenty-over innings against this England attack. And this was the team many had said had been so much better than the home side throughout the summer.

A full toss by Shrubsole mid-way through her second over was the first loose delivery of the innings. Even when Brunt, playing her fiftieth T20 international, was pulled for four by Jess Cameron in the next over she responded with a dangerous yorker and, next ball, fired the ball into the batter's pads. By the end of Shrubsole's third over, Australia had lost two more wickets, the first when Cameron picked up a good length ball off middle stump and lifted it to Wyatt at deep square leg. A couple of balls later, Jess Jonassen chased one that was moving away from her left-handed stance and edged it to Edwards diving forward at short third man. The beaming smile on Lottie's face couldn't help but bring back memories of when her catch had produced the first wicket of the series, a time when so much optimism existed in the England camp. Alex Blackwell, whose pads had been the most used item of equipment in the entire series, survived an immediate lbw appeal and Shrubsole finished the over with figures of 3 for 8, four of those runs having been wides.

The introduction of Becky Grundy saw Australia enjoy their most productive over, Ellyse Perry's swing to long-on helping them take nine from it. Shrubsole and Nat Sciver brought back more control and it needed Blackwell's straight driven four off Hazell to take them to 48 for 4 from ten overs. Perry went in the next over, playing on via the inside edge as Sciver floated one up to her. Grundy pitched a little too short on her return to the attack, but Hazell bowled tightly to her field and Edwards continued to swap the bowlers around effectively. When Sciver returned to bowl the fifteenth over Blackwell sliced a catch to Elwiss at backward point as she tried to force the ball over mid-on and Australia were now 68 for 6 with five overs left.

Hazell seemed to be affected by the intent of the imposing Harris, bowling her a pair of full tosses and seeing the first of them disappear over the mid-wicket boundary. Harris targeted, and found, the same area against Brunt in the next over and slog swept her third six off Grundy. It was when she tried to be a little cute in dabbing Sciver in the direction of fine leg that she came unstuck, chipping an easy catch to Grundy. Her fourteen-ball innings of 24 had at least taken her team into three figures. Sarah Coyte went to the very next ball, driving directly to Shrubsole at mid-off and presenting Sciver with final figures of 4 for 15.

Grundy was entrusted with the twentieth over and was rewarded with two wickets, Greenway completing a catch high above her head on the leg-side boundary to remove Megan Schutt and Healy sweeping her first ball high to a sliding Wyatt in the outfield. Australia had been bowled out for 111, which, as we all knew, was not impossible to defend but represented a third poor effort in the series.

There was no break in the cloud, meaning the batting environment was no better for England than it had been for their opponents. The dismissal of Wyatt to the third ball of the innings – the first she faced – owed little to the overhead conditions, however. She was beaten for pace by a ball that jagged in at her and was clean bowled by Perry. Taylor fell in the second over, trying to guide Farrell through the slips and being ruled to have feathered the ball into Healy's gloves. Sciver was given a couple of leg-side wides to get used to the pace of the pitch before driving cleanly past the bowler for a couple of runs. Twice she was denied a boundary by a matter of inches, but a pair of threes helped her take the score to 22 for 2 from the first three overs.

This now felt like an important innings for Edwards, inconsistent throughout the series, but with the opportunity to play a captain's match-winning knock. Yet whenever she attempted to beat Farrell's off-side fielders she was thwarted and finally she steered the ball at comfortable catchable height to the point fielder, Coyte, and was out for 8.

Sciver and Brunt, England's most aggressive batsmen, found themselves having to protect their wickets once more as the shadow of Hove made its way across the morning's events. Sciver's well-timed clip to the fine leg boundary was the only scoring shot of the fifth over and Brunt was almost run out in a tangle of pads and bat before she eventually got off the mark by lofting two runs off Schutt.

Australia helped out by being wayward in their bowling, the discipline they had found three days earlier dissipating in a flurry of wides. Sciver's composure and confidence grew along with the crowd inside the ground. She steered Blackwell for three and then took one stride down the pitch to land Jonassen beyond the long-on boundary as England took eighteen runs from two overs to reach 63 for 3 at the mid-point of the innings. I happened to be passing Ebony Rainford-Brent just as Sciver unleashed her big hit. 'We need a Surrey girl to see us through,' said Sciver's county cricket boss. 'A bit of Surrey grit.'

Brunt, clearly enjoying the all-rounder's role she had grown into throughout the summer, swept Harris off one knee for four. She played umpire as well, quickly shaking her head when the bowler appealed for leg before off a ball that appeared to be missing leg stump. Sciver brought up the fifty partnership by swinging Farrell's short delivery down the ground for a single, but only one more run was added before Brunt fell lbw to Lanning for 17 as she came down the wicket and tried to turn the ball to leg.

Even with the field set deep and straight, Sciver's hitting was clean enough to find the boundary as she drove Lanning down the ground. Australia looked even more flustered as they gave up a couple of overthrows to Greenway, who moved England closer to their target by swinging Coyte's half-volley through mid-on for four. Sciver would not be there to see her team across the line, though. Her innings ended at 47 off 44 balls, run out by a direct hit by wicketkeeper Healy after being slow to respond to a call for a quick leg bye. She left the field to a deserved ovation and with her reputation enhanced by the events of the summer, which had now included two match-winning innings.

Victory was sealed off the first ball of the nineteenth over. Greenway, whose big hit into the leg side three days earlier had offered Australia their Ashes-clinching moment, was there at the denouement once again, hoisting Schutt to the square leg boundary to take England to a winning total of 114 for 5. The girls hugged in the dug-out, but there were few not thinking how the eventual comfort of this run chase – no more stressful in the end than it had been at Chelmsford – made the failure at Hove even more inexplicable. They had entered the Twenty20 series needing a dominant performance and had been by far the better team in five of the six innings of the series. But, oh, that other one.

'We spoke yesterday about finishing off on a high and getting as much out of this series as possible,' Lottie explained. 'To beat the world champions in the series is a great achievement. We have played brilliantly in this series so it is more frustrating that we have missed out in the run chase in Hove. When we have played our best we have more than matched them.'

'Twenty runs,' sighed David Capel, referring to the margin of defeat three days earlier, as we stood around waiting for the presentations; the consolation prize of the

T20 series trophy to England followed by the one that they really wanted, the Ashes trophy, to the Australians. You could sense the England players trying not to look at the photo backdrop that had been set up bearing the legend 'Women's Ashes Winners' as the ceremonies began.

Sciver took the award for Player of the Match, paying tribute to Shrubsole for advising her to 'bowl it into the pitch'. Anya herself was then honoured as Player of the Series for her seven wickets in the T20 games, stating that 'I love playing in high pressure games because they bring out the best in me'. When it came time for the Aussies to step forward, Lanning admitted that 'we were able to get away with it at Hove'. But no one could deny that the right team were up there claiming their prize. They had played better in the moments that mattered most. Even the England camp knew that, even if their acknowledgement of it was as reluctant as their applause as their opponents celebrated.

For the final time, I followed the girls back into their makeshift dressing room. While we waited for Anya to finish her media interviews, someone reported that 'Nunny got grabbed by the drug tester'.

'Talk about pissing on your parade,' Lydia replied.

Lottie had also been selected. 'Twice in a week,' she sighed as she and Katherine walked in with an anti-drugs official at their shoulders.

'All right, girls, listen up,' said Paul, having done a head count and found everyone present. 'This will be really brief. It's been a really challenging Ashes, as we all know. It's been a real roller-coaster. Today's performance in the context of the Ashes and where we were is outstanding. We have just beaten the world champions in a T20 series. It's important, and Lottie mentioned that, it's really important. But I want to take us back to what Brunty, Lyds and specifically Lottie spoke about a lot yesterday: character, fight, heart, and let's go out there and do ourselves justice. Today you've really, really done that.

'There were eight and a half thousand in the ground half an hour before the game finished and you've made them happy today. You've made yourselves happy, even though I know there is a disappointment in watching them celebrate. But it is really important that we accept the defeat we have had and take it on the chin, which will make us stronger, more resilient and ready to bounce back. Also you look at today and think, "We have done bloody well today." We have shown some fantastic determination to come out there from the situation we were in and win this series after the low at Brighton. So many congratulations for that.

'From our perspective as a management team, it's been tough, we know it has been tough along the way, but we are really proud in terms of the way you have committed to the task you have had to do. It is disappointing. Fine margins have lost us the Ashes, but at the end of the day you have done really well today, a fantastic win. We'll all have a beer together and I think that is important. Well done on your performance. I am proud of you today.'

I joined in the girls' applause. It seemed the natural thing to do and perhaps it was my way of acknowledging them and all they had given me over the previous months. Some of them headed out into the entrance area of the cricket centre looking for family members and I went round saying my goodbyes and thank-yous. 'Are you not coming out with us tonight?' Katherine asked. I declined. They would do just fine without me hanging around like a persistent uncle you can't shake off at a family wedding.

Close to the nets area, a group of the Australian girls were getting impatient, waiting for Lottie to be free of urinal duties. Their designated slowest runner, Villani, had challenged her to a 20-yard sprint. 'If she doesn't show up then she is the slowest,' the Aussie girl warned.

'I think we know she is the slowest anyway,' Heather answered (although Lottie would eventually prove her wrong in a photo finish).

I shook hands with Carl Crowe and said how much I appreciated his assistance over the recent months. 'Are we going to be seeing you with us anymore?' he asked.

'I might get to the T20s in India,' I replied.

But even if I did I knew it would be different. I would be on the outside. I would definitely want the girls to win, but I would not feel part of it. This had been my one shot at experiencing that thrill of triumph from, if not quite the inside, then certainly the fringes. These girls would have other summers. In the case of someone like Lottie, maybe not that many; for others, potentially a decade's worth of Ashes battles and World Cup campaigns stretched out ahead of them. I envied them their opportunities. My own, which I owed to the generosity of so many, was gone.

I went back to find Katherine and Lottie, who was now wearing blue rubber gloves and clutching an empty sample pot.

'I can't wee,' Katherine was still protesting.

'Come on,' urged Lottie. 'Let's get this done. You have to come with me; we have to be joined at the hip.'

Katherine responded with laughing, mock horror. 'I am not showing you my honey as well, Charlotte.'

I doubted I would hear a better line on which to finish. It was time go. Summer was over.

Postscript

'The team is in a really good place. The
foundations are in place, the programme is
in place and I think a hands-on head coach
will take them on to the next level' – Paul
Shaw

THERE was no single moment that pushed him over
the edge; no corrosion of the enjoyment he took from
his employment. Paul Shaw relished the challenge
of moulding the fortunes of England's women cricketers
as much at the end of the summer of 2015 as he ever had.
What he had come to understand, however, was that the
clock had been ticking. The day was approaching when he
would have to make one overseas trip too many, miss one
family birthday more than he could bear or ever forgive
himself for. While the Australians had celebrated in Cardiff
with the Ashes trophy, Paul had set his mind to determining
when he wanted to step away from the job that had been his
life for almost three years. Somewhere between the museums
of Florence and the historic architecture of Rome he made
his decision.

'For the last twelve months I have talked about three or four options,' he explained, 'and in speaking with Clare [Connor] we got it down to two options before the Ashes.' The two courses that were jettisoned early in those discussions were remaining at the helm until after the World Cup in England in 2017, and staying on as a short-term option for the World Twenty20 in India in the spring of 2016. Standing down a month after the Ashes, as soon as he returned from his Italian holiday, was the last potential choice to be discarded. Hence the news released by the ECB that Paul would relinquish his job at the end of 2015 and be replaced by a more traditional head coach.

'There is only so long you can do roles like this where you are constantly travelling around the world,' he argued. 'You are actually away from home quite a lot even when you are in this country. So there is a period of time and mine will not be far off three years by the time I step down. Certainly that is enough for me in that type of role, especially with a young family.'

It had appeared that something was up when Paul had delayed our end-of-series discussions, telling me he needed to go away and 'evaluate', and talk to people who could help him put things in perspective. 'My dad [Paul] has been ill and had an operation for prostate cancer,' he said when he was back in England. 'He is all right at the moment so my brother, Carl, and I took him to Italy to see the places that he absolutely loves. It seemed like the right thing to do. So I bounced things off my brother and dad and talked to Jackie while I was away and I made the decision midway through the holiday. I wanted to make sure that any decision I made was not based on any emotional reaction to the Ashes series. I came back and talked it through with Clare and we agreed that Christmas would work quite well.

'It gives the ECB the opportunity to recruit and restructure while we are still together. Someone still needs to lead the programme. If I went to the T20 in the spring then there is no time to recruit a head coach before we play Pakistan in the summer. This way I can do a proper handover, which is important to me. We can review where we are at and I can make my recommendations for how we move forward. Then they can make their own plan. That is how I always wanted it to be.'

Clare admitted, 'The intention for both of us when Paul was appointed in 2013 was that he would carry on through to the World Cup here in 2017.' But, she conceded, 'With the way Paul works, his intensity and his commitment to spend time with players and staff, the job has taken its toll. There was a realisation before the Ashes that he would not get through to that point.'

If there had been one moment that had hastened his recognition that the job had a finite duration it was when the England women's schedule for 2016 was determined, featuring a tour to South Africa, a world tournament in India, a home summer against Pakistan, followed by trips to Sri Lanka and the West Indies. 'Looking at the tours and the time away from home it became quite clear it would be perhaps a step too far. In the end we thought it would be right for me to step down at Christmas. It was the best time for me and for the team, so they get someone in from a real hands-on perspective going into 2016 for what is going to be a really big year and, I think, a very successful one for them. I think the team will really push on. That is the thinking.'

Paul paused and, with a half-sigh and half-chuckle, added, 'I need to spend a bit more time at home, to be honest. Jackie is looking forward to having me there more. The children are at that energetic stage and they need their dad. Jackie has obviously been aware of the conversations we have had with the ECB for a while and she would back me to the hilt whatever and has always been very supportive. She is the most understanding person I have ever come across, but it is important that she remains supportive.'

The revelation of how long Paul had been considering his future posed me an interesting dilemma as an author: whether or not the narrative of this book should reflect that, unknown to me, he was going into the summer with such an enormous decision occupying part of his mind. In the end I decided that this story was constructed around the way in which I had experienced the Ashes series with the team and that I should remain true to my own timeline. Conversations with Paul over the preceding months would undoubtedly have been different had I been aware of his quandary. To attempt to present them differently in the light of new information would have been unfaithful to my own vérité.

What had been clear during my time with Paul over the previous few months – and which was being underlined now – was that the day-to-day of the dressing room, the detail of the training sessions and what some would see as the adrenalin rush and ego boost of being 'head coach' was not what drove him. His interests lay down an alternate path, not along the vocational route one was required to travel in order to maintain an appetite for year after year on the road, pursuing one series victory after another as a traditional coach. He had always said that cricket was not necessarily where he saw himself in five or ten years' time.

'I think that is fair,' he said. 'I really enjoyed the role; managing the transition from the amateur to the professional era, developing the players, managing the team environment and their values. But lots of those things are generic skills I feel I can use in leadership roles, so from my perspective looking at other areas outside cricket is something I want to do. I am passionate about cricket, but working with other sports and other business is something I am quite excited about and I will be looking at those opportunities as well.

'I have enjoyed every role at the ECB and the challenges that have gone with it. You are right, I am bigger picture. I am strategy. I enjoy that side of things, definitely; building an environment that enabled me to empower Carl Crowe and David Capel to do the vast majority of the coaching and me moving the programme forward. So I was still able to do the bigger picture stuff. I did get pulled into more of the detail, but my role was not a hands-on coaching role.'

Charlotte Edwards had enjoyed a close enough relationship with Paul to know that 'this wasn't going to be a long term thing for him'. She added, 'I knew he never really could commit to 2017, especially with the way the schedule is. It is pretty full on. He was brought in to do a job and I have loved every minute of working with him. It is no coincidence that in the two years he has been involved I have been playing my best cricket. He has really taken the pressure off me. But it is often time for people to move on and I think the ECB are absolutely right in the structure, going to a head coach with many years of experience.'

Clare described the return to a pure coaching appointment as a result of the 'evolution of the programme and what the players now need'. By the time we spoke about the job, it had already been advertised and the search was on for 'someone who has absolutely dreamt of this, who doesn't want to be at a laptop doing spread sheets and business plans, someone who wants to be making a difference to players' techniques, and winning games. The schedule demands it and the players' professional status demands it.

'Because of the skills Paul has, he was just what the programme needed in 2013. We knew that professional contracts were not a million miles away. On reflection, two and a half years on, ninety per cent of what we set out to achieve has been done. He has established a world-class women's cricket programme with a really strong management team and laid good foundations for the players to move on.'

306

The obvious question, of course, was whether Paul would still have been in the job if the Ashes series had gone differently. Criticism of the England performance had been, in some cases, extreme. Journalists and bloggers had suggested changes in the structure, personnel and leadership of English women's cricket and Paul had taken his share of the heat. He was aware that some would assume that he had jumped before he was pushed into unemployment.

'The risk, or the temptation, is if things go really well you get carried along with the emotional high and you go on a little bit longer. But from my perspective we had just got to agree a time when I was going to step down. Whether we had won or lost the Ashes, it was always going to happen.'

Clare stressed, 'People will always look at it however they want, but with the way we lost and under-performed I am pleased that we had those conversations up front. It led to a much easier review when Paul got back from taking a break. I would emphasise that even if we had won the Ashes 16-0 this would be where we would be. There is always a review when you lose a series like the Ashes, but this recruitment process for a head coach is not a product of that review or because of under-performance.'

There was no shying away from the fact, however, that the ECB were looking for the new coach to find ways to return the England team to the pinnacle of the women's game. 'This gives us a huge opportunity and an incredible field of high-calibre applicants,' continued Clare, who had narrowed the candidates down to a shortlist of seven finalists at the time of our conversation. 'People out there knew we were looking for something different. This is a professional environment now that warrants a certain set of experiences, and they are going to come from someone who works in the men's game. It is so different to if we had been doing this, say, two years ago, and credit should go to Paul for taking the team and the perception of the team to another level. I have been bowled over by the quantity and quality of applicants and there will be three or four who will probably feel aggrieved not to get an interview, people who two years ago would probably have got the job. We have had really high quality coaches applying from the men's game in this country and as well as overseas.'[9]

I reminded Clare of our conversation earlier in the year when she had said that it was an advantage for the person guiding the women's team's fortunes to have a grounding in the female game. Yet the applicants for the new position had persuaded her otherwise. 'I think it is less important now,' she said. 'During this process it has become clear that most of the candidates watched the Ashes, know the women's game and there are some consistent themes about where we need to improve, such as critical moment control and playing under pressure and power-hitting. One example someone gave was that Sarah Taylor used to be as good as Ian Bell through and over extra cover, but felt that she had lost that because she is trying to hit everything to leg. Maybe because there has been so much chat about power she has interpreted that differently and lost her super-strength in the women's game, which is going over extra cover – which hardly anyone can do. So my point is that prospective head coaches have seen our games and been able to identify things because of our exposure and visibility.'

---

9   Three weeks later, the ECB named Mark Robinson as the new head coach of the England women's team, ending a ten-year spell in charge of the men at Sussex, during which he had won two County Championships and four limited-overs trophies. 'The fact that we have been able to attract a coach of Mark's calibre is another demonstration that England women's cricket continues to hit new heights,' said Clare. Meanwhile, Robinson offered this verdict on the players he was inheriting: 'From watching this summer, I thought there were times when they didn't realise how good they were. It looked like they didn't quite believe in themselves enough to let themselves go. It looked as if there was doubt in the mind and sportsmen all play best when the mind is free from doubt.'

I also brought up with Clare the notion that perhaps a new coach could give the girls more of the killer instinct that I had rarely seen throughout the summer. 'I would say that has become more apparent this summer and our head of science and medicine has already identified that our psychologist, who only does one day a week with the team, should increase that and work closely with the new coach during training to make sure we are really addressing that bit. The players need a bit more of an edge. It is very difficult, but some of our players need to be more resilient and harder.

'For me, that will be a real priority for the head coach although it is not my expertise, and I don't know how you go about doing that. Maybe training sessions have to come with more consequence. Shawsy was brilliant in his planning because he knew that women in general like to know in advance what the schedule looks like: what have I got to do, and when am I going to have my lunch? He has said that it is very different coaching men. Maybe we shouldn't give them that now, so maybe we want someone who doesn't know women that well and will make them uncomfortable and throw them. Instead of keeping them feeling secure and comfortable perhaps you create some resilience by going off-piste a bit.'

Among those players, Kate Cross confessed that 'we were all shocked when we got the email about Paul just before it was announced publicly' and acknowledged that she now found herself facing an alternative future. 'Obviously I came into the team when Paul was starting so it will be a new thing for me to have a different coach, but I don't think people are nervous about it. We are now in a job where if somebody doesn't take a shine to you that could be your contract over, but I think it is a really positive time for the squad. There is so much to take from the Ashes. I am a massive fan of Paul, he has got me where I am today and I owe him a lot. But equally, and this is not a knock on Paul, it is such a good time for the team to have a new member of staff to take us to the next level. I think Paul has been absolutely brilliant and done absolutely everything he can for us, but maybe he felt it was the right time to go.'

Inevitably, players with one eye on making sure they didn't get off on the wrong foot with a new boss and the other on not upsetting the man who had given them their England opportunity were going to be somewhat appeasing in anything they said. But Kate's comments and, similarly, those of Lauren Winfield reflected Paul's own views that he had reached the appropriate departure time from a role for which he was no longer the exact fit.

'I don't know anyone who can say a bad word against Paul,' said Lauren. 'He is a fantastic guy, but I think there were times in the series when we could have done with a kick up our backsides. I came back to the coach I work with back home and he was just brutally honest with me. There is no point in dressing things up. You have got to do things better at this level. It hurts and you are upset. What do we need to be better next time?

'If we are talking about using this series as a turning point then the change in management would allude to that as well. With a new coach you have to fight your way back into the team and say "this is what I can do" and I think that is going to help with the rocket up the backside we need after this series. It is a challenge because we are used to the way Paul operates and our training regime, but someone new might do things a little bit different. Nobody likes change, but you have to adapt, the same as when you go out to play games. Obviously Paul won back-to-back Ashes, but to take us forward someone new, fresh and exciting with potentially a bit more international playing or coaching experience might be just what we need.'

For all the questions that had been aired over Paul's future as the summer was concluding, there were plenty who had suggested that, in fact, it should be the captain who abdicated her position, some notable cricket correspondents among them. Stephen Brenkley in *The Independent* suggested England needed a younger leader 'more at home with the rhythms of the new, modern women's game and [who] may indeed have ideas about how its rapid progress can be accelerated further'. He suggested she had too often been 'leading according to a pre-ordained plan' while Sky's Paul Allott said bluntly that there was 'no comparison' between Edwards and Meg Lanning over the course of the Ashes series.

The Sun's John Etheridge and Simon Wilde in *The Sunday Times* both used Lottie's lack of mobility as a reason to stand her down. 'Our girls just aren't very athletic,' Etheridge argued. 'You have got to find a way to attract better athletes to the sport. And you have a captain who for all her skill with a bat in her hand is extremely immobile and unathletic and that does not set a great example when the captain is struggling to run between the wickets.'

Late in the series I had asked Clare if her old friend Lottie had been any quicker when she was younger. 'No, she is probably faster and fitter now than ever,' she'd said. Etheridge's ambition to see the best young sportswomen gravitating towards cricket was valid and worthy, but if Lottie had always been a slow-coach it seemed a little harsh to suddenly hold it against her now. Nobody had cared when results were going England's way. Phil Walker of *All Out Cricket* challenged Etheridge on *Cricket Writers on TV* by pointing out that 'great cricketers come in all shapes and sizes'.

'It is disappointing to read and hear anything like that, when people don't feel you are the right person,' Lottie reflected a few weeks after the series. 'I have to look at it in the sense that a lot of these people don't watch a lot of our games and don't have a huge amount of detail around what the women's squad is about. They purely write on what they see at the games and they have not got much background to it. It is slightly disappointing but it comes with the territory to be honest. That is something I have learned this summer – the game is into a whole different world. We are going to have to accept that people are going to write and criticise and want a story and I have got to realise that probably I am going to be one of the biggest stories because I am one of the highest-profile players. That is something I am going to have to be pretty tough and thick-skinned about.

'I would be lying if I said it doesn't upset me. I have not been used to it. In my whole career I have only really had good things said about me. You know you have had lots of blips along the way and they have never been bothered to write about them. It is a bit frustrating. I am very fortunate that I have a lot of people around me who support me and I pay more attention to them than to what I am reading. Alastair Cook is a good person to talk to and take a lot of confidence from when you look at what he has been through in the past eighteen months and the way he has come back.'

As defensive as she was being about her leadership, she knew she had little protection against criticism of her lack of greater contribution with the bat throughout the summer. Apart from anything else, she knew that more runs would have meant less critical analysis of her decisions in the field. 'Captaincy aside, I am there to score runs and that is what I am most disappointed about. People are talking about the captaincy but have forgotten that if I score runs then we are more successful. That probably makes it even harder to deal with; the fact that I have not contributed, which is a big factor in us being successful. But I was probably due a bad series after two years of success. I have played enough cricket to know that even though you want to score runs every time, it is not like that. A couple of unlucky decisions, a few poor shots and you don't have the series you would have liked.'

Lottie forced herself to bear any condemnation of her own performance with a resigned shrug. In her mind, the spotlight of reality that her struggles had thrown on to the England team was more significant and concerning than any personal censure. 'As a batting unit, we have been heavily reliant on a few players over the past few years and this series has probably opened up a few cracks that we have been covering for a while now.'

The shock of defeat and the change of coach would, Lottie ventured, eventually be looked at as important milestones on this England team's journey. 'Possibly for this group of players a setback is what they needed at this point in time. A lot of the younger players have come in and had instant success and haven't suffered any real disappointment. The bad times make you more honest with yourself and about how you are going to improve as an individual and as a team.

'It is going to be a very unsettling time for everyone with a new coach, but it is also very exciting. It is a good time to come in and take on a team that has probably underachieved in the last eighteen months. Hopefully he will really be able to tap in to the talent that I don't think we have seen the full potential of yet. I think me being captain will help maintain some consistency and the girls are going to look to me, so I have a massive role to play to help bring the new coach in and making it a smooth transition. I am really excited by it. This is a great opportunity for me as well. It is a little bit scary, but hopefully it will give the group a new lease of life.'

* * * * *

As I sat one final time in Clare's office, autumn closing in outside her window, I noticed that the walls still bore the signs of the momentous past few months. A poster displaying colour-coded summer fixtures dominated the centre of her notice board, and alongside it was pinned a Women's Ashes advert, featuring eight members of the England team and the legend: 'Smashing Boundaries Together'.

It was the latter towards which Clare pointed as she summed up the summer of 2015. 'It was overwhelming. We had this new pioneering team of professional women cricketers and – you saw the games – it was such a collective ECB effort for the first time. The events department was completely involved, media operations, the commercial team; the integrated collaborative approach across so many departments was just brilliant. If you were at places like Taunton and Hove, the look and feel was like being at a men's game. I sent an email round to the whole organisation at the end of the summer saying, "We haven't won on the field but we have smashed boundaries. It has been a landmark season and we should all be really proud of that."'

Paul Shaw was uncertain when we had our final conversation for this book whether he would continue to be on those group ECB emails. 'There are some potential roles there,' he explained, 'and I have heard from a few people talking to me about stuff I want to do away from cricket. I will work through the options and work out what is important for my life. I want something where I can make a positive difference. That's what really sets the fire burning for me, making a positive difference to people, in whatever walk of life.'

It was those for whom he had been striving to make a difference over the past three years that would leave the biggest hole in Paul's life once he was no longer at the helm at Loughborough. 'I will miss being with the team and with a group of people who are all developing and moving forward. I integrated quite a few of the players into the squad and I will miss that, bringing in young players and integrating them with the older players and creating an environment. I will miss the working relationship I had with the coaches and with Lottie. I have enjoyed some really special relationships.

I will miss the people, to be honest. I won't miss the travel or being away from home.'

I asked Paul about his legacy, how he would like to be remembered and whether going out on the back of an Ashes loss would hurt forever. 'When the dust has finally settled and you look back at things and the bigger picture, it was a tremendous Ashes series. We played some good cricket and beat them in the T20 series, but it is still tinged with disappointment that we did not hold on to the Ashes. But with major crowds, live broadcasts on TV and radio, it was a pleasure to be a part of and something I enjoyed, no two ways about that. It would have been nice to provide the icing on the cake by winning this summer, but if I look at my time as a whole I would look at winning back-to-back Ashes with a young team and be pretty happy with what we have achieved.'

Besides, as he had stressed to me many times, the sport was only part of his story. 'It has been about developing the girls as cricketers and as people so that after they have finished with this great game that we all love they can go on to great things off the field. That is really important. If they can look back and think "during my time with Paul he gave us responsibility, grew us both as cricketers and, more importantly, as people" that, for me, is very important. Going on and doing special things in life is bigger than the game, isn't it?'

Appendix

England Women Results 2015

ENGLAND WOMEN IN NEW ZEALAND
**11 February, 1st ODI (ICC Women's Championship),
Mount Maunganui:** New Zealand 240 for 8 (S.W. Bates
106, R.H. Priest 52; H.C. Knight 4-47); England 173. *New
Zealand won by 67 runs*

**13 February, 2nd ODI (ICC Women's Championship),
Mount Maunganui:** England 194 (C.M. Edwards 65, S.J.
Taylor 45; A.M. Peterson 4-25); New Zealand 104 (A.
Shrubsole 4-36). *England won by 90 runs*

**15 February, 3rd ODI (ICC Women's Championship),
Mount Maunganui:** England 217 for 9 (H.C. Knight 79,
C.M. Edwards 40); New Zealand 219 for 1 off 48.4 overs
(R.H. Priest 96no, A.E. Satterthwaite 76no). *New Zealand
won by 9 wickets*

19 February, 1st T20, Whangerei: New Zealand 60 (H.C.
Knight 3-6, A. Shrubsole 3-10); England 61 for 2 off 11.4
overs (C.M. Edwards 32no). *England won by 8 wickets*

20 February, 2nd T20, Whangerei: England 122 for 5 (L. Winfield 48, H.C. Knight 30); New Zealand 124 for 4 off 19.2 overs (R.H. Priest 41). *New Zealand won by 6 wickets*

24 February, 3rd T20, Lincoln: New Zealand 97 for 9 (S.F.M. Devine 37); England 102 for 5 off 18.4 overs (H.C. Knight 26). *England won by 5 wickets*

26 February, 4th ODI, Lincoln: New Zealand 168 (K.L. Cross 5-24, R.L. Grundy 3-36); England 169 for 1 off 32.1 overs (S.J. Taylor 89no, C.M. Edwards 64no). *England won by 9 wickets*

28 February, 5th ODI, Lincoln: New Zealand 230 for 8 (K.T. Perkins 70no, S.F.M. Devine 58; R.L. Grundy 3 for 36); England 232 for 5 off 45 overs (S.J. Taylor 93, N.R. Sciver 65no). *England won by 5 wickets*

WOMEN'S ASHES, 2015
21 July, 1st ODI (ICC Women's Championship), Taunton: Australia 238 for 9 (E.A. Perry 78, A.J. Blackwell 58); England 240 for 6 off 45.4 overs (N.R. Sciver 66, L.S. Greenway 53). *England won by 4 wickets*

23 July, 2nd ODI (ICC Women's Championship), Bristol: Australia 259 for 6 (M.M. Lanning 104, E.A. Perry 48); England 196 (C.M. Edwards 58, S.J. Taylor 43; M.L. Schutt 4-47). *Australia won by 63 runs*

27 July, 3rd ODI (ICC Women's Championship), Worcester: Australia 241 for 7 (M.M. Lanning 85, E.A. Perry 67); England 152 (L.S. Greenway 45). *Australia won by 89 runs*

11–14 August, Only Test, Canterbury: Australia 274 for 9 dec. (J.L. Jonassen 99; A. Shrubsole 4-63) and 156 for 6 dec. (J.L. Jonassen 54, A.J. Blackwell 47no); England 168 (M.L. Schutt 4-26) and 101 (G.A. Elwiss 46; E.A. Perry 6-32). *Australia won by 161 runs*

26 August, 1st T20, Chelmsford: Australia 122 for 8 (E.A. Perry 30); England 125 for 3 off 17.3 overs (S.J. Taylor 50, C.M. Edwards 39). *England won by 3 wickets*

28 August, 2nd T20, Hove: Australia 107 for 7; England 87 (R.M. Farrell 3-17). *Australia won by 20 runs*

31 August, 3rd T20, Cardiff: Australia 111 (A. Shrubsole 4-11, N.R. Sciver 4-15); England 114 for 5 off 18.1 overs (N.R. Sciver 47). *England won by 5 wickets*

Australia won the Ashes series 10-6

ENGLAND WOMEN'S ASHES AVERAGES
(All formats combined)

BATTING	M	I	NO	Runs	HS	Average	50s
L.S. Greenway	7	7	1	192	53	32.00	1
K.H. Brunt	7	8	3	154	39	30.80	-
N.R. Sciver	7	8	1	175	66	25.00	1
G.A. Elwiss	5	5	1	99	46	24.75	-
C.M. Edwards	7	8	-	159	58	19.87	1
S.J. Taylor	7	8	-	135	50	16.87	1
H.C. Knight	7	7	1	112	38	16.00	-
K.L. Cross	3	3	2	8	4*	8.00	-
A.E. Jones	2	2	-	15	15	7.50	-
L. Winfield	4	5	-	22	12	4.40	-
D.N. Wyatt	3	2	-	7	7	3.50	-
R.L. Grundy	4	2	1	3	2*	3.00	-
A. Shrubsole	7	5	-	5	3	1.00	-
D. Hazell	3	1	-	1	1	1.00	-
L.A. Marsh	2	3	-	0	0	0.00	-
J.L. Gunn	2	1	1	8	8*	-	-

BOWLING	O	M	Runs	Wkt	BB	Average
N.R. Sciver	25	0	158	9	4-15	17.55
A. Shrubsole	84	15	244	13	4-11	18.77
G.A. Elwiss	6	0	24	1	1-11	24.00
J.L. Gunn	12	0	73	3	2-52	24.33
R.L. Grundy	28	0	146	5	2-20	29.20
K.H. Brunt	79	17	290	8	3-48	36.25
D. Hazell	12	0	76	2	1-21	38.00
L.A. Marsh	38	9	120	3	2-42	40.00
H.C. Knight	44.5	2	215	5	2-44	43.00
K.L. Cross	38	5	151	3	1-9	50.33